Autobiographical Writing and British Literature, 1783–1834

Autobiographical Writing and British Literature, 1783–1834

JAMES TREADWELL

OXFORD
UNIVERSITY PRESS

OXFORD

UNIVERSITY PRESS

Great Clarendon Street, Oxford OX2 6DP

Oxford University Press is a department of the University of Oxford.
It furthers the University's objective of excellence in research, scholarship,
and education by publishing worldwide in

Oxford New York

Auckland Cape Town Dar es Salaam Hong Kong Karachi
Kuala Lumpur Madrid Melbourne Mexico City Nairobi
New Delhi Shanghai Taipei Toronto

With offices in

Argentina Austria Brazil Chile Czech Republic France Greece
Guatemala Hungary Italy Japan South Korea Poland Portugal
Singapore Switzerland Thailand Turkey Ukraine Vietnam

Published in the United States
by Oxford University Press Inc., New York

© James Treadwell 2005

The moral rights of the author have been asserted
Database right Oxford University Press (maker)

First published 2005

British Library Cataloguing in Publication Data

Data available

Library of Congress Cataloging in Publication Data

Data available

ISBN 0-19-926297-7

1 3 5 7 9 10 8 6 4 2

Typeset in Sabon by
Cambrian Typesetters, Frimley, Surrey
Printed in Great Britain
on acid-free paper by
Biddles Ltd, King's Lynn, Norfolk

For MEREDITH

Preface

A judge in America famously remarked of pornography that he might not be able to define it, but he knew it when he saw it. That more or less sums up our current state of knowledge about what the title of this book carefully avoids calling 'Romantic autobiography'. Taken on its own, either word in that phrase raises more questions than it answers, and both of them have been subjected to sustained theoretical assault over the last twenty-five years or so. Throw them together, then, and you have a hopelessly perplexing challenge for any would-be literary taxonomist (judges, fortunately, are not (yet) required to decide). And yet, just as the terms 'Romantic' and 'autobiography' have inexplicably declined all invitations (no matter how perfectly worded) to disappear from the vocabularies and the institutions of literary study, so 'Romantic autobiography' still seems to be a point of critical reference: we know it when we see it. And there it is: *The Prelude, Confessions of an English Opium Eater, Dichtung und Wahrheit, Letters Written During a Short Residence in Sweden, Norway and Denmark.* Four books that are in all sorts of ways extraordinarily unlike each other, but all 'autobiographical', and all 'Romantic', and . . .

It is easy enough to see why this line of argument cuts itself off and starts covering its tracks pretty quickly (at least since the 1980s, when we all lost faith in scholarly journeys of that sort). Nevertheless, the texts refuse to sever the frayed threads that seem to bind them together. So, at least, one has to assume from the fact that the phrase 'Romantic autobiography' (or its more self-conscious variants, like the one in my title) goes on turning up in discussions of them, and elsewhere. There is a curious double bind involved. Since we have all but admitted that any attempt to define a Romantic kind of autobiography, or indeed an autobiographical kind of Romanticism (one where texts write about authors' selves), will fall foul of theoretical traps that can no longer be safely disarmed, it follows that the only possible way of thinking about the field is to concentrate on particular texts, rather than trying to talk about a genre. However, the more attention one pays to any given autobiographical-looking document of the late eighteenth or early nineteenth century, the less it is going to look like other such documents; a process which dismantles the very terms one is trying to use to read the text in the first place.

My aim in this book is simple. I have set out to describe what autobiographical writing of the Romantic period actually looked like. It would be nice to say that it 'quickly' became clear that this project could not start by looking at autobiographical texts of the time. In fact, it took the whole course of a D.Phil thesis to discover the proper approach. I am infinitely grateful to my thesis supervisor, Lucy Newlyn, for patiently and tactfully steering me towards a coherent view of the subject, and to my examiners, Stephen Gill and Elinor Shaffer, for encouraging me to pursue these belated insights further. The crucial adjustment was to change 'Romantic autobiography' from a category which one tried to define and explore into a proposition about certain texts made in the context of their publication. That is why my title has the form it does. The book is about certain published documents which were perceived to be 'autobiographical'; and about how that perception came about, and what it meant, in the literary environment of Britain. The years covered define a historical moment when the word 'autobiography' went from being a neologism to a standard generic term, and when the significance of labelling a publication with that word was massively reconfigured by the appearance of Rousseau's *Confessions* in English. The fact that the same range of dates also roughly defines what persists in being called 'Romanticism' is, of course, not quite a coincidence.

It is a little surprising that there has been no general study of Romantic autobiography, under whatever name, until now. (Contrast for example 'Victorian autobiography', a term many scholars are perfectly comfortable with, and a field which has been treated as a separate area of study in quite a few books.) The critical literature of Romanticism has always had a lot to say about subjectivity and its representations in texts; the critical literature of autobiography has always had a lot to say about Rousseau and Wordsworth. This is, however, the first attempt I know of to describe what sorts of things the representation of subjectivity in a text meant to Romantic-period readers and writers, to look at a wide range of the texts where those representations were happening, and to see where readings of the *Confessions* or *The Prelude* might fit into a broader account of the literary and cultural status of first-person writing in the period. (In order not to raise false hopes, I should say straight away that it turns out that *The Prelude* does not fit at all, for the simple reason that it is not a Romantic-period publication.)

The book moves through three phases. Part I, 'Prescription', deals with the idea of autobiography as it made its way into the literary environment: the emergence of a sense of genre, as it were. Part II, 'Prescription/Practice', traces the relations between the conditions in which 'autobiography' emerged and the published texts which present themselves as autobiographies. Part III, 'Practice', turns finally to the texts themselves, exploring some examples of their own representations of autobiography's situation, and considering what sort of readings might be involved when we interpret a given document as an autobiography. There is, then, an overall movement from contexts to texts, from history to literature. However, I have tried to stress that we cannot talk about autobiography in the period without mentioning both at once. If one had to summarize the argument of the book in one relatively manageable sentence, it would be this: In the Romantic period 'autobiography' always describes both a state of a particular text and a relation between that text and the literary public sphere (the wider world in which texts are read, circulated and discussed). Accordingly, Part I contains a chapter devoted to the reception of a single work, while Part III selects two canonical documents which stand in particularly close and necessary relation to the sphere of publication and reading.

There is no separate introduction. The argument begins with the appearance of the word 'autobiography' itself, and tries to account for its subsequent movements as it proceeds. Nor is there a conclusion. The closest I have come to some general propositions about autobiographical writing and British literature, 1783–1834—about Romantic autobiography, if we must—are some remarks at the ends of Chapters 4 and 6. Even those tentative suggestions, I suspect, may have stuck their heads too far above the theoretical parapet, and exposed themselves to deadly flights of empirical arrows. I hope, though, that the book at least shows what we are talking about when we try to talk about 'Romantic autobiography', and what is involved in reading particular texts under that faded and eroded sign.

It is a pleasure to acknowledge the generosity and faith of individuals and institutions, without which the project would have remained deservedly buried in its doctoral state. The Dean and governing body of Christ Church, Oxford, gave me time to start again, and provided a welcoming and stimulating environment in which to do so; my repayment of this deeply felt obligation comes extremely belatedly, but without any lessening of gratitude. The support of the Faculty of Graduate

Studies and Research at McGill University was most welcome at a later stage.

My thinking about Romantic-period writing has been guided, corrected, and deepened by three brilliant and generous teachers: David Bussey, Peter Conrad, and Lucy Newlyn. None can be held responsible for the outcome, but all in different ways have reminded me of why this research felt worth doing. Dr Newlyn in particular has been a, frankly, enviable model of all that is best about scholarship, as well as being a patient and encouraging supervisor of my doctoral research, and a kind supporter of my work since. Briefly but memorably, John Bayley allowed me the benefit of his immense knowledge and courtesy. Equally unselfishly, Zachary Leader has allowed me to exploit his personal and professional wisdom. This would have been a much better book if I had called upon their kindnesses more often.

I was very fortunate to have the assistance of Jennifer Koopman at a stage when the drudgery of browsing through periodical indices seemed close to intolerable. It would have been enough just to have someone else share the work; to see her emerge from the dross with a few gold nuggets was a real blessing.

This book owes its being to four others who took over a different kind of work that otherwise would have swamped my research. My heartfelt thanks to Roz Porter, Chris Holmes, and (especially) Elissa DeFalco, and above all—always above all—to Meredith Hyde. The dedication of this work to her is the poorest of returns, but it comes with an acknowledgement that not a word of it could have happened without her.

Writing it has been by and large a solitary process. Nevertheless, conversations with colleagues and friends have been a regular source of inspiration. It is a pleasure to thank Tim Morton, Tore Rem, Seamus Perry, Robert Maslen, and Kate Bennett for help which at the time they might not have noticed they were giving; the only thing more valuable than their scholarship has been their friendship. At an early stage Alan Hansen helped me focus on the organization of the project, and Gene Wolfe's disciplined but endlessly imaginative suggestions expanded its scope. More recently, I have been grateful to Julie Nimmo and Rodd Christensen for help with (respectively) pedagogical and stylistic matters. Juliet Cadzow helped to keep things moving, and Andrew Agnew provided welcome assistance in imposing order on my work. Confronted with all sorts of unexpected problems, Miles Jupp has been an unfailingly inventive source of solutions.

At a particularly crucial moment the staff of the British Library were very generous with their time and expertise in warding off a crisis. Finally, I would like to thank my editors at OUP. Sophie Goldsworthy's support for the book has nurtured it from unpromising beginnings through to completion, and I owe her a great debt for her willingness to commit to the project when it was nearer beginning than end. Latterly Elizabeth Prochaska has been just as patient and helpful in seeing it over the final hurdles.

J.T.

Contents

I

Prescription

I

The rise of 'autobiography'

'Autobiography' is an invention of the late eighteenth century. Its lexical history, that is, begins in 1797. Various kinds of self-writing, ranging from formal conversion narratives to casual memorandum books, had of course been in existence for centuries before that date, but the word which gathers these disparate and marginal literary practices under a single name makes its first hesitant appearance in a comment on Isaac D'Israeli's 'Observations on Diaries, Self-biography, and Self-characters'. Writing in the *Monthly Review*, the Norwich essayist William Taylor treads warily around unfamiliar ground:

We are doubtful whether the latter word ['Self-biography'] be legitimate. It is not very usual in English to employ hybrid words partly Saxon and partly Greek: yet *autobiography* would have seemed pedantic.[1]

Taylor's uncertainty in the face of his proper but fussy neologism suggests that the practice itself, like the word coined to describe it, was in its embryonic stage. D'Israeli's essay, published in his 1796 *Miscellanies*, was itself the first critical reflection in English dedicated entirely to autobiographical writing, the first sign that the literary public sphere was aware of some new category forming within itself. Thirteen years later, in the *Quarterly Review* of May 1809, D'Israeli had adopted Taylor's word, and with it an acute form of his doubts about 'legitimacy'. The apparently new genre now appeared to have grown with remarkable speed from embryo to monstrosity. Asked to review the *Memoirs* of Percival Stockdale, a clergyman poet and critic much too insignificant (he feels) to be memorialized, D'Israeli becomes far more explicitly concerned than was Taylor about autobiography's threat to literary standards: 'if the populace of writers become thus querulous after fame

---

[1] *Monthly Review*, NS xxiv. 375. See J. Ogden, 'A Note on "Autobiography"', *Notes and Queries*, 206 (1961), 461–2.

(to which they have no pretensions) we shall expect to see an epidemical rage for auto-biography break out'.[2]

By 1835 the same journal could refer to 'the great and increasing proportion which biography, and particularly *autobiography*, appears to bear to the general mass of publications' as 'the most remarkable feature ... in the literature of the present day'.[3] The comment echoes many similar observations emerging from the periodical press throughout the Romantic period. Not all were as disapproving as the high-minded *Quarterly*'s tended to be, but in almost every case the anonymous mouthpieces of contemporary literary authority express their astonishment at the sheer profusion of autobiographical writing in their own time—at the virulence of D'Israeli's epidemic, as it were. 'The malady of memoir-writing continues to rage', as a writer in the *London Magazine* puts it in 1827.[4] At about the time of Taylor's coinage Madame de Staël remarked that 'there is nothing at all in England of memoirs, of confessions, of narratives of self made by oneself'.[5] Yet only three decades later Carlyle in *Sartor Resartus* makes reference to 'these Autobiographical times of ours'.[6] Both statements are to some extent exaggerations, overstated to support a more general point. Nevertheless, the contradiction is not merely a difference of opinion. Public awareness of autobiography, which at the end of the eighteenth century was localized and tenuous, had by the beginning of Victoria's reign become pervasive among the reading classes—just as Taylor's hesitant neologism had become standard usage. Robert Folkenflik writes that

the term *autobiography* and its synonym *self-biography*, having never been used in earlier periods, appeared in the late eighteenth century in several forms, in isolated instances in the seventies, eighties, and nineties in both England and Germany with no sign that one use influenced another.[7]

To this extent Carlyle's view was correct. By the time of *Sartor* (1833–4) 'autobiography' had become the usual name for the kind of writing we

---

[2] *Quarterly Review*, i. 386; cited by Ogden, 'A Note on "Autobiography"', 462. For a summary of the lexical history of 'autobiography' and cognates see Robert Folkenflik (ed.), *The Culture of Autobiography* (Stanford, Calif.: Stanford University Press, 1993), ch. 1.

[3] *Quarterly Review*, liv. 250.

[4] *London Magazine*, NS viii. 221.

[5] Quoted in Folkenflik, *The Culture of Autobiography*, 8.

[6] Thomas Carlyle, *Sartor Resartus*, ed. Kerry McSweeney and Peter Sabor (Oxford: Oxford University Press, 1987), 73.

[7] Folkenflik, *The Culture of Autobiography*, 5. Although Taylor was the first to use 'autobiography' in English, 'Autobiographical' had appeared in a preface to Ann Yearsley's *Poems* of 1786. Taylor's fondness for neologisms was well known to his contemporaries.

now label the same way. An apparently distinct and recognizable genre had naturalized itself in the eyes of readers. Between 1797 and 1834 the times had indeed become autobiographical.

More telling than these rapid lexical and bibliographic developments, however, is the change in tone from Taylor's comment to Carlyle's. During the thirty-odd intervening years the attitude to autobiography has shifted from hesitant enquiry to weary familiarity. D'Israeli's 'Observations' begins by remarking (rightly or wrongly) that 'The art of writing lives has been but lately known', and Taylor's coinage similarly indicates a cautious response to the pressure to recognize and categorize something newly demanding attention. By 1834 this demand is no longer under the control of the critical commentator. Various kinds of books collectively—though flexibly—identified as 'autobiography' have become such a prominent feature of the literary landscape that Carlyle's ironic voice can do no more than grudgingly admit the fact. In such cases the critic is a bystander, unable to police the 'legitimacy' of the word or the genre. He or she is trying to make some sort of literary sense out of what appears to be an economic phenomenon, a fact about the world of booksellers and buyers. Around the turn of the century some accommodation between critic and public might have seemed possible. The emergence of the apparently new genre provoked a series of reflections on its possible values, its uses, the standards of judgement by which it might establish a place in the developing literary public sphere mediated by the proliferating periodicals and the new reading publics of the day. Yet at the time of *Sartor Resartus* the sheer popularity of autobiography seems to have been the only material point. So far from attaining some securely literary status, the only remaining function of such writing is (by 1835) 'that of increasing the multitude of worthless books with which we are overloaded'.[8]

In discussing the rapid rise of autobiography during the Romantic period we are not primarily observing the history of a genre, or a word, but rather the gathering force of a particular pressure on the literary field in general. The raw bibliographic facts are certainly striking. Such evidence bears witness to a widespread taste for these books—though 'appetite' or even 'hunger' might describe it better. Nevertheless, the consumption of autobiography remains largely invisible. It can be deduced from the rapid rise in the number of titles, the number of editions a few of those titles went through, the comments of contemporaries, and so on; but most

---

[8] *Quarterly Review*, liv. 251.

writing and reading of autobiography was ephemeral, intruding only indirectly into the domain of literature—as that domain was circumscribed by institutional forces like the periodical reviews and the authors of aesthetic and belletristic tracts. Yet if the details of its consumption are obscure, the implications and consequences are not. Very few Romantic-period autobiographical texts emerge from the undifferentiated chaos of mass readerships into the institutions of the literary public sphere. The vast majority of such volumes were barely even noticed by the spokesmen of a supposedly refined public, and have been (justifiably) forgotten in the formation of literary canons. As a whole, though—however ill-defined the generic 'whole' might be—they exert a gravitational pull on contemporary men and women of letters. Their total mass created a force that could not be ignored. It is this force whose changing potency is measured by the distance between Taylor's uncertainty and Carlyle's weariness. The arch between their respective comments spans a significant alteration in the *reception* as much as in the *practice* of autobiography; and this is where the story of Romantic autobiography intersects with the history of Romantic literature. More important than the rise of autobiographical writing is the fact that it was felt to be rising. Its increasingly obtrusive presence generates among literary institutions a series of reflections on the translation of selves into texts. These reflections—casual or considered, splenetic or tolerant, polemical or ironic— can speak to us about the situation of Romantic-period autobiography more cogently than any attempt to construct the history of a putative genre.

In a number of different senses autobiographical writing of these years is a highly self-aware practice. A certain interest in selfhood inheres in the books, naturally enough; but the issue of the self as subject is not the first that needs to be addressed. An often more acute self-consciousness is provoked by the act of autobiography itself, the practice of a mode of writing perceived to be unusual, and whose status is uncertain. As the comments of Taylor, D'Israeli, Carlyle, and many others indicate, writing of this sort drew attention to itself. Lacking the stability of genre, or indeed (until about 1815) a widely used name, it could never be confident of its literary place. Genre provides a set of structures which allow texts to assume certain things about themselves, their circulation, their relation to readers, their cultural status, their literary and ethical values. Genre also supplies a newly printed work with a history, a set of ready-made models or counter-examples, and therefore with standards of comparison and judgement. During the early decades of the nineteenth century autobiography only gradually accumulated such markers. Moreover, as the reviewer in the *Quarterly* of July 1835 suggests, the generic position it began to attain was always only marginally literary. In early Victorian culture, as now, it tended to be seen as a mass-market genre, partially redeemed by a few exceptional instances, and by the fact that it was at least potentially available for use by properly literary figures like J. S. Mill, Henry Newman, or Harriet Martineau. At the end of the preceding century, however, even these faint indications of generic respectability were unavailable: the most prominent model (by far), Rousseau's *Confessions*, represented everything that was most troubling about autobiography. Throughout the period, therefore, the mere act of writing autobiographically was contentious. It could never be undertaken innocently.

A particular self-consciousness attaches to the moment of publication. Here autobiographical writing becomes deeply uncertain not only of its literary place but of its broader social place as well. Regardless of the lack of generic foundations, each instance of published autobiography is itself potentially indecorous or offensive, in a way that could reflect (even posthumously) on the character of the author. Public circulation of personal information risks more than one's literary reputation. Writing in *Blackwood's* in November 1829, Mary Busk acidly assigns the name of a social offence in place of a literary practice when she refers to one pervasive autobiographical procedure as 'gossip—we beg pardon, reminiscences, we believe, is the technical term'.[9] Other common accusations, as we will see, decried writers' vanity or egotism. Publication could also be simply inappropriate. A text that might have reflected no opprobrium on the author while in manuscript became ridiculous in print. When a small fragment of Dr Johnson's memoirs, saved by a servant from the fire to which he had bequeathed them, was published in 1805, a disappointed writer in the *Edinburgh Review* lamented its pathetic details of lanced boils and bad dinners. As he pointed out, 'the absurdity of the production consists entirely in its publicity'. The great man's reputation would suffer thanks to the actions of 'common publishers', even though original responsibility for the (now embarrassing) text lies with Johnson himself.[10] Hence anxieties about the act of autobiography are compounded by the translation of that act into print. Its purposes become open to question at the moment of publication. It

---

9 *Blackwood's*, xxvi. 738.
10 *Edinburgh Review*, vii. 436, 441.

can never be a self-explanatory or self-justifying practice; on the contrary, explanations and justifications are positively demanded, and (in the eyes of many censorious commentators) can rarely be adequately supplied. Even manuscript texts show the pressures of this kind of self-consciousness. Thinking of only one reader is enough to make the poet of the early *Prelude* drafts worry about whether any blame attaches to his work: 'Need I dread from thee / Harsh judgments', he asks Coleridge at the end of the first long section of reminiscences completed in 1799.[11] The radical tailor Francis Place begins his long manuscript memoirs with a highly reflective and critical analysis of the value of the task he is committing himself to, and accepts the fact that any future publication of the work would instantly render him liable to 'Harsh judgments': 'no one who chuses to write his own memoirs has or can have any claim for indulgence, should he at any time put his M.S.S. in the form of a book before the public'.[12]

During the Romantic period, then, autobiography is above all a debatable practice. Furthermore, unlike many other subjects of contemporary literary debate, what is being disputed is its actual presence: its nature, its possibility. In a climate of vigorous post-revolutionary contention every kind of writing was to some degree subject to these pressures. In the present case, though, there was no old order to overturn, no widely accepted set of standards to reject or reintroduce. Where Horne Tooke or Wordsworth might propose a revolution in literary language, the procedures of autobiographical writing were called into question by their mere existence; the debate was being made up as it went along. Once beyond the borders of relatively stable categories like travel writing, conversion narrative, or political memoir, each instance of self-writing appeared in the light of a problem.[13] Taylor's hesitation as he adds the now familiar word to our vocabulary is symptomatic of Romantic literary culture's simultaneous awareness of and doubt about 'autobiography'—as a term, as a genre, as a literary act, as a publication practice, as an object of popular taste.

---

[11] *Prelude* (1799), i. 458–9. All citations of the 1799, 1805 (thirteen-book) and 1850 (fourteen-book) states of *The Prelude* are to book and line number in the following edition: William Wordsworth, *The Prelude: 1799, 1805, 1850*, ed. Jonathan Wordsworth, M. H. Abrams, and Stephen Gill (New York: W. W. Norton, 1979). Unless otherwise stated (as here), all references are to the 1805 text.

[12] Francis Place, *The Autobiography of Francis Place*, ed. Mary Thrale (Cambridge: Cambridge University Press, 1972), 8.

[13] This uncertainty has been described in general terms by Laura Marcus, *Auto/biographical Discourses* (Manchester: Manchester University Press, 1994), 11–18.

We cannot therefore read instances of Romantic autobiography without also reading how they instantiate these continuing, unsettled debates. The works themselves are inextricably interlinked with the reviewers and commentators: the gradual emergence of autobiography as a relatively distinct and uncontroversial category arises from the exchange between all these voices, as well as that unvoiced but ultimately decisive power, the consumers. To speak of 'autobiography' in this period at all is to invoke a network of uncertainties. The word looks as if it stands as a collective term for a set of books, but what it really refers to is some fluid, contentious issues raised by those books; questions brought into play not just within the texts, but by the environment in which they circulate, the responses they provoke, the pressures they exert on contemporary notions of what texts do and what they are for. Ultimately, our interest will be in how this wider field of 'autobiography' makes visible within itself what we would now call autobiographies; that is, the aim is to read certain texts as being autobiographies. An attempt to write the history of autobiography in the period would not proceed this way. It would have to be a history of reading, writing, and publishing practices; the 'primary texts' would occupy a small part of its attention, because the formation and development of genre mainly takes place elsewhere. However, once we identify genre not as a goal in itself but as a way certain texts might be inflected, it becomes possible to explore the way texts relate to their environment as a means of understanding what is going on in those texts. To the extent that a work identifies itself as an autobiography it is self-consciously embroiled in the kind of problems exposed by remarks like D'Israeli's or Carlyle's or Busk's: questions about legitimacy, place, the author's public character, and so on. Almost by definition, Romantic autobiographies are self-questioning texts. 'Romantic autobiography' is a categorical description we can now use (albeit with reservations about the coherence of both terms), but the works comprised in that category could not possibly have placed and described themselves so firmly. Like the essays and reviews, they are interested in finding out what autobiographical writing is like, or what it should be like. The first task, then, is to outline the terms of those questions in the literary environments of later eighteenth- and earlier nineteenth-century Britain.

Johnson's famous essay on biography in the sixtieth number of *The Rambler* (13 October 1750) contains what would subsequently become a definitive statement:

I have often thought that there has rarely passed a life of which a judicious and faithful narrative would not be useful.[14]

By the turn of the century this opinion was something of a cliché. Unsurprisingly, it appears in the opening pages of many autobiographical works, as the readiest defence against anticipated criticism. A number of reviewers cite it, sometimes approvingly, sometimes as a stick with which to beat the book before them. An index of its pervasiveness is how often it appears without attribution: 'It has been observed by some author, that if the humblest individual were to relate his own life, the narrative could not fail to be interesting.'[15]

An article in the *Quarterly* of August 1810 begins by quoting the sentence from the *Rambler* and then adds that 'The observation might be made with still greater propriety of self-biography.'[16] Like many others, this writer finds it natural to extend Johnson's dictum so as to make it specifically applicable to his or her discussion of the distinct subject of autobiography. For Johnson himself, though, the area which particularly intrigues Romantic-period writers is not so obviously distinct. Number 84 of *The Idler* (24 November 1759) is largely devoted to considering biographical narratives 'in which the writer tells his own story' (pp. 268–9). As in the *Rambler*, the criterion of utility predominates; Johnson again makes the claim that of all narrative genres biography is 'most easily applied to the purposes of life' (p. 268). In this respect self-written biography is not essentially different from any other kind. The only reason it is 'commonly of most value', Johnson argues, is that it displays the virtues of biography at their best. His essay antedates any terminology that distinguishes autobiography from life-writing in general (the *Oxford English Dictionary* cites D'Israeli's 'Observations' as the first instance of 'self-biography'), and he seems to see no need for any such categorical distinction. The historian of his own life is simply an exceptionally well-informed biographer. Rather astonishingly, Johnson argues that he is also likely to be unusually impartial: 'He that writes the life of another is either his friend or his enemy', but 'he that speaks of himself has no motive to falsehood or partiality except self-love, by which all have been so often betrayed that all are on the watch against its artifices'

---

[14] Frank Brady and W. K. Wimsatt (eds.), *Samuel Johnson: Selected Poetry and Prose* (Berkeley, Calif.: University of California Press, 1977), 182. This edition is hereafter cited in the text by page number only.

[15] *Edinburgh Magazine*, x. 742. The shift from Johnson's 'useful' to this 'interesting', though, suggests that the direct source of this quote may lie elsewhere.

[16] *Quarterly Review*, iv. 104.

(pp. 269–70). Policed by its Enlightenment conscience, this rational subject is in no danger of sacrificing 'the first qualification of an historian, knowledge of the truth' (p. 269) for the sake of mere vanity. (The *Rambler* essay concludes with a similar point about respect for truth always outweighing partiality.) Consequently, autobiography and biography equally are forms of history. They become 'useful' by supplying information, giving knowledge of a particular sort, which Johnson calls 'the minute details of daily life, where . . . men excel each other only by prudence and by virtue' (p. 183). The distinction that matters to him is between these ethically instructive domestic records and the 'useless truth' (p. 268) of classical historiography, history on the heroic scale. Autobiography and biography (as a later generation would distinguish them) provide equal access to the former kind of information, and so there is no need for them to be distinguished.

The emergence of autobiography as an identifiably discrete category runs in parallel with the endurance of Johnsonian assumptions. There is no simple transition from one to the other. What develops during the Romantic period is perhaps best understood as a widening split between theory and practice. The *Rambler* essay is written mainly and the *Idler* essay entirely from a theoretical position, preferring generalities and principles to commentary on particular instances. As the number of autobiographical—and indeed biographical—works in circulation begins to increase dramatically in the last two decades of the century, these principles are more often flouted than confirmed. The most striking case (discussed in detail in chapter 2) was the publication of the first half of Rousseau's *Confessions* in 1782 (a poor English translation followed swiftly, a better one—including both parts—in 1790). This quite widely read and very notorious work radically called into question the worth of knowing Johnson's 'minute details of daily life'. More generally, the slow but steady flow of published autobiographies accumulated into a critical mass, at which point—roughly, the ten years around the turn of the century—they signalled the existence of a textual practice which could then be criticized and theorized in its own right. However, the situation of such criticism was crucially different from Johnson's. It is a response to an existing body of work. Where Johnson proposes abstract formulae, Romantic commentators are at least partially prescriptive; they are attempting to regulate a practice which they know is already proliferating independently of theoretical considerations. For more conservative commentators Johnson's criterion of rational moral usefulness in evaluating (auto)biography represents a powerful tool for prescription. But at the other end of the scale they recognize a very different aspect of the new genre, its habit (in Busk's words) of 'exciting a prurient curiosity that may command a sale'.[17] Theoretical accounts of what autobiography ought to be like have little effect on consumers' irrational, unimproving, un-Johnsonian appetite, a fact which itself supplies a worryingly apt explanation of the continuing rise in the volume of autobiographical writing. Any efforts to reflect critically on this phenomenon are thus shadowed by an awareness of the limits of such criticism. For many Romantic writers autobiography as a distinct concept exists in a strange limbo, between theories of its particular use or value on the one hand and the fact of its embarrassingly vulgar popularity on the other. Either kind of explanation might be invoked to account for its newly evident difference from biography as a whole.

Sustained critical reflections on the practice of autobiography are very scarce during the Romantic period. The huge majority of comments on the subject occur in the context of particular works: as apologetic introductions to autobiographical publications, or at the beginning of review articles. John Lockhart's entertainingly caustic article in the January 1827 *Quarterly* results from a sudden loss of patience: lumping together ten books he would ordinarily have disdained to notice, he uses them as the excuse for a tirade against the principle that 'England expects every driveller to do his Memorabilia'.[18] Nevertheless, this outburst ends up being one of the more extended commentaries the period has to offer. Apart from D'Israeli's brief 'Observations' in his *Miscellanies* (a volume much reprinted in the nineteenth century), the only other reasonably prominent attempt to think systematically on the subject is a long essay 'On a Man's Writing Memoirs on his Own Life', published in the Baptist minister John Foster's *Essays* (1805); the volume was in its sixth edition by 1819. More obscure commentaries include a section of James Stanfield's 1813 *Essay on the Study and Composition of Biography*, and an article 'On Auto-Biography' in the *Edinburgh Magazine* for June 1822. Each of these illustrates how the Johnsonian criterion of usefulness, based on the principles of biography, becomes modified—and partially subverted—by the awareness of autobiography as a somehow fundamentally distinct procedure.[19]

---

[17] *Blackwood's*, xxvi. 738.

[18] *Quarterly Review*, xxxv. 149.

[19] Marcus's *Auto/biographical Discourses* includes an excellent chapter on the anxieties evidenced by nineteenth-century writing on autobiography, and especially on 'contradicting views of the genre' (p. 13). Like most writing on autobiography, though, Marcus's inter-

'The art of writing lives has been but lately known', begins D'Israeli.[20] This is not an inaccurate assertion about the history of biography (which as he knew perfectly well dates back to classical times) but a reference to the discovery of an 'art', which he links to post-Lockean developments in the philosophy of consciousness. He means that the study of individual character has recently become an end in itself, 'as the human mind became the great object of our enquiry' (p. 96). The particular 'art' of life-writing therefore lies in its representation of a person as a private being rather than a historical agent. Formerly biographers assumed that 'he, who had only been illustrious in his closet, could not be supposed to afford any materials for the historian' (p. 95); like Plutarch or Suetonius, they took monumental public figures for their subjects. Eighteenth-century interest in the 'closet'—domestic or private space—has generated the new art D'Israeli identifies.[21] Foster also links the practice of life-writing with the fact that 'Each mind has an interior apartment of its own, into which none but itself and the Divinity can enter', though he construes this space in spiritual rather than psychological terms.[22] Both find the process of textualizing the private space of character (closet or apartment) distinctively interesting. This is true of Johnson, too; *Rambler* 60 argues that 'many invisible circumstances . . . are more important than public occurrences' (p. 183). In Johnson's scheme, however, domestic details attain the status of historical events (hence the word 'important'). They matter because they are a more useful species of history; they 'afford instruction' by exposing the 'similitude . . . in pains and pleasures' of all men (p. 269). (Women are effaced from the *Rambler* and *Idler* essays, as from virtually all these general critiques of autobiographical practice.[23]) By contrast, both D'Israeli and

est is primarily in the concept of the 'self'; she reads the debates over autobiography as a sign of a changing set of ideas that make possible new conceptions of self-writing. My concern is to show how autobiography raises specific problems in Romantic literary culture, and therefore ultimately to see Romantic autobiographies in relation to that culture, rather than as a moment in the history of a genre.

[20] Isaac D'Israeli, *Miscellanies; or, Literary Recreations* (London: T. Cadell, 1796), 95. Hereafter cited in the text by page number only.

[21] The emergence of privacy as an aspect of both social and literary experience from the sixteenth to the eighteenth century is helpfully surveyed in Roger Chartier (ed.), *A History of Private Life, iii: Passions of the Renaissance*, trans. Arthur Goldhammer (Cambridge, Mass.: Harvard University Press, 1989)(see esp. pp. 327–95, 399–445).

[22] John Foster, *Essays in a Series of Letters to a Friend*, 2 vols. (London: Longman, Hurst, Rees, and Orme, 1805), i. 113. Volume i is hereafter cited in the text by page number only.

[23] For an attempt to correct this imbalance by drawing attention to the existence of eighteenth-century female self-writing and to the genderedness of autobiographical subject formation see Felicity Nussbaum, *The Autobiographical Subject* (Baltimore, Md.: Johns Hopkins University Press, 1989).

Foster understand private life as a place of individuation, not assimila-
tion. In their essays Johnson's interest in the telling uniformity of human
nature shades into a curiosity about (to use Foster's words) 'what we call
character' (p. 6). The particular biographical practice whose recent
emergence D'Israeli notes is associated with the idea of writing a life as a
character rather than a history.[24]

This tenuous sense of a difference from prior assumptions enables
D'Israeli to distinguish a subcategory of life-writing:

> There are two species of minor Biography which may be discriminated; detailing
> our own life, and pourtraying our own character. The writing our own life has
> been practiced with various success; it is a delicate operation.   (p. 101)

On its first appearance autobiography is instantly a problem. Once the
process of recording a life becomes an 'art' instead of a historiographical
act, the issue of writers' relationships with their subject makes that art
'delicate', difficult. What D'Israeli calls 'self-biography' is marked off
from biography by the peculiar immediacy of this danger. The 'art' risks
becoming artful: 'To publish one's own life has sometimes been a poor
artifice to bring obscurity into notice' (p. 102). Johnson represents the
autobiographer as the transcriber of his experience, using superior
knowledge to supply an objective account. To D'Israeli life-writing looks
more like the presentation (or publication) of a singular identity, as an
end in itself. Autobiography is therefore suspicious: it raises questions
about motivations, purposes, and, inevitably, about authenticity. 'If once
we detect another deceiving or deceived', he writes, 'it is a livid spot
which infects the entire body' (p. 102). The character of the text as a
whole becomes entangled with the character of the biographical subject;
curiosity about the latter seems to lead directly to anxieties about the
former. These problems do as much to distinguish the category of 'self-
biography' as does the merely formal fact that writer and subject are the
same person. Right from the start the word raises questions as much as
it provides definitions.

For D'Israeli the best response to the concerns he voices is a return to
Johnsonian standards. In order to distinguish the 'poor artifice' of illegitimate autobiography from the proper performance of the genre, the
historiographical model needs to be reapplied. 'There are certain things

---

[24] In her study of the difference between Johnsonian and Romantic biography Cafarelli
points out that in Johnson's own practice biography is a means of reading other texts, not
a 'self' (Annette Wheeler Cafarelli, *Prose in the Age of Poets* (Philadelphia, Pa.: University
of Pennsylvania Press, 1990), ch. 1).

which relate to ourselves, which none can know so well; a great genius obliges posterity when he records them' (p. 102). The first part of the sentence reads like an open invitation to autobiography, but the second clause reimposes hierarchies of use and value, pressing private knowledge into the service of the public interest. A particular form of singularity—the 'great genius'—is elevated above other individuals in order to justify our curiosity. This position is not in itself Johnsonian: *Idler* 84 specifically values autobiography for its levelling function, its power to make all men 'appear equal' (p. 269) on the level of 'the general surface of life' (p. 268). D'Israeli's version still serves the purposes of curiosity more than morality; otherwise he (like Johnson) would be unable to distinguish autobiography from biography at all. Having raised an interest in character, though, his essay imposes what it sees as necessary restrictions on autobiography by prescribing which kinds of character are legitimate objects of curiosity, using Johnson's fundamental standard of utility to construct these hierarchies.

Despite the prescriptive effort, D'Israeli still finds it hard to repress the idea that autobiography's difference or distinctiveness—associated with the singularity of different individuals—has a seductive appeal in itself. The tension is played out through the two examples he cites: Hume's brief *Life* (1777) and (inevitably) Rousseau's *Confessions*. These two works are integrated into an opposition strikingly reminiscent of some familiar constructions of literary history. The 'attic simplicity' or Augustanism of Hume's passionless recitation of his life's central events is contrasted with 'imagination', represented by the rhetorically charged, highly interiorized narrative of Rousseau (p. 102). D'Israeli's worries about 'artifice' underpin his admiration for Hume's text. Here is an unquestionably great man, a significant figure in intellectual history, making available his knowledge of and judgements on his own life with calm, unadorned simplicity. Nevertheless, the opposite pole is hard to resist. D'Israeli's interest in what goes on in the 'closet' is gratified by the man of imagination; most of all by Rousseau's unprecedentedly forthcoming sensibility. The *Confessions* oblige posterity too, but in a very different way from Hume's *Life*, just as Rousseau's greatness and genius are altogether unlike those of his one-time protector and subsequent enemy. (The contentious personal relationship between the two philosophers, a matter of public knowledge and interest in D'Israeli's day, makes his choice of examples all the more piquant.) Artifice seems to be redeemed by the autobiographer of imagination, who will 'express feelings tremblingly alive' and 'effuse his inflammable soul in burning periods' (p. 103). Rousseau's example exposes the appeal of an autobiographical presentation of individual character conceived—via the language of sensibility—as a literary externalization of interior experience ('feelings', 'soul'). Indeed, from this perspective Hume's attic prose also looks like art rather than artless history. Literary style defines at once the character of the text and of the author. Only in autobiography is the equation so direct. The implication is, again, that self-expression is in fact the significant and defining feature of such writing. If so, the Johnsonian criterion of usefulness has been deeply undermined. D'Israeli's focus on literary figures—those whose activity is conducted in the 'closet', not the forum or on the battlefield—raises the possibility that autobiography might be a literary practice, not a biographical (therefore historical) one at all. The essay is quick to retract any such implication: 'What in Rousseau was nature, may in others be artifice' (p. 104). But are the 'burning periods' of the *Confessions* nature? We will see later how many others besides D'Israeli were troubled by the attempt to distinguish truth of character from textual eloquence as they read Rousseau's book.

As autobiography begins to be conceptually dissociated from biography, truth (or knowledge) cannot be identified with historical fact. Correspondingly, other kinds of 'use' come into play for the reader. To know the life of a person is one thing, but autobiography seems to present tantalizing possibilities of encountering the persons themselves. Johnson values intimate detail too, but what interests him is the satisfying congruence between private and public life: the example he gives in *Rambler* 60 is Sallust's description of the conspirator Catiline's uneven gait, indicating the 'violent commotion' (p. 183) of his nature. Knowledge of this sort is valuable 'whether we intend to enlarge our science, or increase our virtue' (p. 183). D'Israeli's essay, however, suggests a kind of knowledge gained from the autobiographical performance itself, rather than primarily from the information it exposes. The text manifests its author's singular personality, which readers can then use for their own instruction or pleasure. A writer in the *Edinburgh Review* of March 1817 commended D'Israeli for 'opening a new species of literary enquiry' by pointing out the 'utility of "deducing the individual character and feelings of authors from their own confessions" '.[25] This utility is however rather nebulous. In what Coleridge had earlier called 'this AGE OF PERSONALITY' it implies a value barely distinguishable

---

[25] *Edinburgh Review*, xxviii. 86.

from institutionalized curiosity, not to say voyeurism.[26] At all events, D'Israeli is credited with discovering in autobiography something which biography had not previously supplied; the new form of knowledge is part of what makes 'self-biography' visible as a discrete practice.

Foster's essay 'On a Man's Writing Memoirs of Himself' situates intimate knowledge within an explicitly Protestant scheme, where judgements are patrolled by conscience and the individual is already 'unerringly recorded' by 'the Divine Judge' (p. 123). His specific interest in autobiographical practice thus begins with the tradition of Christian self-examination. However, his essay has a strong secular bias. Certainly Foster himself was more active, and more successful, as an essayist and reviewer than as a minister. Spiritual autobiographies—especially those of Dissenting Protestants in the seventeenth and eighteenth centuries, which form the most substantial British tradition of self-writing prior to the Romantic period—function primarily as testimonies to the intervention of divine grace in the course of human history (that is, a single human's history). Most characteristically, they narrate a sudden and complete change of direction, after which the individual is presented as a new person, reborn. Foster's model is much closer to the secularized psychology debated by Locke, Berkeley, Hume, and Reid; his interest is in 'the successive states of the mind, and the progress of character' (p. 2) produced by complex interactions with one's environment rather than the dramatic interventions typified by conversion. Like D'Israeli, Foster imagines autobiographical writing as a means of uncovering the nature of the individual. His Christian interpretation of the process acts analogously to D'Israeli's literary evaluation: both are ways of imposing a standard of utility on a practice which otherwise seems to be an end in itself—in other words, ways of converting private experience into public value.

Nevertheless, Foster dwells at far greater length than any of the other commentators—indeed, than any other writer of the period except Wordsworth—on the 'strange emotion of curiosity' (p. 7) attending the autobiographical act. Its distinctiveness derives from the kind of truth the autobiographer offers. Where Johnson assumes that a sufficiently well-informed accumulation of facts will add up to a portrait, Foster rather contemptuously dismisses the notion that the truth about people can be exposed in historical narrative:

[26] S. T. Coleridge, *The Friend*, ed. Barbara E. Rooke, 2 vols. (Princeton, NJ: Princeton University Press, 1969), ii. 138 (October 1809). See also S. T. Coleridge, *Biographia Literaria*, ed. James Engell and W. J. Bate, 2 vols. (Princeton, NJ: Princeton University Press, 1983), i. 41.

As well might a man, of whom I inquire the dimensions, the internal divisions, and the use of some remarkable building, begin to tell me how much wood was employed in the scaffolding, where the mortar was prepared, or how often it rained while the work was proceeding.   (pp. 4–5)

The opening section of the essay organizes itself around the internal–external polarity this simile implies. It is a powerful and significant extension of Johnson's contrast between 'invisible circumstances' and 'public occurrences' (p. 183). The invisible events which (according to Foster) really matter are hidden not by the fact of their privacy or domesticity but by their interiority, their fully inward situation, completely inaccessible to biography. Thus his version of the value of autobiography stresses that 'it is that invisible character, whether displayed in actions or not, which forms the leading object of enquiry' (p. 97). Sensing a disjunction between an individual's nature and his or her history, he sets autobiography the task of representing truths which 'actions' of any sort do not necessarily display. The texts he imagines constitute a unique form of disclosure, different in kind (not, as with Johnson, in degree) from other records of a single life.

Overall, Foster gives a much stronger impression than D'Israeli of a categorically distinct set of reading and writing practices, with its own values and uses. His essay never suggests that its subject is particularly new or contemporary, and he never bothers to use any of the new coinages to refer to it. On the contrary, he describes the instinct to reflect on one's past experience as 'natural' (p. 1) and so presumably universal. It is a moral and psychological phenomenon, not (as D'Israeli thinks) a literary one. Nevertheless, the essay proceeds by hypothesizing a series of memoirs—a misanthropist's, a literary amateur's, an antiquary's, a provincial bully's—and then imagining what a reader might learn from each one. The 'interior apartment' (p. 113) which each mind contains constructs itself, in Foster's reading, through that mind's reflective textual record. Moreover, the 'last asylum of his character' is 'thrown open' specifically because the memoir is 'written on the supposition of being seen by [an] other person' (pp. 114–15). Although Foster says he is 'supposing a man . . . to record the investigation for his own instruction' (p. 96), self-examination is implicated in acts of publication in this essay. He writes more often from the hypothesized position of the reader of memoirs than from the writer's. What intrigues him most about the 'interior character' his essay postulates is the access to it which autobiography opens. His subject, after all, is 'A Man's Writing Memoirs of Himself': a belletristic, not a philosophical or spiritual, topic. Indeed, having described the memorializing instinct as endemic to human nature, he goes on to discriminate sharply—again from a reader's point of view—between those whose self-examinations are of interest and otherwise:

I am supposing, all along, that the person who writes memoirs of himself, is conscious of something more peculiar than a mere dull resemblance of that ordinary form of character, for which it would hardly seem worth while to have been a man. As to the crowd of those who are faithfully stamped, like bank-notes, with the same marks, with the difference only of being worth more guineas or fewer, they are mere particles of a class, mere pieces and bits of the great vulgar or the small; *they* need not write their history, it may be found in the newspaper-chronicle, or the gossip's or the sexton's narrative. (pp. 25–6)

This outburst is worlds away from Johnson's position. The *Rambler* and *Idler* essays imagine narratives circulating among all classes of readers, testifying to the universals of the species: 'those whom fortune or nature place at the greatest distance may afford instruction to each other' (p. 269). For Foster the common currency of mass circulation is of no real value to anyone precisely because it is not invisible. Memoirs ought to record priceless objects, characters marked by dissimilarity, which cannot have the convertible value of 'bank-notes' (this would certainly rule out the tradition of Protestant autobiography, in which each text is a variant of one fundamental plot). The trope reveals how closely Foster's abstract concern with the nature of human experience and the formation of character ties itself to a specific interest in the circulation of texts. Certain kinds of person, like certain kinds of narrative, are universally available, widely disseminated by gossip and journalism. Beyond the range of these vulgar publication procedures are the important characters, whom Foster defines by their exceptional self-consciousness. Interiority is therefore also an *awareness* of interiority. The autobiographical act performs this reflexiveness, bringing into view 'that very *self*, that interior being' (p. 9)—and bringing it into the sight of discriminating readers, as well as of the author's disciplined self-examination. Out of this shared interest in knowing the 'self' arises an implied understanding of autobiography's particular nature and significance as a literary practice.

Like all commentators of the period, though, Foster is ambivalent about the relationship between curiosity and value. Much as he wants to argue that the knowledge provided by proper memoirs is invaluable, he finds it difficult to be sure about what the reader ought to do with that knowledge. Far more explicitly than D'Israeli's 'Observations', his essay suggests that reading texts of the interior self is per se worthwhile. Still, the Johnsonian standard of utility persists in cropping up. As Foster pictures a hypothetical reader eagerly consuming each imaginary memoir, he occasionally converts that reader's sheer fascination with his text into some clear ethical or didactic purpose. More usually, the vocabulary of these scenes avoids referring to usefulness: 'It would be *interesting* to record . . .', 'It would be *curious* to observe . . .', 'It would be *amusing* to observe . . .' (p. 92, 101; emphasis added). In every case, though, this leisurely reading is licensed by the exemplary quality of the story. Most of the memoirs Foster discusses here have, after all, been invented by himself. The atheist's tale is a representative story of how Foster believes godlessness takes possession of the heart; all his other examples work the same way. By predetermining each narrative according to his own conceptions of human nature and progress, he makes them into instructive tales. Curiosity and amusement appear in these imaginary instances to merge into a broadly didactic frame of reading.

The practice of self-examination is thus interpreted from two rather different directions. One aspect of the essay figures it as a literary activity, producing a text valued for the unique possibilities it offers readers. Another presents self-examination in terms of moral discipline and instruction, bringing the self 'within the scope of clear reflection' (p. 8) so that it can be treated in Johnsonian fashion. These alternatives overlap hazily during most of Foster's discussion. They are only brought into stark opposition when he switches from hypothetical autobiographies to real ones. While he is giving the friend to whom the essay addresses itself advice about the idea of autobiographical writing he can present that concept as a tacit compromise between standards of utility and amusement. In the final pages all such equivocations collapse in the face of the actual state of autobiography:

I glance into the literary world, and observe the number of historians of their own lives, who magnanimously throw the complete cargo, both of their vanities and their vices, before the public.   (p. 117)

Neither pleasure nor instruction can be derived, apparently, from an autobiographical practice which is openly, confessedly immoral. Foster's outrage at the 'self-describers who . . . think the publication of their vices necessary to crown their fame' (p. 119) betrays his essentially ideal notion of self-writing. The self-conscious interiority he imagines being shared among discerning students of human nature seems to bear no relation to the prolific dissemination of 'contaminated' (p. 118) personal experience evident to him in 1805. He is forced to admit the existence of a grotesque parody of the natural curiosity defended earlier in the essay:

Yet I own the public itself is to be consulted in this case; for if the public welcomes such productions, it shows there are readers who feel themselves a-kin to the writers, and it would be hard to deprive congenial souls of the luxury of their appropriate sympathies. (pp. 119–20)

Autobiography now becomes the sign of a degraded compact between texts and readers, or a means of circulating their mutual vulgarity through the vehicle of narratives that ought to have remained private. It is as if interiority has become a source of infection rather than instruction. The main problem, one feels, is not so much the mere fact of vice in all its forms (Foster castigates profligates, partisans, actors, playwrights, and women of the town) as the existence of a network of publication and consumption which turns any potential 'compassion' for individual failings into 'detestation of their effrontery' whereby those failings are transformed into texts (p. 119).

As Laura Marcus has observed, though, the line between enlightening self-revelation and indecorous self-advertising is a fine one.[27] Similarly, one might wonder what it is that distinguishes the reading public's appetite from the worthy curiosity of the student of human nature. The contemptible practice of autobiographical writing is not so obviously different in essence from the theory Foster's essay establishes. In fact, his attitude to the burgeoning field of contemporary self-writing exposes a problem in his ideal construction of the genre. As I have argued, the difficulty lies in his tacit reconciliation of Johnsonian principles, whereby autobiography is a form of useful knowledge not essentially different from biography, with an uncertain intuition of another set of standards, according to which autobiography marks itself out to readers as a self-contained and peculiarly satisfying encounter with 'interior character'. When the encounter is quite evidently not a valuably instructive one, the legerdemain of this reconciliation suddenly becomes very clear. Foster describes the subgenre of courtesan memoirs with a horror stemming from his sense of collaborating in the social-sexual negotiations described in such books. The reader's knowledge of the autobiographer here seems equivalent to an illegitimate encounter, as the author relates 'the whole nauseous detail of their transitions from proprietor to

---

[27] Marcus, *Auto/biographical Discourses*, 19–22.

proprietor' (p. 118). Utilitarian history is distorted into explicit details of a prostitute's arrangements: 'the precautions for meeting some person of distinction . . . the hour when they crossed the river . . . the arrangements about money' (pp. 118–19). Such 'invisible circumstances' are at once private and shocking: shocking, in fact, precisely because of the way something which ought to have remained private has been turned into circulated information. The reader stumbles over the confusion of knowledge with curiosity. Neither seems to account for the text. All that is happening is the (illicit, perhaps seductive) encounter with the author, a 'purely' autobiographical meeting that cannot be subsumed under any sort of standard.

Foster's difficulty is made explicit at the very end of the essay, when he considers the only specific example mentioned anywhere in his discussion. Needless to say, the book is Rousseau's *Confessions*, 'a memorable example of . . . voluntary humiliation' (p. 122). He is led into a comment on Rousseau by reflecting on the misuse of the title of 'confession' to describe immoral memoirs. Hence, his approach is determined by a powerful form of the contrast between ideal and actual autobiography, which has already caused him so much trouble. In Rousseau's case, though, he suddenly admits that the sheer representation of interior identity might have a real value of its own, despite the all-too-obvious transgression of autobiographical standards.

If we could, in any case, pardon the kind of ingenuousness which he has displayed, it would certainly be in the disclosure of a mind so amazingly singular as his. We are willing to have such a being preserved, even to all the unsightly minutiae and anomalies of its form, to be placed, as an unique, in the moral museum of the world.   (p. 123)

A footnote adds:

It is very needless to express the admiration, which it is impossible not to feel, of Rousseau's transcendent genius.   (ibid.)

The 'transcendent' self is—in this one instance—admitted to be its own justification. It overrides all the conditions Foster has just asserted: the disgust at inappropriate 'ingenuousness', the wish to keep 'unsightly' privacy out of sight. Autobiography's self-sufficient value thus reasserts itself not just in theory but in practice: indeed, in by far the most notorious instance of self-writing known to the Romantic period. Free of any constraint, Johnsonian or otherwise, the text mediates a disclosure of the self, and this is all readers demand of it. Some such attitude to autobiographical writing is latent throughout Foster's essay, but it is remarkable that it should emerge most explicitly in the very situation (the publication of immoral privacy) which has just startled him into revoking it.

Or it seems remarkable, at least. In fact, Foster's problem here goes on challenging commentators throughout the period. Many other writers simultaneously demand the pleasures of disclosure while imposing standards of judgement. As James Stanfield puts it in his 1813 *Essay on the Study and Composition of Biography*, readers admire 'a bold . . . resolution not to conceal any thing' but also object to 'demeaning propensities obtruded into view'.[28] Still, what these potential confusions really signal is the increasingly widespread understanding that autobiography is a genre of its own (or, to use a word with less difficult implications, a distinct practice), and that it is set apart by the way it privileges disclosure over evaluation. The author of the interesting article 'On Auto-Biography' in the June 1832 *Edinburgh Magazine* assumes that writing of this sort inevitably becomes a revelation of character, whether intended as such or not:

> when a man sits down to write his own story, he unavoidably . . . puts down a full confession on paper, without thinking much of the public to whom it is nominally addressed.[29]

Concerns about criteria of judgement follow the fact of disclosure. By the second and third decades of the century the mere volume of published autobiography had to a large extent normalized the view that (in the same writer's words) readers' 'sensation of curiosity . . . produces altogether a far more intense interest than can arise from any other subject' (p. 742). Prescriptive attitudes had to give way to the primary habits of reading and writing which together visibly constituted the field of autobiography, and which were shaped by non-Johnsonian values ('curiosity', 'interest'). Foster's difficulty accurately predicts the way the rise of autobiographical writing comes to be attended by a persistent unease about what such writing really is, or really does. There is never a consensual definition of the character of the genre. All that can be agreed is that it exists and that it is problematic.

Even when not measured against standards of utility, the notion of disclosure causes trouble. 'There is an unavoidable suspicion attendant on self-biography', as Stanfield observes (p. 34). His concern is not with legitimacy or value, but simply with whether we can believe what we

---

[28] James Stanfield, *An Essay on the Study and Composition of Biography* (Sunderland: George Garbutt, 1813), 38. Hereafter cited in the text by page number only.
[29] *Edinburgh Magazine*, x. 743. Hereafter cited in the text by page number only.

read. In this respect Stanfield is perhaps at the furthest point from the position of *Idler* 84. Any view that sees autobiography as a form of biography must have confidence in its use as a historical record, however much it might be worried about partiality or bias. Stanfield suggests instead that the autobiographical act itself undermines its pretensions to veracity. That is, autobiography is inherently unlike biography not only thanks to its distinctive formal structure but because its claim to provide knowledge is a seductive delusion. It masquerades as a historical narrative, but 'an intention will secretly pervade every portion of the work' (p. 31). It is not what it seems; its very nature is not to be what it seems. The *Edinburgh Magazine* article agrees, though it judges the issue differently. Stanfield (who is after all writing a book on the art of biography) concludes that 'the advantages, which might appear to arise from the certainty of conscious knowledge, are weakened, and often destroyed' (p. 39) by autobiography's particular character. In the *Edinburgh Magazine* the 'self-partiality of the Memoir-writer' (p. 743) becomes an inadvertent means of disclosure. Acutely, this commentator notices that autobiographers give themselves away as much through their suppressions and evasions as through the narrative content of their record. Like D'Israeli, though more systematically, he or she links the character of the text to the author's. The very slipperiness Stanfield regrets can be understood by an alert reader as a mode of knowledge. Reading in this manner involves deliberately sacrificing the text's (historical-biographical) narrative content in order to gauge its real nature, the real nature of the person it represents. It implies that the disclosure for which autobiography comes to be uniquely valued takes place obliquely, at least as much in the process of reading as in the act of recording. The consequent ambiguities are clear enough. One reader's 'inevitable suspicion' is another's 'full confession'. The genre's distinctive deflections from the straight and narrow path of history could equally be seen as what makes it valuable or what makes it worthless, even if one's aim is restricted to finding out about the autobiographical subject, without enforcing moral or utilitarian standards.

It is hard to generalize about critical attitudes from a small body of evidence, most of which seems to have been produced fairly casually, without any sign that it is representative of opinions held more widely in the literary public sphere. Nevertheless, the persistence of certain issues and problems in this small group of texts tallies with the characteristic concerns of the reviewers and writers of autobiography, at least in so far as autobiography impinges on the terrain where literary values were debated in print. If there is no consistency within this 'higher' print culture over how to understand the genre, one can at least argue that the mere fact of its recognition as a category tends to be accompanied by a fairly distinct set of concerns about the principles of categorization. Broadly speaking, autobiography appears in the eyes of Romantic-period commentators to invite the kinds of critical standards appropriate to non-fiction (instructiveness, informativeness, and so forth); but at the same time the qualities that make it recognizable as a separate mode of writing suggest that its function is not use, and its object is not truth. Its generic nature, that is, contradicts its generic presuppositions. This explains why the prescriptive tendencies that emerge from the critical remarks usually find themselves to be hopelessly incongruent with the practice of autobiographical writing. Romantic observers anticipated late twentieth-century theorists by intuiting that the genre is inherently untheorizable.

The closest thing to a critical consensus achieved in the early nineteenth century is an application of the old Horatian formula from the *Ars Poetica*, pleasure and use.[30] The classical cliché is almost too fundamental in modern European aesthetic thinking to count as a standard of judgement; it could be—and, especially in the eighteenth century, was—freely applied to virtually any field of cultural endeavour. Nevertheless, Romantic writers adapted it comfortably to autobiography, especially when (as so often) they approached the subject along Johnsonian lines, as a variant of biography. This is how it is treated in the *New Annual Review* for 1817. A long section taking stock of the literary character of the age reflects on the 'strong tendency, we had almost said rage', for biographical publication.[31] Near the end of the century's second decade it is virtually inevitable that autobiography should be mentioned as a specific strain of this disease. The author singles it out using conventional terminology:

There is still another species of Biography, on which we must say a few words: we allude to Self-biography. In some respects, this is even more interesting and instructive than the Biography. (p. 63)

The twin criteria of entertainment and utility seem to describe such writing very well. For Johnson they effectively overlap. He begins *Idler* 84 by identifying biography as an unusually harmonious marriage of the

---

[30] See *Ars Poetica*, 343: 'omne tulit punctum qui miscuit utile dulci' (he who mingled the useful with the pleasurable won all approval).

[31] 'Literary Retrospect', 1817, *New Annual Review*, 63.

classical principles: of all the forms of 'narrative writing', it is the 'most eagerly read, and the most easily applied' (p. 268). Eagerness blends smoothly into usefulness. Readers' nosy curiosity about other people's private lives naturally causes them to reflect on their own. Citing the same formula, the *New Annual Review* points out the added piquancy of self-writing. Interest is presumably heightened by the greater degree of intimacy between author and reader, while instructive reflection is aided by the autobiographer's superior knowledge of the facts. The formula neatly controls any anxiety about the 'rage' for publicizing such intimate information. Its respectable classical symmetry frames these reading and writing practices within canonical ideas of textual value. Even when (as in the case of autobiography) other, less permissible relationships between reader and writer might appear to obtain, the standard of amusement and instruction can simply be applied in a higher degree.

A review in the *Quarterly* a year later shows the same principle at work:

MEMOIRS may, we think, be called the most instructive of the amusing and the most amusing of the instructive departments of literature: they combine individual characters and feelings with public transactions.[32]

This writer has only the loosest sense of the generic distinctions which had begun to crystallize by 1818. The general comments at the beginning of the article apply sometimes to all forms of biography, sometimes to the personal and anecdotal life-writing suggested by the word 'memoir', and sometimes to the added intimacy of autobiographical literature. This particular instance of the Horatian pairing bears most heavily on the latter species of writing, as the qualifying clause indicates with its reference to individuality and inner experience ('feelings'). As elsewhere, instruction and amusement result from the juxtaposition of a book's public and private modes; and (as in the *New Annual Review*) the pitch of both classical criteria is heightened in proportion to the nearness of the juxtaposition. Such critical principles are, superficially at least, fairly uncontroversial. It is not hard to see how they relate to the broadest contemporary assumptions about literary value. An essay in the August 1824 *Edinburgh Magazine* sounds almost perfunctory: 'BIOGRAPHICAL Memoirs are generally perused with avidity, often with much pleasure, as a fruitful source of amusement and instruction'.[33] By the time of her

---

[32] *Quarterly Review*, xix. 460.
[33] *Edinburgh Magazine*, xv. 153.

Blackwood's article of 1829 Mary Busk can take for granted a basic consensus along these lines. Despite being distant from Johnson in her clear sense of a separate genre, she begins by testifying to a 'common' principle he would certainly have shared:

AUTOBIOGRAPHY is allowed, by common consent, to be one of the most universally agreeable kinds of reading, combining utility with amusement.[34]

Where does she find this consensus? The statement refers far more to the critical environment, the community of Johnson and D'Israeli, than to the texts themselves, Rousseau's or De Quincey's or (the article's particular *bête noire*) Harriette Wilson's. It appears to be speaking for a consensus of readers, but it is really about a theoretical tradition. The classical tag is invoked as a self-evident proposition about autobiography in the abstract. Utility and amusement again provide a form of official sanction for the indisputable popularity of such writing. This is the critical vocabulary that comes most naturally and readily to hand—so much so that Busk can rely with apparent confidence on her readers' assent to it. The implication is that an unproblematic understanding of the nature and value of the genre was shared among readers in 1829 in much the same form as Johnson described it seventy years earlier.

However, the Horatian formula not only raises more problems than it answers, but begs those very questions which Romantic-period writers found as impossible to answer as to ignore. Amusement and utility are the two terms whose interrelationship becomes so confusing in the field of autobiography as that field becomes discrete. Horace's terms translate exactly into the alternative reading practices—curiosity and knowledge—that seduce D'Israeli, confound Foster, and alarm Stanfield. Instead of allowing them to remain the mutually supporting props of classical literary theory, autobiography makes each cast doubt on the other, with the subversive force already noted. It distorts the standards of literary judgement as if in a curved mirror. Entertainment and instruction are both still there, but the former has become prurience, voyeurism, or gossip, while the latter is made trivial and ephemeral, if not (as in Foster's account of courtesan memoirs) actually immoral.

One would be justified in interpreting Romanticism's periodic recourse to the classical formula as a prescriptive manoeuvre masquerading as a descriptive one. Pleasure and use might look like a straightforward, self-evident way of talking about autobiographical writing, but in

---

[34] *Blackwood's*, xxvi. 737. Hereafter cited in the text by page number only.

fact the phrase is a demand, or a plea. It illustrates the degree to which all discussions of autobiography in the period, however casual or conventional, carry a prescriptive charge, simply because the contemporary understanding of what 'autobiography' refers to is unformed, and therefore continually in debate. Even as late as the moment of Busk's article the apparent assumption that 'autobiography' already exists and can be generically criticized conceals an attempt to determine the conditions of a genre a priori. Here, again, is the problem worked out so extensively in Foster's essay: the more a critic tries to describe what autobiography is, the more he or she tends towards an idealizing conception which seems increasingly remote from any recognizable textual condition.[35]

Busk's rather reactionary article develops symptoms of this problem very quickly. Having presented, and claimed consensus over, the basic nature of the genre, she not only fails to find any actual examples, but laments the absence of the very standards she has just claimed 'common consent' for: 'This has long been the brilliant condition of autobiography, but . . . we doubt whether the era of its splendour is rapidly passing away' (p. 738). In the light of all that has been said about the apparent newness of autobiography the statement is surprising. (One might however note Busk's sense of an autobiographical canon, an idea increasingly readily available in 1829 but not formulated at the end of the previous century.) Given that contemporaries like Carlyle saw their age as one of unprecedentedly prolific self-writing, where in the past does Busk locate this golden age? Like other golden ages, hers is surely fabular. Her classicized vision of 'universally agreeable', diverting, utilitarian autobiography is displaced into an imaginary literary utopia. Revealingly, she cites no examples. Her Johnsonian theoretical principles are forced to confess their divergence from autobiographical practice, despite their looking not only uncontroversial but universal. The 'brilliant condition' of autobiography which they underpin is equivalent to Foster's series of hypothetical narratives, a fictional genre acting as a kind of negative image of actual contemporary reading and writing habits. Such double vision is entirely characteristic of Romanticism's views of autobiography. Busk and others tend to find themselves talking about two things at once, or using different critical languages at the same time. In so far as they imagine a genre, a coherent literary domain subject to definition, it appears to them both as a set of normative,

---

[35] Cf. Marcus, *Auto/biographical Discourses*, 37–8.

prescriptive criteria and as a network of readers and texts where the rules seem not to work properly.[36]

For conservatives like Busk the doubleness presents itself as a polar opposition: good theory versus bad practice. The situation need not be so obviously contentious, though. In their different ways Foster and D'Israeli move uncertainly between prescriptive and pragmatic approaches, negotiating conflicts between the two as they become aware of them. The 1822 *Edinburgh Review* piece, in contrast to Busk's, sees very little difficulty, and ends by affirming the conventional judgements. The writer hopes that it has 'in some measure' explained

the reason why Auto-biography at once excites such a strong and enduring interest as it has done, and is the source of so much valuable instruction with regard to the latent springs of human character. (p. 745)

Here the threat of risky disclosure is reconciled with the principles of amusement ('interest') and utility. Even in this more positive version, though, a pronouncement about generic value needs silently to impose certain hierarchies in the ranks of both literature and 'human character'. The author cites Rousseau and 'the Poetical Confessions of Lord Byron' as instances of works which are 'of the nature of a written soliloquy'; but among what he or she then calls 'numberless other memoirs' (p. 743) are texts in which the ideal of poetic self-presentation would surely seem less obvious to enlightened literary and psychological study. By mapping Johnsonian criteria on to Romantic conceptions of interior character, the writer sets out a standard for the genre as prescriptive in its way as Busk's. It is a more tolerant standard, because it values the act of confession independently of the particular things confessed, and is therefore likely to welcome a wider range of autobiographical writing. Nevertheless, representing the autobiographical act as sublime Byronic self-revelation quietly ignores the gregarious interchange of curiosity and information among readers and writers. The article sees no tension between its lofty model of the genre and the kinds of 'interest' and 'instruction' readers are said to gain thereby, but—potentially at least—these are different ideas. There is no guarantee that reading practices will echo the soliloquizing text by focusing on interior selfhood. On the

---

[36] Recent interest in Romantic-period conceptions of genre recognizes their mobility. Genre is understood to 'produce the subject in a shifting conjunction of past usage(s) with present appropriation ... they are not so much fixed "positions" in the socioliterary system as "transpositions" ' (Tilottama Rajan and Julia M. Wright (eds.), *Romanticism, History, and the Possibilities of Genre* (Cambridge: Cambridge University Press, 1998), 6.

contrary, the circulation of confessional memoirs would seem to publicize and socialize an author; hence the reference to Rousseau and Byron, both objects of popular fascination but fetishists of social exclusion and icons of solitary Romantic genius.

On the whole, theoretical reflections on autobiography are more likely to acknowledge openly the split between theory and practice. The *Edinburgh Review* article stretches the principle of amusement and instruction as far as it can perhaps be taken, in order to endow the genre with a value which accommodates its alarming aspects to respectable terminology and to discriminating readers. Other writers, equally sympathetic to autobiographical writing in general, admit that its ideal state bears little relation to what actually goes on between such texts and the public. A review in the *Quarterly* of August 1810 follows the characteristic trajectory:

> Let any man, who has in a common degree mixed with the world, delineate a true picture of himself . . . and he could not fail to produce a work, in which many would take a lively interest, and from which all might draw matter of instructive reflexion.
>
> But, unluckily, there are no instances in which self-biography has fully answered this purpose, and very few in which it has done so in any tolerable degree. It may perhaps be said, notwithstanding all professors to the contrary, that no one ever published memoirs of himself, entirely for the benefit of others.[37]

Like Stanfield, this writer suspects that there is a worm in the core of autobiography, always preventing it from being what it ought to be and doing what it ought to do. The prescriptive formula is straightforwardly Johnsonian-Horatian, but here it is confessedly only an ideal, distorted by an impurity in the act of publication. Indeed, the last tentative sentence hints at a different way of defining genre. Perhaps what distinguishes autobiographical writing is not a set of formal qualities but a particular way of deceiving the reader (or, more charitably, a particular imbalance in the relation between author and public). The reviewer slyly offers this as an alternative rule, to compete with Johnson's famous blanket assertion of biography's utility. Moreover, the autobiographers' own protestations of selfless devotion to the public spirit—these are the 'professors to the contrary'—represent the reverse of the truth. The genre is most suspect at the very point where it claims classical, utilitarian value; but then again it is most distinctive because of its false claim.

---

[37] *Quarterly Review*, iv. 104.

Comments like these indicate both the persistence and the limitations of prescriptive attitudes to autobiography in the Romantic period. Criticism is inevitably provoked by the sheer volume of autobiographical material crowding the literary market place, and it brings its own presuppositions to its consideration of this apparently unprecedented phenomenon. It would however be a mistake to take the prescriptive vocabulary emerging from this critical discourse as the language in which autobiography was understood at the time. Even at the level of its most basic assumptions, the discourse is slightly out of step with its subject. Prescription becomes so insistent as the nineteenth century proceeds because it knows it has not brought autobiographical practice under control; this ultimately accounts for the weariness of commentators like Carlyle, surveying the literary battlefield and recognizing that autobiography has managed to hold its lines against the assault of critical judgement. More importantly, prescriptive attitudes prove unable to evaluate—or even define—autobiographical writing. The genre emerges as a set of practices, a series of books, whose relationship to any formal or theoretical concept is always contentious.

Rather than seeking some central Romantic pronouncements about autobiography, then, we are more likely to understand contemporary attitudes by tracing the anxieties, confusions, and missed expectations exposed by the literary sphere's encounters with particular texts. Prescription occurs, by definition, because of a disequilibrium between expectations and events. Writing about autobiography is most revealing when it testifies to this gap; its more confident conclusions are less reliable. The Johnsonian position is critically stable, but only because it has no interest in recognizing autobiography for its own sake. In the unsettling shock of that recognition, as it comes about during the Romantic period, the very failure of existing critical vocabularies offers the clearest approach to understanding what autobiography was thought to be.

2

The case of Rousseau

Prescriptive attitudes are always shadowed by defensiveness. Their unease is usually well concealed, if not kept altogether invisible, because their judgements by definition lay claim to a priori authority, setting out rules and marking boundaries in advance of any specific critical decisions. By speaking in terms of universal standards and generalized criteria they present themselves as pronouncements of a transcendent intellectual order which cannot be disturbed by the vagaries of ordinary incidents. Nevertheless, this stance is specious, because prescriptivism actually occurs as a response to the threat of change; it reacts to the particular events which it then claims to precede. Doing so allows change to be defined as error. A set of standards is retroactively codified on the basis of the point from which change seems to have departed. Despite its pose of lofty theoretical primacy, prescriptivism is really a reaction to the messiness of history. Its standards are inevitably shaped by the actual instances of error it wishes to suppress; in effect, its judgements are the result of those errors, and 'universal' standards are in fact produced by the action of change itself.

This is a helpful principle to bear in mind when thinking about the concept of the 'genre' of autobiography. Best understood as a temporarily stable convergence of reading and writing practices, genre can sometimes appear instead in the guise of an a priori structure, whose given boundaries then either include or exclude particular textual instances. The structure is not defined by formalist considerations: internal evidence alone is insufficient to locate a text (especially in the case of autobiography: Is 'I wandered lonely as a cloud' an autobiographical sentence?). The most persuasive theorists of the genre have noticed the kind of negotiated exchanges between texts and their publics which in various contexts define what constitutes 'autobiography'. To borrow Hans Robert Jauss's term, genre appears as a 'horizon of expectation'.[1] In

---

[1] See Hans Robert Jauss, *Toward an Aesthetics of Reception*, trans. Timothy Bahti

late eighteenth- and early nineteenth-century Britain, as I have argued in the preceding chapter, certain expectations began to crystallize within the world of letters in order to recognize and then standardize something that looks like a distinctly *auto*biographical practice. Jauss's 'horizon' is meant to enclose the range of possible readings available to a particular document at a particular moment. In the present case, as we have seen, that limit is best represented by the classical values articulated so influentially in Johnson's essays on life-writing. The Romantic period's understanding of autobiography as a genre is thus largely formed within such expectations, and Romantic autobiography (as a practice) needs to be read in those terms. However, like the prescriptive formulae which attempt to lay down the rules of a genre, generic expectations and assumptions are heavily dependent on what they exclude as well as what they include. The formation of relatively coherent reading and writing practices is, as we have seen, always accompanied by anxiety about what is really going on. What this ambivalence tells us is that the boundaries of genre (such as they are) are to a great extent defined by the way they are tested and transgressed. Rather than forming a neat border drawn around the outline of an accumulating body of texts, they appear in reaction to troubling changes and innovations. An extension of Jauss's metaphor illustrates the point: when it comes to genre the 'horizon' is not in fact the limit of perception, but something more like a line of defence, a way of choosing not to look at what lies outside it. Genre emerges after the fact; and therefore we also need to explore those prior, disruptive events in order to read Romantic autobiography. The forces that prescriptivism exists to contain (or deny, or render improper) are as important as the terms it establishes.

Remarkably, those forces can for our purposes be accurately identified with a single book, whose first sentence famously declares the shattering of expectations and the impossibility of incorporation into a

(Brighton: Harvester, 1982), 23–34. Jauss's theory aims 'to conceive the meaning and form of a literary work in the historical unfolding of its understanding' (p. 32), rather than directing attention to the reception context itself as a separate object of enquiry. Nevertheless, its implications for understanding 'the borders of a genre-structure' (p. 23) are clear. Given the problems of achieving any useful formal definition of autobiography, it is no surprise that reception theory has been productive for theorists of the genre. Two particularly cogent accounts of autobiography based on its implicit and explicit positionings of its readers are Elizabeth W. Bruss, *Autobiographical Acts* (Baltimore, Md.: Johns Hopkins University Press, 1976) and Philippe Lejeune, *On Autobiography*, ed. Paul John Eakin, trans. Katherine Leary (Minneapolis, Minn.: University of Minnesota Press, 1989). Equally helpful on a smaller scale is Jonathan Loesberg, 'Autobiography as Genre, Act of Consciousness, Text', *Prose Studies 1800–1900*, 4 (1981), 169–85.

genre: 'I have entered on a performance which is without example, whose accomplishment will have no imitator.'[2] There are no predecessors, there will be no followers, the book is *sui generis*. This ostentatiously dramatic gesture opens part I (the first six books) of Rousseau's *Confessions*, posthumously published in 1782 and first translated into English in 1783. It also supplies the most powerful—and the most ambivalent—impetus for the accumulation of autobiographical writing into something like a genre over the subsequent half-century. Paradoxically, Rousseau's assertion of the absolute uniqueness of his enterprise came to look like the archetypal version of an increasingly widespread practice (everyone wanted to be unique like Rousseau, as it were). Romantic-period commentators often saw the transgression of social and textual norms in the name of individuality as autobiography's mark of Cain. This is, essentially, the gesture to which the prescriptive effort reacts; it is the negative image of institutional efforts to outline and evaluate the domain of autobiography. The gradual formation of a genre is thus founded on (and against) the principle that autobiographical writing cannot be a genre, the principle of inimitability or absolute singularity. This fact perhaps makes it easier to understand why the critical discourse surrounding such writing during the Romantic period is so contentious and confused. It is not simply a matter of competing versions of what autobiography is for or what it ought to be about (we will look more closely at those arguments in Chapter 3). Rather, the mere possibility of making such general claims seems itself to be in tension with the texts they are supposed to police.

My focus here is accordingly on the reception of the *Confessions* in Britain, not on a reading of the work. Whether or not Rousseau's claim is true (either for his own practice or in relation to anyone else's) does not matter. The aim is to determine how this declaration of independence becomes an essential part of the conception of autobiographical writing as a distinct field, in acrimonious dialogue with the prescriptivists' consequent efforts to reassert a normative, communal set of standards. Rousseau's defiant assertion of the differentness of himself and his book appeals ultimately to a notion of inviolable (though exquisitely

---

[2] Jean-Jacques Rousseau, *The Confessions of J. J. Rousseau, Citizen of Geneva: Part the First*, 2 vols. (London, G. G. J. and J. Robinson, 1790), i. 1. I cite this edition because (along with the accompanying volumes of part II) it marked the first appearance of the whole of Rousseau's text in Britain. Part I had been published in English translation in 1783, and reactions to the publication date from that year, but the 1790 version was the main conduit for Rousseau's autobiography in Britain.

vulnerable) selfhood. British responses to the *Confessions* recast the idea of uniqueness in less transcendentalized terms. The author himself is said to be 'an aggregate of contradictions', 'that most irreconcilable . . . of all human characters', a compound of 'eccentricities so singular and so opposite'; and his book—'this most extraordinary work'—is still more obviously defined by its disorienting strangeness, a 'mad confession of . . . mad faults', 'a dwelling with pleasure on what never ought to have been recollected, at least never ought to have been written'.[3] It is this intuition of uniqueness which is relevant to the state of Romantic autobiography, not the outworn and misleading question of whether the Rousseauan self is the seminal model of Romantic identity.[4] To British readers (as indeed to late eighteenth-century readers all over Europe) the *Confessions* had a meteoric quality, brilliantly and inexplicably unlike anything they had encountered before. 'Mais que dire des Confessions? Je suis fort embarrassé a en parler'.[5] Their responses show how an enormously influential instance of autobiography resisted and then contravened the efforts of commentators like Foster or Busk to put such texts in their place. Following on from the work of Edward Duffy, my initial task here is to draw out the implications of those responses, so as to specify the problematics of autobiography's emergence, the difficulties glimpsed in the vague nervousness of the commentators.[6]

[3] *Monthly Review*, lxvi. 533; *Monthly Review*, NS lxx. 468; *Critical Review*, lxx. 205; *Gentleman's Magazine*, liii(2). 775; Edmund Burke, *A Letter From Mr. Burke to a Member of the National Assembly* (London: J. Dodsley, 1791), 34; *New Review*, i. 374.

[4] The critical history of autobiography since the fifties shows a persistent interest in Rousseau's place as the father or founder of modern autobiography, and by extension (in some arguments) of modern conceptions of interiorized, autonomous selfhood. A good example from the early years of the serious academic study of the history of autobiography is John N. Morris, *Versions of the Self* (New York: Basic Books, 1966); see also Karl J. Weintraub, *The Value of the Individual: Self and Circumstance in Autobiography* (Chicago, Ill.: University of Chicago Press, 1978), Heidi I. Stull, *The Evolution of the Autobiography from 1770–1850* (New York: Peter Lang, 1985), and Thomas McFarland, *Romanticism and the Heritage of Rousseau* (Oxford: Clarendon, 1995). Recent attention to different autobiographical traditions has helped decentre Rousseau; by recentring him I do not mean to reinstate him at the head of a tradition, merely to draw attention to the historical fact of his pre-eminence as a problem for contemporary readers and writers.

[5] The reaction of a writer in the *Journal helvétique*, June 1782, cited in Catherine Beaudry, *The Role of the Reader in Rousseau's 'Confessions'* (New York: Peter Lang, 1991), 29.

[6] Amid the enormous volume of scholarship on the *Confessions* a few works provide excellent documentation and analysis of the British reception. For an encyclopedic listing see Jacques Voisine, *J.-J. Rousseau en Angleterre à l'époque romantique* (Paris: Didier, 1956). Huntingdon Williams, *Rousseau and Romantic Autobiography* (Oxford: Oxford University Press, 1983) focuses on the different forms of self-writing in Rousseau's literary career as a

Is it really justifiable to single out Rousseau as the focus of all contemporary concerns about autobiographical practice? He has been given pride of place in so many histories of canonical autobiography that some suspicion must be warranted. Romantic-period readers certainly did not find themselves completely without points of comparison; he could be placed in relation to other autobiographers whose works were circulating at the same time. His title positively invited comparison with Augustine's *Confessions*, newly translated in France in 1762 and in England by Bishop Challoner in 1739, although such comparisons were likely to make him look still more startlingly unique, since they drew attention to his already conspicuous failure to frame his acknowledged crimes and errors within the overarching redemptive narrative implied by 'confession' in the sacramental sense. Nevertheless, one of the first British reviewers of part I of the *Confessions* cited Augustine to prove that 'ROUSSEAU is mistaken, when he says, at setting out, that he has formed an enterprise without example'.[7] Looking back from the vantage point of 1790, when part II appeared in English translation (having been published in France in 1789), the *Critical Review* refused to join the general condemnation of Rousseau as a pathologically extreme and eccentric case. 'The publication of confessions was not a new design', it reminds the public, and goes on to place this instance on a generic scale: 'The Confessions of Rousseau give us a pleasure probably less pure and unadulterated than those other works.'[8] No 'other works' are actually cited, but the tenor of the rest of the review suggest that the writer is thinking of eighteenth-century memoirs of public life. Rousseau is a prominent public figure and therefore entitled to his autobiographical platform, his mistake being to drag in 'the foibles and weaknesses of his friends'.[9] Some sense of genre is at work here, suggesting that Rousseau need not be differentiated entirely from other scandalous autobiographers like Constantia Phillips or even Colley Cibber, nor ought one to take seriously his claim that his book is beyond the scope of literary regu-

series of models or possibilities for other autobiographers. The major debt of this chapter is to Edward Duffy, *Rousseau in England* (Berkeley, Calif.: University of California Press, 1979). Duffy's interest is in the transmission of the figure of Rousseau as a whole; however, his excavations of scattered reactions to the *Confessions* (which he finds to be the most important of Rousseau's works for English readers) have been invaluable for my argument.

[7] *Monthly Review*, lxvi. 531.
[8] *Critical Review*, lxx. 202.
[9] Ibid. Referring to the work of Bernard Gagnebin, Beaudry mentions that Rousseau's indecorous revelation of the private lives of others as well as himself was frequently noted in hostile reviews of the *Confessions* (Beaudry, *The Role of the Reader*, 30).

lation or comparison. The *European Magazine* managed to contain the volumes published in 1783 within the most conventional 'horizon of expectation'. Admitting that the *Confessions* might appear strange at first, its reviewer assured readers that the book 'may afford not only entertainment but profit' (amusement and instruction). He or she anticipates Foster's approach to autobiography by interpreting Rousseau's story as an exemplary—or at least characteristic—portrait of the consequences of a certain type of sensibility: 'a young man, endowed by nature with the most lively fancy and the most violent passions', forced by circumstances to depend on his own 'imagination, passion, and pride'.[10] Rousseau's distinctiveness is absorbed among a Theophrastian gallery of portraits, an approach which comfortably accommodates individuality to some inclusive concept of genre.

We should remember, however, that even Foster—who reads individual lives as instructively exemplary documents—located Rousseau in a gallery all of his own, 'an unique, in the moral museum of the world'.[11] No other journal managed to retain the *European*'s relative equanimity, not even the sympathetic *Analytical*. Its notice of part II of the *Confessions* (probably contributed by Mary Wollstonecraft) strives for a Johnsonian universalism and pragmatism: 'a description of what has actually passed in a human mind must ever be useful'.[12] This, however, is an attempt to excuse the bizarre quality of what went on in this particular human mind; it makes no attempt to deny Rousseau's claim of singularity. A more typical response would be the opening of the *Monthly Review*'s notice in the appendix to its 1782 volume:

WHO is the man (we were going to say miscreant) that has exposed to the light of noon-day this strange mixture of secret, personal history, with the wild but sometimes ingenious effusions of an over-heated brain? They rather deserved oblivion, and if poor Rousseau was foolish enough to write them, no honest or humane man would have been sordid or malignant enough to publish them.[13]

The degree of incredulous astonishment produced by the *Confessions* is evident in this reviewer's doubt over their authenticity. Many readers were inclined to be suspicious—even in 1790 the *Monthly* worried about the new volume's 'genuineness'[14]—despite the work's unmistakably

[10] *European Magazine*, iv. 276.
[11] Foster, *Essays*, i. 123.
[12] *Analytical Review*, vi. 386. Duffy notes that the radical *Analytical* had been Rousseau's most consistent champion in England (Duffy, *Rousseau in England*, 48).
[13] *Monthly Review*, lxvi. 530.
[14] Ibid. NS ii. 564.

Rousseauan eloquence and its abundance (overabundance, even) of precise personal detail. Their scepticism was instinctive, not based on any evidence for suspecting a fraud; the publication of the *Confessions*, with its embarrassingly frank admissions of masochistic eroticism, compulsive onanism, opportunism, and dishonesty, simply did not make sense. Sympathetic and hostile readers alike testified to the kind of confusion typified by the *Monthly*'s outburst. In so far as genre locates the public place and function of a particular text, no generic category could *explain* Rousseau's book, and most commentators felt that it had no place in the world of letters.

Two conclusions followed, in many ways closely linked to each other. The first and most obvious was to say that it ought not to exist at all, as the *Monthly*'s shocked contributor protests. There was literally no place for such a performance. An alternative response, however, encouraged by Rousseau's own rhetoric, assigned his book a unique place of its own. Transgressing any existing assumptions about the purpose and value of life-writing, it demanded to be recognized as a new phenomenon. Rousseau's notoriety—reinforced after his death by the Revolution controversy, which perpetuated discussion of his social criticism and his status as an author of the principles behind the new French Constitutions—guaranteed that the *Confessions* would not be discarded as a mere eccentricity. Moreover, many readers bore witness to the fascination of the narrative even as they disapproved of it. Henry Maty's *New Review*—one of many publications to pronounce that the *Confessions* 'never ought to have been written'—was willing to concede that Rousseau's apparently complete frankness entitled him to 'indulgence'; the *Critical* agreed that 'his faults are almost excused by the candor of the confession'.[15] Though not particularly well served by the translations of either 1783 or 1790, Rousseau's famously enchanting prose also mitigated the offensiveness of his lurid narrative. For a sympathetic reader like Wollstonecraft the *Confessions* could be read as a movingly expressive tale, stylistically congruent with the sentimental eloquence of *Julie*; her review in the *Analytical* speaks of 'the effusions of a warm heart'.[16] Such responses move towards the strangely double-edged judgement that the book's scandalousness was also grounds for its justification: the extremity of its frankness or effusiveness is both shocking and inviting. It is this sort of confusion which above all characterizes eighteenth-century

---

[15] *New Review*, i. 374; *Critical Review*, lv. 346.
[16] *Analytical Review*, vi. 385.

British reactions to the *Confessions*. The reviews are littered with references to the book's strangeness, its mixed or paradoxical quality, its difference from anything else: 'this strange and motley performance', 'this singular work'.[17] In 1813 the *Monthly* returned to Rousseau in the course of an article surveying eighteenth-century French literature, and its description again typifies the usual bewildered response, which three decades of familiarity have apparently failed to soften:

we come to that strangest, that most irreconcilable, that most repulsive, yet most fascinating (in the original sense of fascination) of all human characters, Rousseau . . . we will march to his *heart* directly through his *Confessions*.[18]

Fascination in this original sense refers to a malign magical enchantment, a Circe-like compulsion; it is a neat summary of the intimate mingling of horror and interest surrounding Rousseau's autobiography. In this crucial sense the *Confessions* genuinely was unique. This is not to say that there were no other works beside which it could be evaluated. The significant fact is that it *appeared* singular, incomparable, utterly eccentric. Its rupture of a 'horizon of expectation' single-handedly gave that limit clearer and more explicit definition while also pointing to the existence of a literary domain beyond it; and thanks to this double effect 'autobiography' began to form itself along both sides of the now permeable border.

Taking an obviously and admittedly exceptional document as an index of the wider literary environment is risky, as critics of the last two decades in particular have pointed out; it is the kind of assumption which led scholars to describe all early Romantic literature in terms of Wordsworth, or all Romantic irony as Byronic. In this case, though, the exceptional status of the *Confessions* is not a problem. Uniqueness, rather than representativeness, is the central claim. Romantic autobiography emerges in doubts over the normative standards of life-writing, and those doubts are raised to their most acute level by Rousseau. The *Confessions* is in no sense typical (the opening declaration is accurate to that extent at least). We are not witnessing the maturation of a genre through the publication of its primary and exemplary document, its archetype. What develops after Rousseau is the *sense* of a genre whose terms are defined not by what the *Confessions* is like but by the standards its abrupt singularity suddenly makes explicit. No other autobiographical writing of the period, except

---

[17] *Monthly Review*, lxix.148; *Critical Review*, lxx. 207.
[18] *Monthly Review*, NS lxx. 468.

the 'poetical confessions of Lord Byron', came anywhere close to generating the volume and persistence of commentary provoked by
Rousseau.[19] The fact that all this commentary is distinguished by controversy (much of it political, of course, in the wake of Rousseau's posthumous association with revolutionary thinking) serves to reinforce the
book's role as an impetus, if not as a model, because (as I have already
argued) the category of autobiography is always defined as much by its
contentiousness as by any generic coherence.

Romantic-period writers themselves certainly did not hesitate to see
Rousseau as a starting point. We have noted how general discussions of
autobiographical writing submit to the 'fascination' of the *Confessions*,
tending to give the work a central place—whether as climactic instance
or representative problem. The name of Rousseau also slips casually into
all sorts of less formal discussions of the subject. He can be the uniquely
satisfying standard of an otherwise degraded literary practice, as in a
notice of Richard Cumberland's 1806–7 *Memoirs* in the *Edinburgh
Review*—

Authors, we think, should not be encouraged to write their own lives. The genius
of Rousseau, his enthusiasm, and the novelty of his plan, have rendered the
Confessions, in some respects, the most interesting of books[20]

—but his singularity (of both character and 'plan') is here incapable of
imitation. Or he can be the progenitor of the autobiographical rage, as in
the *Monthly*'s review of De Quincey's *Confessions*:

we thus find that, from the time of Jean-Jacques up to the present Opium-Eater,
the world has been fond of assuming the character of a father-confessor, listening to the sins and errors of its votaries, and perhaps giving absolution with a
kind and merciful spirit, providing that the detail be sufficiently instructive and
amusing.[21]

Autobiographical writing like De Quincey's, with its unusual stress on
inner experience and its highly rhetorical register, was of course most
likely to bring Jean-Jacques to mind; Hazlitt's anonymous erotic confession of 1823, *Liber Amoris*, was similarly read in the shadow of Rousseau.
Nevertheless, this reviewer is ready to align a recent habit of extreme
autobiographical disclosure with the classical cliché invoked at the end of
the sentence. The *Confessions* here sits happily within either an orthodox

---

[19] *Edinburgh Magazine*, x. 743.
[20] *Edinburgh Review*, viii. 108.
[21] *Monthly Review*, NS c. 288.

or a transgressive reading of the genre. More significant is the way Rousseau is made to mark the origin of a distinct phenomenon, however understood. George Darley says in a footnote to his pseudo-Spenserian long poem the *Errours of Ecstasie* that 'since the time of Rousseau, it has been customary for authors to write their own history in their works'.[22] When this literary habit discovered its most spectacular popular and accomplished exponent in the first-person poetry of Byron, many readers instantly thought back to Rousseau as a point of reference.[23] As late as 1834 the dilettante of letters Egerton Brydges could look back over the *copia* of life-writing and still single him out:

His Confessions, true or false, are a wonderful book; and amid the hundred memoirs, biographies, and autobiographies, which have been published since, not one have [*sic*] disclosed the secrets of the bosom with the same thrilling interest.[24]

It would not quite be accurate to say that Rousseau's book became metonymic for whatever was understood by the term 'autobiography'. Even in relation to the particular area of that domain distinguished by the language of expressive interiority, other points of reference could sometimes be cited; most importantly, the tradition of sentimental narratives by women best represented by Mary Robinson's posthumous *Memoirs* (1801). The *Confessions*, though, demonstrates its continuing pressure on the discourse of autobiography by cropping up in that discourse for so long, and in so many different guises: exemplary or counter-exemplary, as origin, standard, point of comparison. No consensus about it was ever reached, but nowhere in the period is there any doubt that it overshadowed the whole field.[25]

This is partly explained by the work's unusually wide distribution. Its sheer notoriety has been sufficiently demonstrated by Voisine and Duffy. Further confirmation appears in the early British reviews. A correspondent in the *Gentleman's Magazine* for May 1782 wrote that 'No work has

[22] George Darley, *The Errors of Ecstasie* (London: G. and W. B. Whittaker, 1822), 48.
[23] See Duffy, *Rousseau in England*, 74–5.
[24] Sir Egerton Brydges, *Imaginative Biography*, 2 vols. (London: Saunders and Otley, 1834), i. 275.
[25] W. J. T. Mitchell points out an apparent exception: Wordsworth's *Prelude*, a thoroughly self-conscious autobiographical project, makes no reference to Rousseau at any stage. Interestingly, he argues that this means Rousseau has been repressed in, not that he is absent from, Wordsworth's understanding of autobiography (see Mitchell, 'Influence, Autobiography, and Literary History: Rousseau's *Confessions* and Wordsworth's *The Prelude*', *ELH* 57 (1990), 643–64).

ever excited the curiosity of the Learned more than the *Vie privée de J. J. Rousseau* ... now printing at Geneva'; a year later the *Critical* could say that 'The work itself is, at present, well known', and by the time part II appeared in 1789–90 the existence of a public and familiar 'Rousseau controversy' was taken for granted, even before Burke's diatribe in his *Letter to a Member of the National Assembly* (1791) sharpened the political edge of the dispute.[26] Thus the *Critical* began its account of the 1790 volumes by noting that a review of Rousseau's character and writing would be superfluous: 'public opinion has ascertained their real value with sufficient accuracy'.[27] At a time when autobiographical writing was widely ignored as a sub-literary practice of merely local interest, if not entirely ephemeral, the *Confessions* entered the world of letters with unprecedented and unmatched emphasis. The manuscript had been the subject of curiosity since 1771, when Rousseau had given public readings in one of the Paris salons, so its publication had been widely—and in many quarters anxiously—anticipated before 1782. Apart from this, the author's literary prominence ensured tremendous interest in his confessions, reaching well beyond the circles that were already to some degree familiar with the contents. Still further beyond the immediate literary environment of the text were readers all over Europe who had been captivated by the effusive sentiment of *Julie* and were eager to confirm their inclination to identify those sentiments with their supposed 'editor', to discover in Rousseau the authentic pattern of Saint-Preux.[28] The *Confessions* came with a huge ready-made readership, by contemporary standards. Even after the language of sentiment had lost its currency and the controversy over Rousseau's political significance had faded, they continued to provide by far the readiest lodestone for autobiographical discourse.

Despite due caution, then, it is probably impossible to overstate the force of Rousseau's posthumous influence on the formation of 'autobiography' up to the 1830s. What form did that pressure take? How did it engage with contemporary prescriptive tendencies? Merely citing Rousseau as the origin of Romantic autobiography misses the need to ask these questions. It is never a case of autobiographical writing somehow becoming Rousseauan; on the contrary, in Britain at least Rousseau's claim to be inimitable looks relatively plausible. The practice

---

[26] *Gentleman's Magazine*, lii(2). 235, *Critical Review*, lv. 346.

[27] *Critical Review*, lxx. 201–2.

[28] See Robert Darnton, *The Great Cat Massacre* (Harmondsworth: Penguin, 1985), 222–44.

of self-writing is however only part of the story. The wider standards and assumptions surrounding it, whose rough coalescence into a permeable 'horizon of expectation' represents the best approach to genre, are fundamentally shaped by the challenges of accounting for the *Confessions*.

Many responses to Rousseau's book are disguised as responses to Jean-Jacques. Even the most sympathetic of these acknowledge a paradoxical quality in their own sympathy: 'It is impossible to peruse his simple descriptions without loving the man in spite of the weaknesses of character that he himself depicts.'[29] The ambivalence is not usually expressed so mildly. A more typical response is Thomas Green's. Green, an occasional writer, testifies in his 1810 *Diary of a Lover of Literature* that 'Rousseau is a character who has by turns transported me with the most violent and opposite emotions.'[30] At the nadir of the scale of personal judgements lies Burke's character assassination, in which the more usual alternation between positive and negative responses becomes instead a diagnosis of pathology. For Burke in his 1791 *Letter* Rousseau is insane, driven by 'deranged eccentric vanity' to publish his 'mad' book.[31] The tension between the sublime honesty claimed by the author of the *Confessions* and the sordid details of his narration often directed readers towards double-sided interpretations of his character; those unwilling to go as far as Burke, or to pursue their quarry so systematically, wondered nevertheless at the spectacle of 'this odd mortal'.[32] (Evidence suggests that plenty of readers took as extreme a view of Rousseau's eccentricity as did Burke, even before 1789 or the still more acute politicizing of the issue in October 1794 when Rousseau's monument was installed in the Pantheon.[33]) When the *Monthly* announced in its 1813 article that 'we will march to his *heart* directly through his *Confessions*', it echoed a basic assumption about the subject of autobiographical writing, one naturally inherited from the eighteenth-century view that autobiography was a subset of biography.[34] The text in this view documents a person's character; hence, any confusion experienced in reading is explained by the grotesquely 'irreconcilable' nature of the author himself. So the *Confessions* offered polemically minded readers the last word on the

[29] *Analytical Review*, xi. 528.
[30] Quoted in *Quarterly Review*, iv. 155.
[31] Burke, *Letter*, 33, 34.
[32] *Monthly Review*, lxvi. 533.
[33] See Beaudry, *The Role of the Reader*, ch. 1.
[34] *Monthly Review*, NS lxx. 468.

controversial author of *Émile* and the *Discourses*. Duffy confirms that the
'*ad hominem* argument against Rousseau . . . became a standard item in
the arsenal of anti-Jacobin propaganda'; on the other side,
Wollstonecraft saw in the *Confessions* a touchstone of emotional sincerity and warmth, believing she 'should never expect to see that man do a
generous action, who could ridicule Rousseau's interesting account of
his feelings and reveries'.[35]

Once the *ad hominem* reading of the *Confessions* becomes explicitly
motivated by political considerations, its investment in reaching a final
judgement on Rousseau personally is obvious. His private character (so
the argument goes) confirms the moral ignominy or integrity of the
whole man, and by extension of all his works as well. Similar debates
over the private character of the Revolution were everywhere in the
1790s: the terms in which Burke and Wollstonecraft dispute Rousseau
are very much the same as in the contention over sympathy between
Helen Maria Williams's *Letters Written in France* (1790) and Burke's
Reflections of the same year. Nevertheless, no reading of the *Confessions*
in the period could confidently claim that it testified to a single version
of the 'real' (that is, inward) Rousseau. However much polemicists tried
to adduce the book as final evidence, it remained recalcitrantly peculiar
and irreconcilable. The assumption was that it contained the authoritative depiction of the contentious public figure. In fact, though, all the
comments on the oddness of the real Jean-Jacques bear witness to the
oddness of his book. Arguments over Rousseau continue partly because
of the endurance of political factionalism, but partly also because his
autobiography fails to supply the definitive evidence the public expected
to find therein. Strangeness, eccentricity, and madness are the usual
conclusions of the *ad hominem* interpretation; but they have been
projected as biographical judgements about the author after originating
as judgements about the text. Those first bewildered responses of the
1780s reveal the impossibility of accounting for the autobiographical act
itself. This fundamental confusion persists as the root of the Rousseau
controversy. Take, for example, an article in the *Anti-Jacobin Review* of
September 1805. Ostensibly a review of the 1786 *Memoirs* spuriously
attributed to Madame de Warens (famous as Rousseau's 'Maman'), it
begins with a telling survey of the continuing—and clearly undecided—
arguments over the real character of her protégé and lover, worth quoting at length:

MUCH has been done by the disciples of Rousseau to justify the 'confessions' of their master. Some have applauded them with boldness, and others have defended them with diffidence: some have regarded them as a proud monument of his magnanimity, and others as an irrefragable proof of his modesty: some have admired them as the efforts of a hero who, undaunted by vulgar prejudice, and in defiance of popular opinion, courageously comes forth to avow his errors and his faults, and others have approved them as the declarations of a sage who, actuated by the love of truth, and regretting his aberrations from the path of rectitude, unveils the recesses of his heart to expose his most secret failings: none condemned him, but all were satisfied with his acknowledgment; and, though none praised him for extraordinary virtue, yet all joined in palliating his misconduct, and all believed that, as his weaknesses were only these which are inseparable from our nature, no one possessed more integrity than Rousseau.

His admirers and the world, however, judged differently. The honest, the honourable, the just, and the wise, those who preferred the eternal dictates of sound reason and true religion to the treacherous doctrines of a vain and false philosophy, felt in their own bosoms an indignant refutation of the plea on which his conduct had been vindicated; and, while they condemned the follies, the vices, and the wickedness of which he had been guilty, wondered at the hardihood and the effrontery with which they had been avowed; and all the best and most estimable among mankind who saw in those 'foiblesses' which he considered as 'a l'apanage de l'humanite' [*sic*], the characteristics of a selfish, depraved, and unprincipled profligate, behold in his public confession of them a gross outrage of decency, an audacious contempt of morality, and a most impudent insult to the virtuous part of the community.[36]

As one would expect in this journal, the overriding purpose of the survey is to align the camps of the *Confessions*' friends and enemies with the opposition of 'false philosophy' to 'true religion'. It is curious, then, that the issue is left open. The article goes on to condemn Rousseau roundly and confidently on the basis of having exposed others' secret lives as well as his own, but it is unable to be so categorical about the value of the autobiographical act itself, although its opinion is perfectly clear. The author is fully convinced that the true Rousseau was a monster of vanity and appetite. He is not however able to deduce this from the content of the *Confessions*, the acts of Rousseau's private life. The argument whose two sides he summarizes is instead over the act of confession. Rousseau's private nature is judged by the character *of* his book, not the character *in* it. In this case it is clear how the *ad hominem* interpretation is in fact a disguised extension of a critical reading. The first camp bases its praise

---

[36] *Anti-Jacobin Review*, xxi. 476–7.

of Rousseau on the way that the autobiographical act redeems error and vice by translating them into the 'integrity' signalled by full and frank self-exposure, while the opposed camp—which the *Anti-Jacobin* in its partiality calls 'the world'—understands that same self-exposure as a more heinous crime than any of the predilections it narrates. For both sides Jean-Jacques's nature is read '*in* his public confession', in the quality of the act.

The confusion of moral categories which leads to the verdict of Rousseau's personal strangeness is also contained in the autobiographical act, rather than in the ethical inconsistency of his confessed deeds. Despite the *Anti-Jacobin*'s huffing and puffing, the story of the *Confessions* exemplifies neither heroic virtue nor criminal vice. However startling it may have been to see them in print, Rousseau's errancies were not of the sort to put him entirely beyond the range of sympathy (as the reception history of the *Confessions* clearly shows). Where the issue becomes confused is in the weird alchemy by which the work apparently changes the public proclamation of error into the mark of virtue, so that autobiography transmutes vice into honesty.[37] This unsettling effect is well described by the author of the review of French literature quoted in the *Monthly* for August 1813: 'There is something . . . extraordinary in the success of such an enterprize: namely, in the author's having persuaded men that he was virtuous while he told them how he was not so'.[38] Persuasion and telling—narration, that is—are the fields in which the moral evaluation of Rousseau takes place. Once again, the antithetical judgement of his character is really a reflection of the strangeness of the work.

The *Confessions* anticipates and authorizes this slippage in the book's famous opening paragraphs, as Rousseau identifies himself with his volume:

Whenever the last trumpet shall sound, I will present myself before the sovereign Judge with this book in my hand, and loudly proclaim, thus have I acted; these were my thoughts; such was I.[39]

---

[37] This aspect of the *Confessions* has been extensively discussed. It is not my purpose anywhere in this chapter to deal directly with the work; the classic account of the issue is Jean Starobinski, *Jean-Jacques Rousseau: Transparency and Obstruction*, trans. Arthur Goldhammer (Chicago, Ill: University of Chicago Press, 1988), esp. ch. 7. See also Thomas M. Kavanagh, *Writing the Truth* (Berkeley, Calif.: University of California Press, 1987). An excellent account of Rousseauan transparency in the sphere of revolutionary politics is Gregory Dart, *Rousseau, Robespierre and English Romanticism* (Cambridge: Cambridge University Press, 1999).

[38] *Monthly Review*, NS lxx. 469.

[39] Rousseau, *Confessions: Part the First*, i. 2.

Yet if this gesture is supposed to declare that the text is a transparent window on to the identity of its author, its effect is something like the reverse. The scene of judgement becomes a literary one; the uniqueness readers encountered in this opening flourish is really the uniqueness of a textual performance lying well outside their existing horizons.

Since responses to the *Confessions* are primarily based on critical rather than ethical considerations, we ought to describe the pervasive bafflement in terms of reading strategies, rather than following Burke (and others) into evaluations of Rousseau's character. The first stress exerted on implied generic assumptions comes through a complication of the idea of truth. This notion of course underpins contemporary approaches to life-writing, albeit (as argued above) with an awareness that not all truth is per se valuable. Rousseau, however, shifts the emphasis from truth to sincerity. The documentary value of his memoir is close to nil: in fact one could call it a negative value, in that he supplies information about himself and others which is all the worse for being true (the sexual laxity of Mme de Warens's household, for example, or the difficulty of persuading Therèse to consent to the abandonment of their children). In Bruss's terms, 'truth-value' is replaced by 'act-value': the heroic sincerity of the confession transcends the worrisome content.[40] Rousseau explicitly addresses this move:

I should be continually under the eye of the Reader, he should be enabled to follow me in all the wanderings of my heart, through every intricacy of my adventures; he must find no void or chasm in my relation, nor lose sight of me one instant, lest he should find occasion to say, what was he doing at this time? and suspect me of not having dared to reveal the whole.[41]

Only sincerity, that is, can make the autobiographical act valuable; any hierarchical distinction between different kinds of truths would damage its moral integrity. Hence, the 'unexampled minuteness' of his record, which intrigued and troubled so many commentators, is embedded in the nature of the project.[42] The only worth his narrative can have is the value contained in the moment of narration, the readiness to bare all. For most early readers of the *Confessions*, apparently, the result was a disturbing sense that life-writing had here willingly surrendered its claim

---

[40] See Elizabeth Bruss, 'Eye for I: Making and Unmaking Autobiography in Film', in James Olney (ed.), *Autobiography: Essays Theoretical and Critical* (Princeton, NJ: Princeton University Press, 1980), 294–312. This article extends the arguments about the literary genre made in Bruss, *Autobiographical Acts*, 4–17.

[41] Rousseau, *Confessions: Part the First*, i. 109–10.

[42] *Critical Review*, lv. 346.

to documentary value. Rousseau's vaunted sincerity was frequently interpreted as mere self-importance—after all, what other sort of importance could minute and trivial private details have?

This was the man whose vanity and presumption so imposed on his understanding, as to lead him to imagine that mankind would lend a ready ear to the most trifling, to the most dull, to the most impertinent, to the most disgusting relations, because they concerned ROUSSEAU![43]

By treating the claim to integrity as mere vanity, such remarks highlight a rupture in the reading strategies appropriate to confessional autobiography. Truth is still the basic standard of judgement, but it has divorced itself from utility, reaching for an autonomy which makes truth itself look egotistical. (A more sympathetic reviewer commented that 'a number of minute circumstances which appear uninteresting to the reader, are almost inseparable from a work, in which the author is his own hero'.[44]) The *Confessions* made purposeful or functional reading impossible. There could be no *reason* to know things which it alone was able to tell. If, as the rhetoric of sincerity implies, truthfulness is its own justification, that reason seems pertinent only to the individual author (compare the closed-circle self-interrogation of *Rousseau juge de Jean-Jacques*). Readers have no obvious way of making Rousseau's transparency matter to them. Even sympathetic sensibility, the readiest model for reading the *Confessions* in the late eighteenth and early nineteenth centuries, reaches a limit here, since Rousseau positively denies fellow feeling at the moments when he accuses himself of negligence and error.

The only recourse left is to appreciate singularity itself. As with Foster's metaphor of the 'moral museum', the truth about an individual person might be interpreted as a proper object of interest (something more studious and analytical than simple gossipy curiosity). Wollstonecraft's review uses this approach to bypass the problem of autobiographical sincerity and restore a standard of utility:

Without considering whether Rousseau was right or wrong, in thus exposing his weaknesses, and showing himself just as he was . . . it is only necessary to observe, that a description of what has passed in a human mind must ever be useful.[45]

Henry Maty is thinking along the same lines when he admits, despite his obvious distaste for the *Confessions*, that it supplies 'some food for the Moralist'.[46] This approach follows Rousseau's lead by indicating that

---

[43] *Monthly Review*, lxix. 150.   [44] Ibid. NS ii. 571.
[45] *Analytical Review*, vi. 386.   [46] *New Review*, i. 374.

truth has an inherent significance distinct from its details. Knowledge is itself valuable—a position we should expect to find in the pages of the *Analytical*, published by Joseph Johnson and closely associated with the radical rationalism theorized in Godwin's *Enquiry*. Enlightened readers might find in Rousseau's autobiography materials for studying the operations of the passions, the connections between early habits and their later consequences, the distinctive character of a man of 'genius', and other such clichés of Romantic-period psychology.

Nevertheless, Wollstonecraft's defensive tone—the work, she admits, has been 'treated with great contempt'[47]—suggests how hard it is to adopt this strategy in the case of the *Confessions*. Again, the question of uniqueness is what creates difficulties. If the individual is to be treated as a kind of case study, what are the prospects for instructive generalization? Rousseau's claim to singularity naturally denies that anyone else might be like him: 'I am not made like any one I have been acquainted with, perhaps like no one in existence; if not better, I at least claim originality'.[48] Glorying in eccentricity, his narrative continually frustrates a reading which searches for laws of human nature. The narrative keeps returning to feelings and situations which are interesting (to the author) precisely because they are inexplicable. Erotics and paranoia—the two major psychological themes of the *Confessions*, respectively dominating the first and second parts—both powerfully challenge the idea of the text as an instructive case study, because they both rest on the impenetrable opacity of fundamental causes. They show the self in fascinated or bewildered conflict with itself. Rousseau does not know why he responds to certain sexual situations as he does, just as he cannot account for the 'abyss of evil' constructed by his enemies. In fact, the language he uses to describe the conspiracy he thinks is directed against him might also refer to sexual excitement (given his confessed pleasure in being spanked): 'I feel the blows reach me, without perceiving the hand by which they are directed, or the means it employs.'[49] Things happen indirectly, inexplicably. For all its professed sincerity, then, the narrative cannot be transparent to itself. It can record experience in exhaustively minute detail, but always with a sense that what matters about those experiences—what constitutes the uniqueness of the subject—is the way that no generalizing synopsis can account for them. Rousseau says he wants to leave

---

[47] *Analytical Review*, vi. 385.

[48] Rousseau, *Confessions: Part the First*, i. 1.

[49] Jean-Jacques Rousseau, *The Confessions of J. J. Rousseau, Citizen of Geneva: Part the Second*, 3 vols. (London, G. G. J. and J. Robinson, 1790), ii. 248.

such judgements to the reader: by faithfully recording the particulars of his history, someone like Wollstonecraft 'may form a judgment of the principles that produced them'.[50] Some contemporaries could take this as an invitation to a model reading of autobiography. Yet the particular, singular history recorded in this case obscures any such 'principles'— hence the vocabulary of astonishment pervading contemporary responses. The principles, the causes, the directing hand—these are hidden by Rousseau's transparency.

Another possible response to the singularity of the *Confessions'* subject is sheer interest or pleasure. As we saw in Chapter 1, this aspect of reading autobiography is closely woven into the emergent awareness of the genre, always accompanied by a degree of anxiety. Rousseau exposed the temptations of voyeurism very clearly. Too clearly, in fact: no commentators openly admitted to enjoying the intimacy his book permitted. (One might argue that transparent self-exposure defeats the pleasure of voyeurism, which depends on a prurient interplay between the desire and the difficulty of access.) Complaints about the tediously close-grained record of Rousseau's private life turn up far more frequently than satisfaction at being allowed an unprecedentedly close view of an individual life. In a more subtle sense, though, the *Confessions* did seem to invite a reading based on entertainment (in the classical formula, the counterpart to Wollstonecraft's appeal to utility). According to the aesthetics of sensibility, Rousseau's passionate sincerity could free itself completely from the notion of truth, and appear instead as the highest pitch of expressiveness. This implies an almost theatrical approach to autobiographical self-representation: its value depends on the quality of the performance, which in Rousseau's case was admitted to be matchless by all but the most sternly moralistic or intransigently polemical commentators. The resulting pleasure is never purely aesthetic, of course. Rousseau's rhetorical intensity—his 'burning periods'—is described as 'the effusions of a warm heart', and the proper reaction is therefore a similarly spontaneous agitation of the feelings.[51] His sincerity may not be useful but (from this perspective) it does at least call forth a sympathetic response, which becomes sufficient justification for the reading experience.

[50] Rousseau, *Confessions: Part the First*, i. 317.

[51] D'Israeli, *Miscellanies*, 103; *Analytical Review*, vi. 385. The conventions of reading practice in the literature of sensibility are well described in Janet Todd, *Sensibility: An Introduction* (London: Methuen, 1986). For a study more specific to the immediate context of the *Confessions*, see C. B. Jones, *Radical Sensibility* (London: Routledge, 1993).

However, Rousseau's self-proclaimed singularity compromises this approach as well, because the passions inhabiting his narrative tend not to invite reciprocation. He often describes his sensibility as a contradictory, anarchic impulse, appealing to the reader's laughter more than his or her sympathy. His passions are disproportionate: he speaks of 'the excess to which my heart is subject to be heated by the most trifling incidents'.[52] He sees himself as the victim of a tendency which carries 'sensibility to extravagance'.[53] Sensibility's value is thus ambivalent at best: 'A sentiment takes possession of my soul with the rapidity of lightning, but instead of illuminating, it dazzles and confounds me.'[54] In all sorts of ways the *Confessions* challenges an unequivocally enthusiastic reading of its effusiveness. For one thing, it foregrounds the erotics of the body which impassioned writing more conventionally sublimates.[55] Readers are allowed to see how the language of feeling serves the practice of sex; this threatens to turn a sympathetically responsive reading back into uncomfortable voyeurism. More disturbingly, the warmth of Rousseau's heart as represented in sentimental episodes sits uneasily with his offhand treatment of the domestic sphere. His pragmatic treatment of Thérèse in the *Confessions*, and still more his decision to abandon their children, demonstrate the limits of sensibility at the very point where it would conventionally carry the greatest charge. Contradictions like these prevent the work from being read in terms of a reciprocal exchange of feeling between author and reader based on sympathetic identification (a reading very widely adopted in the case of *Julie*, as Robert Darnton's essay shows).[56] Those wishing to celebrate the sheer expressiveness of the performance had to deal with finding themselves watching it from the point of view of astonished observers rather than friendly collaborators. Such considerations may well account for the fact that very few British contemporaries were willing (in print at least) to give the *Confessions* credit for the eloquence of its language of feeling. Sincerity ends up interfering with sensibility by intruding the ambivalent character of the autobiographical subject into his expressive voice. Without this interference readers might have read the work as they read *Julie*, enraptured by second-hand passion. Instead, they always risked being betrayed into the position of a reluctant witness to the eccentricity of a singular figure.

---

[52] Rousseau, *Confessions: Part the First*, i. 183.
[53] Ibid. i. 137.   [54] Ibid. i. 206.
[55] Duffy observes that after the *Confessions* 'even the English Left often felt forced to look on the celebrated Rousseauean sensibility as something more candidly called sensuality' (Duffy, *Rousseau in England*, 49).
[56] Darnton, *The Great Cat Massacre*, ch. 6.

Since utility and entertainment are equally unable to account for the experience of reading the work, something has to take their place. The August 1813 *Monthly*'s word for it is 'fascination'. Individual critics' and readers' reactions were of course as various as that huge readership itself, but the total picture—the environment in which 'autobiography' emerges—presents an oscillation between approach and withdrawal, interest and disgust, which governs the pervasive and continuing reference to the *Confessions*' strangeness. To be fascinated is, as the writer in the *Monthly* implies, to experience attachment and horror at the same time.[57] Attraction and repulsion become disturbingly mixed within one's own response (in today's cliché, like watching a car crash). Even Burke's splendidly abusive assault betrays a degree of fascination, defined as the inability to avert one's gaze; why else should an attack on the politics and principles of the National Assembly centre itself on the figure of Rousseau? The constitution of the Assembly, as well as its actions, horrify him so much that he claims scarcely to be able to observe them, even while his essay lingers on the subject. Rousseau, cast as 'the insane Socrates of the National Assembly', embodies this ghastly 'false and theatric' presence as much as he stands synecdochically for the false philosophy of revolutionary France.[58] The theatre of the *Confessions*, where vice is inexplicably paraded as virtue, shares a stage with the theatre of the Assembly, where hypocrisy and brutality call themselves patriotism; yet Burke is an enthralled spectator of both pantomimes. In less extreme versions, many different responses to Rousseau resolve themselves finally into some such mixed experience of reading.

Attraction and repulsion are not in themselves problematic ways of encountering the autobiographical subject. In fact, they can be understood easily enough as equivalents in the field of reading to two quite conventional—even foundational—conceptions of life-writing: the individual as model and as counter-model. It was not just openly exemplary narratives like the spiritual autobiographies of the seventeenth and eighteenth centuries which invited this stance towards their subject. In all sorts of manifestations the idea of judging the life, and the principle 'go thou and do likewise/otherwise', were fundamental to biographical and autobiographical representations. Rousseau confronts these assumptions with typical gusto, inviting every reader in the world to gather at the seat of ultimate judgement, and then turning their stance against them and daring them to come to a conclusion:

[57] See *OED* s.v. 'fascinate', 2b.   [58] Burke, *Letter*, 34, 36.

Power eternal! assemble round thy throne the innumerable throng of my fellow-mortals, let them listen to my Confessions, let them blush at my depravity, let them tremble at my sufferings; let each in turn expose with equal sincerity the failings, the wanderings of his heart, and, if he dare, aver, *I was better than that man*.[59]

By referring to his 'Confessions', Rousseau invokes the most judgemental version of the autobiographical act, in which the narrative of the self is dedicated to exposing its errors in order to receive authoritative absolution. In this scheme the confessor (the recipient of the narrative, that is) need not be 'fascinated' by the confession, because he is empowered to interpret the act of self-exposure sacramentally, as the beginning of a sufficient expiation for any sins disclosed. Rousseau's book privatizes, and so secularizes, this response. Every reader is personally invited to weigh his or her own 'failings' against Rousseau's. Like so many invitations to the reader in the *Confessions*, though, this one is double-edged. It appears to revert to a relatively straightforward solution to the issue of how to read this text. The singular self is there as a moral benchmark. If not exactly a model (or counter-model), it does allow readers to reflect on their own moral nature, making them wonder how confidently they will approach the throne of 'Power eternal'. In this light, the absolute distinctiveness and originality it claims and the reactions of sympathy or revulsion to the particular episodes it narrates can both be interpreted according to the conventional scheme. One cannot be entirely like (or by extension entirely unlike) Rousseau, but one can take his story as a prompt to consider whether one wishes to be more or less like him at particular moments. This, however, is as far as those mixed feelings of attraction and repulsion can be rehabilitated as elements of a familiar approach to life-writing. It is an extremely limited compensation. The real weight of the passage just quoted falls on the challenge to all those 'fellow-mortals'. Ultimately, it is not a challenge to decide whether they are better or worse than Rousseau, but a challenge to speak at all; the clear rhetorical implication is that no one will dare respond. This is indeed what happens in the extraordinary coda to the *Confessions*, the brief last paragraph of book XII which follows the end of the narrative proper (it refers to Rousseau's marathon readings of his manuscript given in the Paris salons in 1771):

---

[59] Rousseau, *Confessions: Part the First*, i. 2. The passage provoked many accusations of blasphemy from contemporary reviewers.

Thus I concluded, and every person was silent, Madame d'Egmont was the only person who seemed affected: she visibly trembled, but soon recovered herself, and was silent like the rest of the company. Such were the fruits of my reading and declaration.[60]

Muteness here might be interpreted as astonishment or outrage or an excess of sympathetic passion: the point is that silence prevents such choices from being explicit. Unlike the confessor, formally obligated to respond by imposing penance and granting absolution, those sitting in judgement on Rousseau find their authority disabled. All they have is a private reaction to an individual who can be read as neither model nor counter-model: he is just *there*, his text communicating the singular fact of his identity apparently unencumbered by any scheme of judgement. Attraction and repulsion have a strangely intimate air, as if reading the *Confessions* were a personal encounter (or, more worryingly, a vaguely sexual one), where moral evaluation of the work is no longer relevant.

All this suggests that the root of the *Confessions'* strangeness lies in an unaccountable convergence of intimacy with publication. When reviewers and commentators blustered that the book should never have seen the light of print, they were not just taking offence at the intrusion into public notice of sordid details of private life. More essentially, they revealed the disturbance caused by the circulation of privacy itself, an individuality whose appearance in print could not be explained with any reference to its public function or place. 'If poor Rousseau had satisfied himself with *auricular confession*', the *Monthly* remarked, 'he would have done much better'; publishing the autobiographical act is the real disaster.[61] (For Burke also, the height of insanity is his decision to 'publish'.[62]) Since he loudly declares his difference from everyone else in his opening paragraphs, Rousseau's relation to the public sphere is by nature one of opposition, of separation (this is explicitly thematized in the *Reveries of a Solitary Walker*, which were published with the first part of the *Confessions* in 1782–3). Yet, by virtue of the book's distribution, the relationship is simultaneously one of all but universal 'fascination'. Rousseau's self-proclaimed uniqueness circulates, replicates itself in translations and new editions, and indeed for all its inimitability ends up looking like the originating moment of a new literary habit. If so, however, it is not because of the *Confessions'* emphasis on a new degree

[60] Rousseau, *Confessions: Part the Second*, ii. 397.
[61] *Monthly Review*, lxvii. 233.
[62] Burke, *Letter*, 34.

of intimacy or privacy. What makes the book such a force in the construction of 'Romantic autobiography' is the availability of that privacy for public consumption, and nothing but consumption. The result is a prominent and unsettling overlap of public and private spheres, or a reconfigured relationship between them, in the literary field. 'Autobiography' (as a Romantic-period term) is to a large extent a name for that reconfiguration.[63]

Far more than any other late eighteenth-century document, the *Confessions* makes readers notice that the moment of publication is the key to the problem of autobiography, and therefore effectively the defining feature of 'genre'. The book confronts the public with autobiographical writing in all its raw fascination, independent of prescriptive or theoretical models. Prescriptivism contains and delimits; the *Confessions* is habitually about excess and the rupturing of boundaries. In the contemporary commentary the favourite trope for this aspect of autobiographical writing is unveiling or disrobing. Here again Rousseau is exemplary, thanks to the persistently erotic tenor of his narrative. There is a great deal of undressing in the *Confessions*, literal and figurative (needless to say, reviewers loved to focus their outrage on these passages). Most of the erotic encounters in the narrative are enacted obliquely, in the tantalizing way Rousseau confesses he enjoys; so these episodes, however risqué, were partially veiled by the (admittedly semitransparent) 'gauze' of 'a certain decency of phrase'.[64] Nevertheless, the veil is there to be removed. No readers felt themselves screened from the frank sensuality clothed by the language of sensibility or romance. These erotic episodes, though, are symptoms of a more pervasive exposure which is autobiographical not sexual. As the *Monthly*'s review of the 1783 translation notes, Rousseau's disrobing is a moral and intellectual habit. He

observed no measure with the world when he broke through its shackles . . . he scorned accommodation with fashion; and instead of taking off unnecessary appendages with coolness and decorum, he rent the garment in sunder, and tore it into rags, in order to get rid of the whole at once.[65]

---

[63] Marcus observes that anxieties about autobiography are closely related to anxieties about contact between the self and the world, 'with the boundaries between "inner" and "outer", "private" and "public", becoming the sites of greatest concern' (Marcus, *Auto/biographical Discourses*, 15).

[64] *Monthly Review*, lxvi. 533.

[65] Ibid. lxix. 149.

Publication—becoming public—here ceases to be modelled on any form of social behaviour (the more ordinary template for how to exist in the public domain). Instead, it is a crazily incongruous transgression of the borders between self and world: not just washing one's dirty linen in public but removing it in public as well. This, I suggest, is the true 'fascination' attached to the *Confessions*. Ordinarily, both attraction and repulsion are moderated by screens between the viewer and the object. What makes the mixing of the opposed responses so acute in this case is the apparent absence of those screens. Rousseau makes readers unprecedentedly aware of their discomfort at the prospect of torn and discarded garments, a discomfort which tends to present itself as disgust, or perhaps as mingled interest and condemnation, but which is most characteristically manifested in the sheer sense of strangeness.

Highly charged metaphors of unveiling appear often enough in Romantic-period writing on autobiography to indicate that Rousseau's nakedness seemed alarmingly typical. An openly Rousseauan effort like Hazlitt's weakly anonymous *Liber Amoris* (1823) produced very much the kind of reactions the *Confessions* had caused: 'what a veil is here rent away!'.[66] Its reviews were more political even than Rousseau's, deploying admiration of or disgust at the autobiographical act in the service of partisan critique of Hazlitt's public character. Still, the torn veil was their starting point: Hazlitt's embarrassing infatuation, as told in the brief narrative, is no more significantly grotesque than the fact that he has made its details public. For John Wilson, also writing in *Blackwood's*, 'tearing away that shroud' which ordinarily interposes itself between public and private spheres is an act ruinous enough to damn even Coleridge's *Biographia Literaria* (1817), a less than racy autobiographical performance by any standard.[67] Less polemical observers might not go so far in their censure, but would still agree that autobiography disturbed a balance which those shrouds and veils existed to preserve. The great risk run by all life-writing, says an essayist in the *Edinburgh Magazine* in 1824, is the danger of

forgetting that there are attitudes and positions in which we may allow ourselves to appear before a very intimate friend, at the moment when restraint is banished ... but which a sense of decorum would paint as an indecent exposure, should we be thus seen by the public.[68]

[66] *Blackwood's*, xiii. 645.
[67] Ibid. ii. 3.
[68] *Edinburgh Magazine*, xv. 154.

So even a figure as magisterial as Goethe is lowered by the publication of autobiographical material: 'He strips himself stark-naked, and empties his pockets inside out into the bargain.'[69] Foster's *Essays* call on an icon of 'indecent exposure', making an analogy between these apparently shameless autobiographers and 'the Lady Godiva'.[70] In fact, the parade of exposure might be the only distinguishing mark of such writing, uniting sexual profligates like Hazlitt and Rousseau with an eminently respectable memoirist like Edward Gibbon—whose posthumous autobiography exhibits him in a 'state of simplicity and nakedness', according to the *Monthly*.[71] Across the range of autobiographical writing, from elaborate narratives to casual and ephemeral publications, a response like Foster's is always not only possible but likely. Whatever sense of genre there might be is thus founded on a fascinating disturbance in the way reading happens. Nothing seems as characteristic of autobiography to contemporaries as the threat (or promise) of unveiling, whether or not it is carried through in any specific publication.

Rousseau was not the first to provoke these anxieties but his book certainly brought them to prominence and intensified their ambivalence. After the *Confessions* the world of letters contained a permanent association between autobiographical acts and the set of concerns the book so consistently raised. Indeed, Dennis Porter has argued that Rousseau was singly responsible for intruding privacy into the literary public sphere in a new and enduring way, thoroughly 'establishing a new and more intimate relationship with the work's reader'.[72] Returning to Jauss's term, then, the notion of a 'horizon of expectation' gains a double significance. As I have already argued, the *Confessions* straddles this horizon, extending it and (in the same process) making it visible as a prescriptive limit. The work thereby mobilizes the forces which begin to define 'autobiography' in the Romantic literary environment. At the same time, though, the *Confessions* repeats at a basic thematic level this same pattern of transgressing and so reinforcing a limit. Rousseau also straddles the horizon of privacy, removing a veiling barrier in front of his readers and so making them acutely conscious of the line that he has so

[69] *Edinburgh Review*, xxvi. 314.

[70] Foster, *Essays*, i. 118.

[71] *Monthly Review*, NS xx. 79.

[72] Dennis Porter, *Rousseau's Legacy* (New York: Oxford University Press, 1995), 32. Porter's interesting discussion is not centred on the *Confessions*, though it certainly could have been. He wants to show that 'Rousseau's combined sociopolitical and autobiographical project' (p. 69) reaches well beyond issues of self-representation, and influences far more than just the history of autobiography (see ch. 1).

energetically breached. In other words, the *Confessions* systematically performs the transgressive gesture which is the condition of autobiography's emergence as something like a genre. It is not a question of the book's direct influence on other autobiographies, or of his originality or primacy in one branch of literary history. Rousseau's book is fundamental to Romantic-period autobiographical writing because, in exposing itself, it exposes the place which appeared to be allotted to the practice, and reveals the unsteadiness of that situation. The 'fascination' of the *Confessions* is also the fascination of autobiography in general, the fascination which defines how autobiography comes to be.

3

Autobiography and the literary public sphere

So far we have been tracing the 'rise' of autobiography, the features of Carlyle's 'Autobiographical times', via a historical rather than formal understanding of genre; not, that is, as the literary mode corresponding to expressive Romantic individualism, but in terms of a field forming among the general circulation and consumption of texts. Two aspects of the story stand out. First, the fact that 'autobiography' belongs to the arena of reading as well as writing, emerging in the form of prescription as well as inscription, its 'conditions and limits'—Gusdorf's seminal phrase—set by reviewers and commentators as well as autobiographers.[1] Second, the endemic instability of its boundaries, which seems to make every recognition of autobiography an anxious one and every judgement of it as ambivalent as Foster's of Rousseau. These two points need stressing before we turn to look more closely at the criteria used in the period to think about autobiographical writing. Otherwise, one might be tempted to treat those criteria as if they were definitions: as if the terms used to discuss the emergent genre—terms like veracity, impartiality, public interest or eminence, historical value, and so on—told us what autobiography was, or is. Alternatively, one might isolate the autobiographical documents themselves from the confused babble of surrounding discourses, assuming that 'Romantic autobiography' equals Rousseau and Equiano and Mary Robinson and Wordsworth and De Quincey, without reference to the disputed and often trivial- or banal-looking reactions they generated in the world of letters. The former of these mistakes is to lend too much authority to contemporary commentators' voices, the latter to lend them too little. Autobiographical texts

[1] Georges Gusdorf, 'Conditions and Limits of Autobiography', in James Olney (ed.), *Autobiography: Essays Theoretical and Critical* (Princeton, NJ: Princeton University Press, 1980), 28–48.

were always in dialogue with the criteria by which they were read, often explicit dialogue (Rousseau's direct address to the reader is much more nearly the rule than the exception); but those criteria were never a priori standards, though they often wished they were, nor were they consistent or even certain of themselves.

What were they, though? When prescriptive attitudes closed ranks to protect the good order of the literary public sphere, how did they typically present their claims? Marcus summarizes early nineteenth-century anxieties as the 'fear of public transgression, symbolized by an extension of the autobiographical franchise and of the debasement of the literary coinage'.[2] The genre, that is, signifies a levelling of identity and a democratizing of authorship.[3] Among the guardians of the developing institution of 'literature' the idea of autobiography certainly provokes this sort of reaction. That institution does, after all, partially found itself on the possibility of distinguishing between what would eventually be called 'high' and 'low' (or 'mass') culture; and a genre like autobiography, with suspiciously sensationalist popular appeal and theoretically open to writers who were in no other sense authors, would be placed below the dividing line (De Quincey's *Confessions*, notes the *Monthly Review*, has 'met with a degree of attention and applause that is seldom accorded to auto-biographies').[4] It is a different matter, though, to ask how Romantic-period commentators react when confronted by actual autobiographical practice. Marcus again rightly observes that a feature of the critical discourse at the time is its habit of contrasting the actual state of autobiography with its ideal conditions, always of course to the disadvantage of the former: compare Busk's reference to the long-lost 'brilliant condition' of the genre, or Foster's horror when he turns his critical gaze to the publications mushrooming up around him.[5] Nevertheless, my aim is to read the discourse of autobiography in close relation to its practice, since thinking about genre means thinking about its ideal and actual versions together ('autobiography' being both a concept and a set of texts). This means closing the gap between the two, however insistent contemporaries were on preserving it as a shield. Otherwise, we are left

---

[2] Marcus, *Auto/biographical Discourses*, 38.

[3] Nussbaum's work on eighteenth-century autobiographical writing, though much less interested in the literary public sphere, and critical of the universalizing assumptions behind the formation of the autobiographical subject, reaches similar conclusions: autobiography rests on an 'ideology of the individual as an instance of human nature' (Nussbaum, *The Autobiographical Subject*, 56).

[4] *Monthly Review*, NS c. 289.

[5] Marcus, *Auto/biographical Discourses*, 17; *Blackwood's*, xxvi. 738; Foster, *Essays*, i. 117.

with a set of purely ideal terms which will not easily be accommodated to the process of reading autobiographical texts (Marcus's book is a study of writing about autobiography, not autobiographical writing). As is suggested by the response to Rousseau's *Confessions*, appeals to the ideal state of the genre are often prompted not just by the 'fear of public transgression' but by a sense of a specific transgressive moment: theory is subsequent, not antecedent, to the offensive act (text). Moreover, the riskiness of autobiographical writing is as likely to produce 'fascination' as it is to prompt a retreat into prescriptive theorizing. However alarming the genre's proliferation looked, the books still exerted a widespread attraction, and not only on those who could be presumed not to know any better. In this chapter I will sketch out the challenges attendant on autobiography as they appeared in relation to those autobiographical acts. In the most straightforward terms the question is: What exactly did people object to? By preserving a close relation between critical criteria and actual texts we will get a better sense of the place of autobiography in the literary public sphere, because the conversations and disputes which constitute that sphere can be heard at their loudest, rather than from the relative distance created by the more reflective stance of theorizing commentators like Johnson, D'Israeli, or Foster.

For this reason, most of the evidence offered here is drawn from review periodicals. In many ways this is an unrepresentative and perhaps misleading sample. The journals had their own agendas, and of course they institutionalized certain conceptions of what counted as 'literature', filtering out all but a tiny fraction of autobiographical writing (in defiance of the genre's evident popularity). Furthermore, however fiercely they differed with each other politically, they shared some fundamental interests. Their proprietors, contributors, and readers were largely educated middle-class men; and even if many were not, the public sphere they mediated was one that absorbed differences of interest into a broad uniformity very like the rational, respectable, polite, bourgeois, 'classical' public sphere described by Habermas.[6] Subsequent historians have pointed out that Habermas's account of the late eighteenth-/early nineteenth-century public sphere as a space defined by enlightened, moderately progressive, rational critical intersubjectivity represents only one aspect of the contentious publics of the period, and perhaps a hegemonic

[6] Jürgen Habermas, *The Structural Transformation of the Public Sphere*, trans. Thomas Burger with the assistance of Frederick Lawrence (Cambridge, Mass.: MIT Press, 1989), 27–43.

one at that. Even if one is thinking only of literary public spheres—the arenas of textual publication and circulation—the model Habermas proposes was, as Jon Klancher says, more a representation than a reality.[7] By drawing on reviews of autobiographical writing from the *Monthly Review*, the *British Critic*, or the *Edinburgh Review*, one is restricting oneself to a set of criteria that may well be specific to a narrow (though disproportionately influential) social and cultural stratum. This is a pertinent consideration since, as I will shortly argue, readings of autobiography invoke the decorums of middle-class, gentlemanly social intercourse. There is a risk of losing sight of other reading and writing practices which manifested different attitudes to the genre: Low Church or Dissenting religious publics, scientific and other professional publics, the 'counter-public spheres' of women readers or radicalism, and so on.[8] As noted in Chapter 1, one of the features which struck contemporaries most strongly was the insinuating breadth of autobiography's popularity. It called attention to the existence of the threateningly amorphous and democratically constituted 'reading public' over which the spokesmen of the institution of literature poured so much contempt.

It is very difficult, though, to recover those wider readerships' responses to and prescriptions for autobiography. Only in the major review periodicals can we see the genre being read and written about with any consistency, and they are thus the best available window on to the encounter between the world of letters and specific autobiographical acts, despite all the factors limiting the way they imagined such texts being read. Furthermore, it would be unhelpful to try and provide a full survey of all forms of autobiographical reading and writing in the period. The genre that occupies us here is the one that could be imagined to include *Biographia Literaria* or the essays of Elia or *Childe Harold*: a catholic enough embrace, but recognizably restricted to the field of 'literature'. Correspondingly, the literary public sphere within and around which such a genre formed is the one which included Coleridge (semi-professional man of letters, the son of a country priest), Lamb

---

[7] See Jon Klancher, *The Making of English Reading Audiences, 1790–1832* (Madison, Wis.: University of Wisconsin Press, 1987), 18–26.

[8] The term developed among critical reactions to Habermas's work: see especially Rita Felski, *Beyond Feminist Aesthetics* (Cambridge, Mass.: Harvard University Press, 1989) and Oskar Negt and Alexander Kluge, *Public Sphere and Experience*, trans. Peter Labanyi, Jamie Owen Daniel, and Assenka Oksiloff (Minneapolis, Minn.: University of Minnesota Press, 1993). In a printed response to a series of papers on Romanticism and its publics Orrin Wang makes an interesting case for retaining Habermas's model (Wang, 'Romancing the Counter-Public Sphere', *Studies in Romanticism*, 33 (1994), 579–88).

(India House drudge, son of a scrivener), and his Lordship. Without doubt, the primary forum of that sphere was the review periodicals, which advertised publications, defined readerships, and employed authors; which created the space in which 'literature' was created, circulated, and discussed. Their concerns about autobiography are very close to the anxieties displayed within many autobiographical texts themselves, as we will see in Chapter 4. This fact implies that the interrelations and exchanges between inscription (texts) and prescription (commentaries) which shape the emergent genre are at their most intimate in the major monthlies and quarterlies. Carlyle's 1834 reference to living in 'Autobiographical times' comes from a view of the literary field which was almost entirely supplied for him by those periodicals. The accumulating mass of autobiographical ephemera would never have made its way to the farm in rural Dumfriesshire where he had been living for the previous six years; it was his regular access to the *Edinburgh* and the *Quarterly* that allowed him to scan the features of the world of letters and characterize the spirit of the age. However distorted such a perspective was, it defined the arena of literary production and reception more effectively, and perhaps also more widely, than any other.

Throughout the period between Rousseau's *Confessions* and the comment in *Sartor Resartus* one word appears far more prominently and persistently in relation to autobiography than any other: egotism. Here one can be completely confident that the review periodicals reflect the literary environment as a whole, for accusations (or at least mentions) of egotism appear everywhere, attached to autobiographical writing like its shadow. Any volume sullied with the mark of self-writing is liable to be reviewed this way. James Lackington's popular *Memoirs* (1791), although hardly Rousseauan in their self-absorption, maintain a fairly consistent focus on the history and opinions of the author, so it is no surprise to find the *Monthly Review* referring to the writer of 'a volume wholly written about himself and his own affairs' as 'a sly egotist'.[9] It is more disconcerting to see the miscellany of *Biographia Literaria* described in *Blackwood's* as being 'all about [Coleridge] himself and other Incomprehensibilities', and therefore 'poisoned by inveterate and diseased egotism'.[10] The proliferation of such publications in the early decades of the nineteenth century clearly did nothing to accommodate

---

[9] *Monthly Review*, NS vii. 208.
[10] *Blackwood's*, ii. 9, 5. The *Edinburgh* agreed, accusing Coleridge of 'indulging his maudlin egotism' (*Edinburgh Review*, xxviii. 515).

most reviewers to this aspect of the genre. Charges of egotism are as much a reflex in the 1820s as in the 1790s. Nor is it only spokesmen for the proper conduct of the literary public sphere who use the word. The strength of its hold over the domain of autobiography is best illustrated by the way many autobiographers themselves acknowledge—defiantly or apologetically—the egotism of their enterprise. Their own gauge of the literary world's habitual attitudes is likely to be more accurate than any retrospective view, and perhaps also less partial than the reviews, since they have in most cases no institutional investment in the propriety of that sphere; they are concerned simply with how they expect to be read, not how they ought to be (or, at least, the latter concern is always contingent on the former). As the introductory chapter to *The Life, Adventures, Pedestrian Excursions, and Singular Opinions of J. H. Prince* observes, they expect the charge of egotism as a matter of course:

It has also been objected, that the narrator of his own life must necessarily be guilty of so much egotism as to make his work preposterously ridiculous, and insufferably disgusting.[11]

Guilt is not just attached to worries about publication and reception. Egotism is so intimately associated with autobiography that it can just as easily seem to inhere in the act of writing. Sounding curiously like one of the caricatures of false modesty in a Jane Austen novel, Richard Cumberland writes: 'I am sure I never took delight in egotism, and now behold! I am self-devoted to little else.'[12] The novelist John Galt forces himself to compromise with his self-disgust: 'Egotism is at all times an odious habit', his preface admits, and he adds that 'It is certainly not a very gentlemanly occupation to write one's own life.'[13] So pervasive is the term that in the *Monthly*'s notice of Cumberland's *Memoirs* it effectively becomes a label for the genre. Commenting more generally on the practice of self-writing, the reviewer refers to the figure of 'the egotistic biographer', meaning what we would call an autobiographer.[14] It is as if the recently coined word could have incorporated Latin *ego* (I) as comfortably as Greek *autos* (self), the genre (or subgenre of biography) being as well defined by the sign of the first-person pronoun as by reflexivity or self-reference.

[11] J. H. Prince, *The Life, Adventures, Pedestrian Excursions, and Singular Opinions of J. H. Prince* (London, 1807), 22.

[12] Richard Cumberland, *Memoirs of Richard Cumberland* (London: Lackington, Allen, 1806), 21.

[13] John Galt, *The Autobiography of John Galt*, 2 vols. (London: Cochrane & McCrone, 1833), vol. i. pp. ix, 1.

[14] *Monthly Review*, NS l. 226.

'Egotism' indicates that the pronoun itself is at stake. The word has come to denote a quality of character; its meanings currently lie in the domain of psychology or personality. In the Romantic period, though, that aspect of autobiographical writing was labelled 'vanity' (the second most frequent term found in the reviews), a judgement directed specifically at the character of an author and referring to the habit of 'obtruding their own merits on their readers' which a notice of De Quincey's *Confessions* calls the 'besetting sin of those who write or tell their own tales'.[15] Referring to a 'sin' indicates a moral failing, exactly as reviewers of Rousseau tended to diagnose the *Confessions*' self-exposure as a flaw in its author's moral constitution. 'Egotism', however, is a significantly different problem. It is to do with grammar, and therefore with writing, not psychology; it is a problem about the circulation of texts/selves in the public sphere. The word denotes an excessive use of the pronoun 'I' itself. In fact, it need not imply excess: it can simply be a neutral, descriptive term for the act of saying or writing 'I', though never without at least a nimbus of hazy disapproval. One autobiographer, for example, distinguishes egotism proper, 'the frequent and natural use of a pronoun, which consists of one poor letter', from 'any arrogance or presumption in writing'; the accusation he fears is not egotism itself, the 'natural'. vocabulary of self-writing, but the more personal charge of 'a *propensity to egotism*' (emphasis added).[16] Prince's introduction claims an impeccable authority for autobiographical vocabulary, St Paul, who (he says) 'used as much egotism as any man'—citing an epistle where 'the pronouns I and me [are] used no less than eight times in one verse'.[17] For a hostile reviewer of the first volume of Hazlitt's *Table Talk* it was enough to note 'an expense of the capital *I*, enough to exhaust the stock of the first printer in London'.[18]

The prominence of the word 'I' itself is therefore at the root of this most ubiquitous autobiographical anxiety. A review of the *Biographia* in the weekly *Literary Gazette* praises William Beloe's ramblingly anecdotal memoir *The Sexagenarian* of the same year (1817) for evading the issue by adopting 'the unchallenging third person', unlike 'the bolder I, chosen by Mr. Coleridge'.[19] That a simple grammatical evasion should

---

[15] *Monthly Censor*, ii. 356.
[16] Percival Stockdale, *The Memoirs of the Life, and Writings of Percival Stockdale*, 2 vols. (London: Longman, Hurst, Rees, and Orme, 1809), i. 4–5; ii. 1.
[17] Prince, *The Life*, 22, 23.   [18] *New Edinburgh Review*, i. 104.
[19] Donald H. Reiman (ed.), *The Romantics Reviewed*, 3 pts. (New York: Garland Publishing, 1972), pt. A, 592.

count as a successful strategy indicates how much concern egotism could generate. Self-writing becomes a technical challenge, given that the boldness of the 'I' is more likely to look barefaced than courageous. 'There is no doubt', a writer in the *Edinburgh* acknowledges, 'but that a person who writes his own life, must be allowed to put himself in the foreground.' Admitting the existence of a genre means allowing for its distinctive grammar. Nevertheless, the same review goes on, 'A great many devices and artifices must be resorted to, before the repetition of the hateful pronoun can be rendered at all tolerable to the reader.'[20] Whether it is the pronoun itself or the repetition that is 'hateful' is not altogether clear; the mere typographical presence of the word 'I' seems in this critique to signal a propensity for its overuse, as if any instance of self-writing is at some very literal level a sign of the disease of egotism in the modern sense. Hence the need for 'devices and artifices', techniques of writing allowing the text somehow to veil the inevitable insistence of the pronoun. This review dates from 1816, but its attitude is very much the same as Coleridge's in the preface to his 1796 Poems: 'With what anxiety every fashionable author avoids the word I!'[21] The fashion evidently did not change much over the two decades. If 'fashionable' can be taken to denote the mores of the literary public sphere in its Habermasian 'classic' aspect—the sphere of readers and writers of a broad middle class that was coming to think of itself as the 'public'— then Coleridge's remark confirms the link between egotism and autobiographical writing in that environment. Indeed, its vaguely radical veneer of insouciant indifference to the decrees of fashion is paper-thin. Coleridge's preface acknowledges that 'Compositions resembling those of the present volumes are not unfrequently condemned for their querulous egotism', but the existence of the defensive introductions refuting this charge is of course a mark of the 'anxiety' about writing 'I' which he wants to ridicule as mere modishness.[22] Even taking into account Coleridge's personal tendency towards apologetic and defensive glosses on his own work, the preface testifies to a pervasive, even normative, assumption that first-person writing is above all a problem of literary decorum. The printed 'I' is itself a point of contention; it is not just a metaphor for the presumed sin of authorial pride.

---

[20] *Edinburgh Review*, xxvi. 314 (a review of Goethe's *Dichtung und Wahrheit*).

[21] S. T. Coleridge, *Complete Poetical Works*, ed. E. H. Coleridge, 2 vols. (Oxford: Oxford University Press, 1912), ii. 1136.

[22] Ibid.

Frequently though vanity and egotism are linked, therefore, the reviews recognize (if only implicitly) a distinction between the moral culpability of vain self-centredness, which can always be mocked and condemned outright, and the risky practice of writing 'I', which ought to be controlled by 'devices and artifices'. Vanity is error. Egotism, the language of autobiography, is a matter of how the writing and written self presents itself to the community of readers. This is why a notice of Gilbert Wakefield's *Memoirs* (1792) in the *Analytical* calls it a 'figure in rhetoric'. The review begins, as so many do, with some general thoughts on the practice of what was just coming to be called autobiography:

THERE is certainly no figure in rhetoric so difficult to manage as that of egotism. So few people, either in speaking or writing, succeed in the use of it, that some critics have proscribed it altogether. 'I would allow no man, says lord Chesterfield, to speak of himself, unless in a court of justice.' But such a limitation as this would be too rigorous a restraint upon the natural propensity which every man has to talk of himself, and would deprive many of no small share of amusement in peeping into the bosoms of others. If by writing of himself a man can at once indulge his own feelings, and gratify his reader's curiosity, why should he not be at liberty to make himself the hero of his tale? For the same reason that the letters of eminent men, written without disguise from the present impulse, are always exceedingly interesting, a narrative of the principal occurrences in the life of an individual, drawn up by himself, is commonly read with eager attention.[23]

The paragraph slides easily from the technical rhetorical problem of egotism to the familiar intuition of a popular autobiographical genre. It is a version of the ambivalent response to Rousseau: on the one hand the literary public sphere is a place of 'curiosity', 'eager attention', and 'amusement', enthusiastically consuming self-writing, while on the other hand its protocols demand that the first person be managed in order to 'succeed'. In a pattern that we have already noticed in Foster and D'Israeli and which will crop up over and over again, egotism is welcomed and yet restrained. As the *Monthly Literary Register* commented in response to the second volume of Hazlitt's *Table Talk*, 'Egotism is amusing when managed with tact.' (The reviewer 'bluntly' advises Hazlitt to 'put out of his head a puerile emulation of his unfortunate model, Rousseau'.[24]) In theory at least, there is some way of accommodating the iteration of the 'hateful pronoun' to the demands of

---

[23] *Analytical Review*, xiii. 394. I am most grateful to Jennifer Koopman for drawing my attention to this review.
[24] *Monthly Literary Register*, ii. 66.

a public community, some correct management of the unavoidable rhetorical figure. The *Monthly*'s review of Wollstonecraft's 1796 *Letters Written During a Short Residence* puts it in terms of a subjugation of author to readership which mitigates the self-centredness of writing 'I': 'She claims the traveller's privilege of speaking frequently of herself, but she uses it in a manner which always interests her readers.'[25] As the *Analytical*'s remarks in the Wakefield review also show, it is a question of aligning egotism with the interests and uses—in Horatian terms, the requirements of amusement and instruction—proper to a public sphere. The critique of autobiographical writing, then, depends not so much on the genre's exposure of individual character as on the correctness (or otherwise) of its management of the relation between individual and public.

Egotism is, after all, originally the name of a social offence. The reviews are effectively imagining the literary public sphere as a room for conversation; intrusive repetition of the 'hateful pronoun' on the page is exactly analogous to individuals who break the decorum of conversation by obtruding themselves and their interests on the gathered community. The writer in the *Analytical* could be talking about 'either . . . speaking or writing' until he or she turns the discussion explicitly to printed genres; in the 1790s especially, before the expansion of print media finally gave writing the status of a clearly separate domain of activity, literate and conversational practices could seem very closely equivalent. One memoir reviewed in the *Edinburgh* is said to have 'an unfortunate resemblance to the conversation of a professed talker'.[26] The *Critical*'s less sympathetic review of Wakefield's *Memoirs* finds in them 'a degree of self-conceit as is wholly incompatible with that deference which we ought to have for men of different talents and opinions', implying an ideal of restrained, tolerant exchange apparently envisaged in a debating room or a salon as well as in print.[27] This equivalence again accords closely with the general model Habermas proposes in *The Structural Transformation of the Public Sphere*. Habermas argues that in the eighteenth century the quasi-conversational forum established in the world of letters represented the initial phase in the creation of a relatively open sphere where individual opinions could be freely exchanged and debated in such a way that its participants came to understand themselves as a 'public'.[28] The development of a reading public, that is, acts as a model

[25] *Monthly Review*, NS xx. 252.　　[26] *Edinburgh Review*, viii. 108–9.
[27] *Critical Review*, 2nd ser. vi. 38.　　[28] Habermas, *Structural Transformation*, 51–6.

for the rise of a civic public sphere. Habermas's argument is made with very broad strokes, but even if one dissents from his linear chronology and his interest in only one public sphere it is still important to recognize how the world of letters imagines itself as the mirror of rational, polite society. If Habermas's theory is in the end a partial fiction, it is nevertheless the same fiction as the one governing the major periodicals' sense of their critical standards, and determining writers like J. H. Prince's or Coleridge's worry over what was 'fashionable' and proper.

Via this conversational metaphor the charge of egotism links writing with decorum: autobiographies are texts that do not know how to behave in public. Reviewing the second part of *Poetry and Truth* (*Dichtung und Wahrheit*) in 1817 the *Edinburgh* sniffs that Goethe 'appears to us to be always deficient in literary good-breeding—in literary decorum'.[29] The last phrase is striking: more explicit than the *Analytical*'s reference to managing figures of rhetoric. Texts need more than technical management, according to the Goethe review: they need breeding, manners, propriety in the social sense. Here again (as in the case of Rousseau) autobiography's transgressiveness both marks a quality of the texts and defines the arena in which they were read. That is, the egotism of autobiography offends against 'literary decorum', but in doing so it helps define the parameters of the 'literary' by introducing an equation between circulating texts and polite social circles. A great deal of autobiographical writing is thus marginalized, written out of the equation: all texts whose concerns seem merely local—sectarian religious testimonies being the most obvious example—are ignored, because their interests never overlap with what the *Anti-Jacobin*'s remarks on Rousseau call 'the world'.[30] Unpublished diaries, public legal testimonies, instructive accounts meant for a small, specific readership, all such forms of self-writing fall out of the sphere of autobiography in the 'literary' sense. Their purposes and problems do not impinge on the generic idea of 'autobiography', because egotism is not a problem if a speaker has not been admitted into conversational circles in the first place. When Marcus writes of the threat of 'an extension of the autobiographical franchise', therefore, it should be noted that the sheer range of this expansion is not itself the decisive factor in making contemporary commentators uneasy. To take one example from a highly varied field, *The Life of Jonathan Martin* (published in Barnard Castle in 1826) at one level exemplifies Marcus's point. The author, brother to the painter John

[29] *Edinburgh Review*, xxviii. 86. [30] *Anti-Jacobin Review*, xxi. 476.

and the eccentric philosopher William Martin the 'Anti-Newtonian', had a career in no way qualifying him for inclusion in an elitist (or even meritocratic) world of letters. Minimally educated, he was pressed into the Navy in his early twenties, converted to Methodism, suffered from apocalyptic delusions, was confined at least twice for insanity, and eventually set fire to the roof of York Minster. His autobiography appears to have been quite popular, an instance of the broadened 'franchise' which in principle alarmed observers like Foster or J. H. Reynolds, whose article 'Fleet-Street Biography' in the *London Magazine* of April 1824 remarks that 'Every keeper of an apple-stall might unstore his "fruits of experience" . . . each sweeper at a crossing might give a trifle to the world'.[31] But if 'the world' was troubled by the idea of a levelling profusion of autobiography, in practice it simply ignored a book like Martin's. Because he is excluded from the conversational sphere of 'literary decorum', his eccentricity, assertiveness, and egotism never register as offences, however widely they might have circulated among other kinds of readers. It is only when a writer from the excluded classes adopts the formal manners of the literary public sphere that the issues surrounding autobiography come into play. Martin's *Life* is simply not 'public' in any sense that the self-policing institutions of the literary environment would have recognized. Other reading publics would of course look at it differently, but their concerns would be different also: consumers of prophetic literature or readers with a local knowledge of Martin's exploits would not care about the 'decorum' of the performance, nor probably would they be thinking about the state of autobiography as a genre.

Concerns over autobiography therefore occur in relation to fairly specific, fairly exclusive social and cultural practices—practices which are also constitutive of the literary field as it was constructed in the Romantic period (and, it bears repeating, it is the literary field which concerns us throughout this study). To return to the questions proposed at the start of this chapter, then, the basic criteria applied by prescriptive discourses must be understood primarily as social ones. The writing self is expected to conduct itself properly. To an extent (though, as I will shortly argue, a more limited extent than is often assumed to be the case) it is judged by its right to a place in the conversational gathering: Is the author the kind of person who deserves to be admitted and listened to? Egotism always begs for an excuse. If the 'I' is going to monopolize

---

[31] *London Magazine*, ix. 417. The phrase quoted alludes to the title of Joseph Brasbridge's autobiographical volume of 1824.

conversation, it has to be worth listening to, by virtue of possessing unusual knowledge which is in the public interest (as is the case with travel narratives, for example). Alternatively, it has to have a 'natural' (that is, culturally sanctioned) right to speak, derived from eminence or talent—in other words from being what D'Israeli's 'Observations' call a 'great genius'.[32] There are other admissible possibilities too. As long as authors stay within a proper and appropriate position, they are observing 'decorum'. Women writers, therefore, are admitted in so far as their self-writing is visibly determined by appropriate sociocultural roles. So Mary Robinson's *Memoirs*, posthumously published in 1801, keep well within the conventions of victimized female sensibility, and are correspondingly reviewed in the *Monthly*: 'We are not desirous of commenting upon instances of this kind: but when ladies write their own memoirs, we must perform our task with as much mildness and delicacy as possible.'[33]

The specific challenges of reading autobiographical writing by women have been a source of much debate. Since feminist scholars first began to point out that women were excluded from histories of canonical autobiography, and that women's experience was ignored in most theoretical definitions of the genre, the arguments have been complicated by a desire on the one hand to register the effects of sexual difference, while on the other to avoid falling into binary categorizations of 'male' and 'female' modes of self-writing. In her exemplary 1987 study of the issue Sidonie Smith rightly justified her attempt to sketch out a distinctive poetics of women's autobiography by pointing out that pre-twentieth-century women writers are inevitably aware of being read by men and compared with them: 'the autobiographer reveals in her speaking position and narrative structure her understanding of the possible readings she will receive from a public that has the power of her reputation in its hands'.[34] The problems begin when she elaborates this understanding in terms that are meant to specify an exclusively female position within a gendered literary public sphere:

Since the ideology of gender makes of woman's life a nonstory, a silent space, a gap in patriarchal culture, the ideal woman is self-effacing rather than self-promoting, and her 'natural' story shapes itself not around the public, heroic life, but around the fluid, circumstantial, contingent responsiveness to others that,

[32] D'Israeli, *Miscellanies*, 102.
[33] *Monthly Review*, NS xxxvi. 345.
[34] Sidonie Smith, *A Poetics of Women's Autobiography* (Bloomington, Ind.: Indiana University Press, 1987), 49.

according to patriarchal ideology, characterizes the life of woman but not auto-biography . . . From that point of view, she has no 'public' story to tell.[35]

As we have begun to see, this is simply not a situation which can be mapped on to a binary gender divide (Smith's more recent work indi-rectly acknowledges as much).[36] Writing by men as well as by women is subject to—and knows itself to be subject to—judgements about whether the story it recounts is properly 'public'; writing by men as well as by women can depict a life of circumstantial events and social rela-tions. In the last fifteen years or so a consensus has emerged that any categorical scheme will be reductive in the face of the heterogeneousness of autobiographical documents, or more simply (in Shari Benstock's words), 'Women's writings are as individual as women themselves'—and, one can therefore add, as men.[37] Linda Peterson's illuminating recent study has historicized the whole notion of women's autobiogra-phy. Noting that critical studies of such documents tend to 'have assumed that the experience of gender determines the form of a woman's life writing or at least that it motivates a woman writer to seek a separate autobiographical tradition', she discovers that this tradition appears as a distinctive feature of the early Victorian writing of literary history, inscribed within gendered critical discourses; and she demon-strates different texts' resistances to the overdetermined equation of autobiographical representations with gender positions.[38]

Questions of class may be treated the same way. As a category, it does not override the wider prescriptive considerations of autobiographical propriety. Stories of industrious self-improvement fit comfortably within the requirements of 'decorum', as long as they are presented with sufficient modesty. More challenging positions occupied by working-class autobiographers can also enter the literary public sphere, as long as the challenge is presented in something approximating the correct language. The West African ex-slave Olaudah Equiano models himself in his autobiography as a pious and diligent citizen, and so is easily admit-ted into the conversational exchange by 'passing' as a white middle-class

[35] Smith, *A Poetics of Women's Autobiography*, 50.

[36] A more nuanced account, based on the idea that gender as well as autobiography is a performative act (not a fixed state), is outlined in Sidonie Smith, 'Performativity, Autobiographical Practice, Resistance', *A/B: Auto/Biography Studies*, 10 (1995), 17–33.

[37] Shari Benstock (ed.), *The Private Self: Theory and Practice of Women's Autobiographical Writings* (London: Routledge, 1988), 4.

[38] Linda H. Peterson, *Traditions of Victorian Women's Autobiography* (Charlottesville, Va.: University Press of Virginia, 1999), 2. Peterson's first chapter is an excellent account of the problems of trying to differentiate a 'women's autobiography'.

Briton.[39] Henry 'Orator' Hunt's 1820 *Memoirs*, unapologetically radical in stance and content, provide a more confrontational example, but he uses the language and rhetoric of mainstream (that is, recognizably 'literary') autobiography, to the extent of professing the Horatian-Johnsonian creed: he would not write at all, he says, if he did not think that 'almost every part of my life may prove instructive, as well as entertaining, to my fellow creatures and the rising generation'.[40] Gender and class are the most obvious axes along which the 'autobiographical franchise' was expanding, but it is important to realize—against much current writing on autobiography, which sees them as determining factors—that they are not themselves the main causes of institutional anxiety about autobiographical practice in the period. The literary public sphere was perfectly capable of extending itself to include female and lower-class autobiographers—under the right circumstances. It follows that questions about how prescriptive attitudes operated are not essentially to do with gender and class, but with those circumstances: the general conditions of proper management of the figure of egotism, whether the self-authoring 'I' belongs to man or woman, labourer or lord.

This is not to deny the existence of a general assumption that literary decorum, like its social counterpart, belongs by right to certain kinds of people, more probably lords than labourers. The *Edinburgh*'s metaphor of 'good-breeding' shows clearly enough that managing the 'hateful pronoun' is supposed to come more naturally to those who are born to inclusion in polite conversation. Both authorial egotism and readerly curiosity are somewhat mitigated within the higher circles of that sphere. A review of Philip Thicknesse's *Memoirs and Anecdotes* in the *European Magazine* for December 1789 strikingly demonstrates the sense of an exclusive social stratum within which legitimate autobiography occurs:

THERE is not perhaps in the whole circle of literature any species of writing which excites the curiosity of the public more than the lives of men, with whom many of us have been either personally acquainted, or have received some interesting accounts of them in the general intercourses of society.[41]

The confident reference to 'us' indicates that publication is here simply

---

[39] On the concept of 'passing' in relation to Equiano see Marion Rust, 'The Subaltern as Imperialist', in Elaine K. Ginsberg (ed.), *Passing and the Fictions of Identity* (Durham, NC: Duke University Press, 1996).
[40] Henry Hunt, *Memoirs of Henry Hunt, Esq.*, 3 vols. (London: T. Dolby, 1820), i. 394.
[41] *European Magazine*, xvi. 408.

an extension of those 'general intercourses'. This is because the intercourses are not general at all: the 'many of us' cited are obviously a
fraternity small enough to guarantee that nothing out of the ordinary is
happening when the lives of its members become the subject of writing
rather than personal acquaintance. Likewise, the 'public' whose curiosity is aroused by such books must consist of a restricted circle of readers
already familiar with the objects of its gossipy interest. Thicknesse, an
officer and a gentleman (the summit of his career was a post as a colonial administrator), apparently belongs in the same sphere as the
reviewer and the *European*'s subscribers. Justifications for autobiography along these lines are fairly common in the period. Clearly, the
notion they depend on is a hierarchical arrangement of the right to be
heard. If it is never entirely acceptable to force the 'I' on the public
notice, however narrowly the public is conceived—and Thicknesse is
criticized in the *European* for speaking too freely of its other members
and so levelling 'all distinctions of rank and character'[42]—rank nevertheless endows the self with an inherent worth which some observers
find reason enough for its appearance in print. Compare the list of criteria cited in a review in the July 1835 *Quarterly* as now forgotten standards
of life-writing:

The eminence of the person—the splendour or utility of his or her life—the
information it may convey, or the lesson it may inculcate, are by no means—as
they used formerly to be—essentially conditions in the choice of a subject.

Alongside the usual Johnsonian references to utility appear 'eminence'
and 'splendour', purely hierarchical values. In this case the reviewer is
talking about biography in general, but the principle is the same: knowledge of private experience, and therefore by extension the act of self-
writing, is acceptable when the self occupies an elevated social place. The
article interprets the loosening of these criteria as a sign of decay in the
public sphere overall, 'indicative of some degree of deterioration in the
public taste, and of abasement in the literary character of our times'.
When 'the lives of second or third rate persons' share the stage with first-
raters, autobiography obviously becomes the sign of a mismanaged
social and literary environment, just as Marcus describes in her brief
account of the period's prevailing anxieties about the genre.[43]

---

[42] *European Magazine*, xvi. 410. I am grateful to Jennifer Koopman for locating this
review.
[43] *Quarterly Review*, liv. 250.

The standard of 'eminence' is not as straightforward as it seems, though. If it could simply be equated with 'distinctions of rank' it would legitimize autobiography according to broad social rules; but there are other kinds of eminence than good breeding. Rousseau is an obvious example, becoming a proper subject of a restricted public's interest from talent, not birth. Rank is no guarantee of gentle treatment in the reviews, either: a baronet like Sir Egerton Brydges can be accused of rampant egotism as readily as anyone else. While the language of the periodicals certainly implies a hierarchical division between those who deserve a hearing and those who have no right to say 'I' in public, it is surprisingly muddled about the scale that measures the difference. (To some limited extent this is a function of the different political stances of the journals, but their broad consensus around a gentlemanly public sphere certainly overrides their disputes over qualifications for social eminence.) Everyone seems to recognize that the public status of a person is not a matter of class. Instead, the reviews resort to phrases as suggestively vague as D'Israeli's 'great man'. Lamenting the exposure of private detail in Richard Edgeworth's 1820 *Memoirs*, the *Edinburgh* comments: 'It is only of Great Men that we are greedy to preserve such relics.'[44] Who are these capitalized worthies, though? As the same journal's review of the 1806 *Memoirs* of Dr Joseph Priestley notes, it is thanks to Priestley's notoriety as a public figure that 'we have perused this miscellaneous volume with more interest than we have usually found excited by publications of the same description'.[45] Or again, with reference to James Northcote's biography of Sir Joshua Reynolds, the *Edinburgh* exempts from a general assault on the dissipating triviality of life-writing 'the histories of those lives, which have been successfully devoted to the cultivation and improvement of the useful and elegant arts'.[46] Talent, accomplishment, or sheer fame turn out to be at least as effective as rank in determining prescriptive attitudes to the autobiographical franchise.

In fact, it appears that the qualifications of 'Great Men' can only really be understood in terms of public interest. Those figures—women as well as men—who have been subjects of conversation, whose names crop up in 'the general intercourses of society', are legitimate objects of public curiosity and therefore are endowed with a kind of right to speak of

---

[44] *Edinburgh Review*, xxxiv. 123.
[45] Ibid. ix. 136.
[46] Ibid. xxiii. 263.

themselves in published form. Usually public interest is construed in the sense of benefit rather than mere curiosity (that which concerns the interests of the public, not just that which piques its interest). So a notice in the *Monthly Critical Gazette* argues that the only lives worth reading are those connected with 'the march of nations, the progress of science, and those arts which enable men to surmount the obstacles of nature'.[47] However, the distinction is not maintained easily. Once the justification for autobiographical writing is transferred from the status of the author to the interest of the public sphere, it finds itself mirroring the debased criterion of curiosity: whatever interests the public is in the public interest, and therefore any instance of egotism is proper as long as there is an audience for it. This spectre of undiscriminating prying consumerism is, as we have repeatedly seen, the most disturbing (or fascinating) aspect of the 'rage for auto-biography'.[48] The worth of 'Great Men' threatens to shift from their own achievements to their prominence, their visibility, their currency as subjects of society's 'intercourses'. With the completion of this shift, greatness or eminence is indistinguishable from notoriety or fame. The legitimate authors of autobiography would therefore be those whose lives are perused with interest—who are already in the grip of the greedy, nosy public sphere. As much as the reviewers presume that eminence authorizes egotism, they cannot avoid the implication that eminence itself turns out to be a function of (not a precondition for) general curiosity.

'Great men' are supposed to transcend the ordinary separation of private individuality from the public sphere. Their autobiographies are acceptable, even valuable, because their greatness makes them common property (just as their egotism is acceptable because greatness is allowed to hog the conversational limelight). Once, however, the concept of greatness is aligned with mere fame, private experience is everywhere vulnerable to the incursion of an interested audience. This kind of disintegration of social boundaries is at the root of John Lockhart's splenetic outburst in his article 'Autobiography' from the January 1827 *Quarterly Review*. He begins with the usual sarcastic survey of what Marcus calls the extended autobiographical franchise:

Modern primer-makers must needs leave confessions behind them, as if they were so many Rousseaus. Our weakest mob-orators think it is a hard case if they cannot spout to posterity. Cabin-boys and drummers are busy with their commentaries *de bello Gallico* . . . thanks to 'the march of intellect,' we are already rich in the autobiography of pickpockets.[49]

Lockhart is picking on very easy targets by deigning to notice works that would normally be unlikely to receive notice in the periodical press. He pulls ten autobiographies out of the circulating mass in order to pick apart their authors' pretensions in detail: but, as he remarks, 'we might easily have graced our table with twice as many of the same kind, all produced within the last two or three years' (p. 149).[50] The real object of his critique, needless to say, is the 'kind' itself, the genre. He assaults each of the volumes at hand with characteristic gusto—'His power of *boring* seems to have been enormous' (p. 155)—but in each case the author's inflated notion of his or her own public significance stands for the essential effect of the genre, to wit:

that it emboldens beings who, at any period, would have been mean and base in all their objects and desires, to demand with hardihood the attention and the sympathy of mankind, for thoughts and deeds that, in any period but the present, must have been as obscure as dirty. (p. 164)

To this point the critique is obviously based on hierarchical distinctions of class, as Lockhart makes explicit by writing that 'few great men—none of the very highest order—have chosen to paint otherwise than indirectly . . . the secret workings of their own minds' (ibid.). Gradations of 'order' are clearly in inverse proportion to autobiographical proliferation: at the top there is none at all, at the bottom it spreads like a plague. However, he goes on to shift his attention to the interaction between classes—to the structure of the relatively open middle-class public sphere, that is:

The mania for this garbage of Confessions, and Recollections, and Reminiscences, and Aniliana, 'is indeed a vile symptom.' It seems as if the ear of that grand impersonation, 'the Reading Public,' had become as filthily prurient as that of an eaves-dropping lackey. (ibid.)

The inappropriate self-importance and egotism of nobodies finds its match in the degraded appetite of the literary public sphere, which

[49] Ibid. xxxv. 149. Hereafter cited by page number only. '*de bello Gallico*': on the French war (alluding with heavy irony to Julius Caesar's account of his first-century BC campaigns).

[50] A very conservative estimate: he could easily have quadrupled the number. Some sense of the scale of autobiographical increase in the first two decades of the nineteenth century can be gained from looking at the index to Matthews's bibliography (William Matthews, *British Autobiographies* (Berkeley, Calif.: University of California Press, 1955)).

worsens the problems of class by levelling everyone into a community of undifferentiated listeners. Socially worthless autobiographers can simply be ignored, as Lockhart's ten selected victims otherwise largely were, but autobiography itself is less innocuous because it creates the conditions for lackeys to listen at the doors of their betters. In this situation the author's rank or eminence makes no difference. Silencing the 'mean and base' in favour of great men is no answer; what has happened is a sudden permeability of the borders separating one class from another. The lackey eagerly laps up his master's private experience; and this unstoppable, universal circulation of privacy in public means that the conversational sphere no longer has any 'decorum', any social mores. It is instead compounded of nothing more than 'I's and ears. Lockhart calls the 'Reading Public' an 'impersonation' because it has no actual social coherence, therefore no identity of its own. It is not in his view a public—a specific constituency—at all, since it apparently comprises everyone equally and consumes everything indiscriminately. Autobiography testifies particularly well to this morass of undifferentiated speakers and listeners. Hence Lockhart identifies it as a threat to social interaction itself. '[T]he effects of it will, ere long', he writes, 'be visible elsewhere than in literature. An universal spirit of suspicion will overspread the intercourse of society' (pp. 164–5). He concludes by recommending that the higher circles of society lock the doors, plug the keyholes, and keep their mouths shut, tightening the limits of privacy by refusing to admit 'the companionship . . . of farce-wrights and professional buffoons' (p. 165) who might relay anecdotes to the ear of a mass readership.

What makes the article so interesting is the way it never touches on the issue of what autobiographical texts ought to look like. It offers no prescriptive indications, nor any suggestion that the books under review might have been conducted differently. As he says with reference to Joseph Brasbridge's memoir *The Fruits of Experience* (1824), an author this garrulous, trivial, and self-satisfied 'has put parody out of the question' (p. 165).[51] Individual instances do not call for analysis or criticism. Lockhart understands instead that as a genre autobiography is about the nature of social space as it is reproduced in the literary public sphere. The fact that he prophesies the complete collapse of social conversation is perhaps partly to do with the periodicals' tendency towards extreme

---

[51] The general tenor of Brasbridge's book may be gathered from one fairly representative phrase: 'I recollect the first broad-wheeled wagon that was used in Oxfordshire' (Joseph Brasbridge, *The Fruits of Experience* (London, 1824), 233). (No offence is intended to scholars of the history of agricultural technology.)

positions. (As the world of letters discovered with the appearance of the *Edinburgh* and the *Quarterly* in the first decade of the nineteenth century, exaggerated polemic makes for livelier journalism.) Nevertheless, his reactionary splutterings are founded on a powerful understanding of autobiography's capacity to fill the public sphere with inappropriately (or at least confusingly) 'private' gestures and representations; to turn all conversation into eavesdropping.

The problem is not just that autobiography gives cabin boys and drummers the same platform as a Caesar or a Wellington. Satire of Lockhart's sort can easily distinguish (on its own terms) the worthlessness of one next to the other. More disturbing is the way such writing threatens to confirm its levelling pretensions by addressing a level of private experience where, as Dr Johnson suspected in *Rambler* 60, people are not so different from one another. Compare a review in the *London Magazine* of March 1828:

> The desire to pry into the private actions of illustrious persons has perhaps become a disease of our times . . . the great object of all the writers of scandalous memoirs, and the great point of gusto with all the readers, is, that the commonest order of minds shall be upon a level with the highest, in having cognizance of their vices and foibles; in other words, that all the countless thousands who derive wit and wisdom from circulating libraries, shall degrade every 'hero' or man of genius, into a very common-place fellow, by being, with reference to his habits, in the condition of his 'valet-de-chambre.' This is the secret of the attractive memoir-writing of the present day.[52]

Though the vocabulary of class distinction predominates, it is not the crucial point here. Rather, as with Lockhart's lackey, the review recalls that no one is a hero to his valet; given sufficient access to the private self, all the achievements of rank or eminence are levelled. It is a question of knowledge ('cognizance'); Burke invokes class distinction the same way in his famous outburst in *Reflections on the Revolution in France*, where he praises the 'pleasing illusions' that clothe the private state of greatness in the veiling trappings of aristocratic magnificence.[53] Social intercourse depends on keeping certain things out of the public arena. Once those private matters are known (and circulated), what is occurring is no longer conversation but (as Lockhart's image of a greedily prurient ear suggests) mere consumption. Egotism is complicit in this process, needless to say.

---

[52] *London Magazine*, x. 410.
[53] Edmund Burke, *Reflections on the Revolution in France*, ed. J. G. A. Pocock (Indianapolis, Ind.: Hackett, 1987), 67.

As in the always paradigmatic case of Rousseau, excessive self-publication is more or less an invitation to readers to gorge their inquisitiveness. The louder the 'I' relates itself, the more it damages conversational exchange and forces the audience into voyeurism. Hence, autobiographical writing can come to signify a nightmare version of Habermas's intersubjective public sphere; it appears to turn the whole conversational environment where texts circulate into a gigantic whispering gallery of prying and eavesdropping. Instead of the rational exchange which Habermas describes as constituting the very notion of the 'public', intersubjective relations in this space occur behind closed doors—with a keyhole left permanently open for the convenience of any listener happening to pass by.

In the end, then, gradations of class and distinctions of gender are largely irrelevant to the fundamental prescriptive attitude, or at least not primary considerations within it. The essential yardstick for autobiographical publication is decorum, manners (which in theory are available to anyone, though of course determined by gentlemanly and masculine notions of propriety). Compare a comment in a broadly sympathetic review of *The Spirit of the Age* in the *Monthly*:

Perhaps the ungentle and deformed character of many of Mr. Hazlitt's portraits is one of the many objections that may be urged against contemporary memoir-writing, to which authors who have strong and impetuous feelings should never addict themselves.[54]

Intersubjective relations in print need to be maintained with polite calm and tolerance. Personal writing is inherently threatening here. In particular, a Romantic, Rousseauan interiority—'strong and impetuous feelings'—seems incompatible with the social standards this reviewer takes for granted. Inwardness of that sort is, again, a private matter, and in so far as autobiographical writing draws thereon it does not belong in print.

So the prescriptive demands say, at least; but the attitudes encapsulated in Lockhart's article always coexist with the recognition that it is precisely autobiography's power to open closed doors which makes it not only entertaining but instructive—which gives it value, that is, according to the ubiquitous criteria. As I have already argued, this is largely what turns autobiography into a visible genre. Reviewing the *Anecdotes of the Life of Richard Watson* in 1818, the *Edinburgh* identifies a specific reading practice (or horizon of expectation): it refers to 'those

---

[54] *Monthly Review*, NS cvii. 14.

who chiefly prize such books [note the indication of genre] for the secret history which they develop, or the particulars which they detail of private life and conversation'.[55] The eavesdropping lackey here metamorphoses into a scholar and historian. The review goes on to imply a contrast between readers of this inquisitive class and 'men of enlightened minds', but without dismissing the value of secrecy unmasked and privacy published.[56] Its assumptions are similar to those of the high Tory *Imperial Magazine*'s notice of De Quincey's *Confessions*, which guesses that a reader's reaction to the author's unburdenings 'will depend on the interest he feels in tracing the mysterious operations of a deeply-culti-vated mind'.[57] From the point of view of Lockhart's article, such 'inter-est' is no better than ill-bred meddling and prying. Yet it is widely assumed in the periodicals that what Foster calls the 'interior apartment' of individual experience is a legitimate field of knowledge and interest. In this light, reading autobiography is simply another way of acquiring information, and the egotist is a useful authority.

These ought to be contradictory positions. On one side stands the Burkean position that in certain fields knowledge is a positive evil, that certain privacies should be inviolate. In the other view knowledge of 'secret history', 'private life', and 'mysterious operations' is a particularly prized resource. The opposition superficially mirrors the period's funda-mental political dispute between rational enlightenment—Burke's 'new conquering empire of light and reason' which 'strips away all decorous veils'[58]—and reactionary traditionalism. In practice, however, the differ-ent attitudes not only coexist but overlap. (There is certainly no correla-tion between the politics of any given periodical and its tendencies when reviewing autobiographical works.) The literary public sphere, after all, functions as a site for opening and distributing all kinds of intellectual and cultural material. If private experience seems from one perspective to be excluded almost by definition from a public sphere, it is also possible that there is no such thing as 'private' experience in (to use Coleridge's term again) an 'AGE OF PERSONALITY'; the barriers Lockhart wishes to reinforce are breached by the very medium he is operating in, the literary sphere itself.[59] Publication permits any egotistical voice to occupy a niche in that environment. (The economics of the market control this to some

[55] *Edinburgh Review*, xxx. 206.   [56] Ibid. 207.
[57] *Imperial Magazine*, v. 93.   [58] Burke, *Reflections*, 67; ironic, naturally.
[59] Eighteenth-century constructions of the sphere of privacy have recently been studied at length: Patricia Meyer Spacks, *Privacy: Concealing the Eighteenth-Century Self* (Chicago, Ill.: University of Chicago Press, 2003).

extent, but many autobiographical books of the period were privately published: as Lockhart acidly remarks of one of those he reviews, he is 'pretty sure that no bookseller encountered the risk of the adventure'.[60] This indiscriminate access upsets literary decorum, but at the same time creates an alternative conversational model, an intersubjectivity governed by the fascination of exposure rather than polite discursive interchange. Even Lockhart writes that the 'only legitimate object of the private autobiographer is to give the public the cream of his personal experience', recognizing some kind of licit transition from private/personal to public spheres.[61] There is no clear, systematic distinction between filthily prurient eavesdropping and a licensed, worthy circulation of personal experience. Autobiographical writing signals the reconfiguration of the relations between what happens behind closed doors and the open arena of textual circulation. The question of how the new relation works out—which is also the question of how to manage the figure of egotism, the individual speaking of him- or herself in public—remains negotiable and uncertain. It is, once again, a matter of proper management, however much prescriptivist stances imply that absolute rules can be applied. The periodicals show the literary establishment reacting to autobiographical acts case by case, each instance in practice often generating unexpected or contradictory responses even as the reviewer pronounces on how autobiography ought to be. With a particular volume open before them commentators often find that the new kind of knowledge or access it provides becomes its own justification. 'It is impossible to justify the composition of such biography better than has been done by Mr. Gibbon himself'; 'if by fastidious delicacy this [spontaneous and forcible expression of personal feelings] should be thought a defect, it is amply compensated by the undistinguished disclosure of an enlightened and contemplative mind'; 'characters may sometimes arise of such manifest importance to the world, to their country, or to themselves, that the noble daring which plunges them into the hazards of egotism, is not only to be justified, but even to be admired';

NOTWITHSTANDING the disadvantages necessarily attached to the biography of a man's self, we are still disposed to listen with much attention to narrative of events, in which the author played a conspicuous part. As time passes on, the traits of egotism are softened down, we forget that the writer is the hero of his

---

[60] *Quarterly Review*, xxxv. 154.
[61] Ibid. 157.

own tale, and at the same time we enjoy the rich stores of information, to which his own peculiar circumstances had given him access.[62]

Repeatedly commentators' sense of transgressed literary decorum comfortably overlaps with their interest or pleasure in watching privacy enter the arena of publication—a less highly charged version of the characteristic reaction to Rousseau.

A closer look at the central prescriptive assumptions illustrates their difficulty in containing the discourse of privacy. Bearing in mind that the readiest way for Romantic-period writers to talk about the value of nonfiction was the amusement-and-instruction formula, it is obvious that amusement is the riskier of the two terms, since the pleasures of autobiography might seem all too straightforwardly akin to those of the eavesdropping lackey or the greedily prurient public ear. We can get a better sense of prescriptivism's struggles from the question of instruction. Referring to autobiography's utility offers commentators a clearer chance to define its value in an unambiguously public sense: to assert its 'public interest', that is, without drawing attention to the overlapping of privacy and publicity which Lockhart rightly sees as its major threat. The readiest route to interpreting self-writing along these lines (as Johnson's essays show) is to imagine it as a form of historiography, a documentary resource. Two basic assumptions are at work here: first, that the factual narrative content of the book is its most important feature, and, second, that the author's stance towards that content is relatively dispassionate and detached. We might call these the criteria of truth and objectivity respectively. Together they turn autobiographical writing into something very like reportage. An 1818 review in the *Quarterly* makes the equation explicit. The writer laments that the age of newspapers has caused the decline of memoir-writing (he is thinking in terms of historical records of prominent people and events): 'the curious, instead of writing the memoirs of their own time, now content themselves with filing and preserving the *Morning Post*'.[63] Journalism, he or she thinks, has taken over the function of autobiography by supplying a more convenient conduit for documentary truth and objectivity. So straightforwardly pragmatic an understanding of the genre is unusual in the commentary (the fact that this review speaks of a decline in the volume

---

[62] *Monthly Review*, NS xx. 78 (reviewing Gibbon's posthumously edited autobiography); *Monthly Review*, NS xx. 251 (on Wollstonecraft's *Letters Written During a Short Residence*); *British Critic*, NS xv. 629 (on Hazlitt's *Table Talk*); *British Critic*, NS xi. 88 (on the 1817 publication of a Scottish political memoir of the early eighteenth century).

[63] *Quarterly Review*, xix. 461.

of memoir-writing shows that it is not really referring to the proliferating kind of writing that was coming to be called 'autobiography'). Still, it suggests a basic idea of instructive value which was widely shared.

The truth criterion, curiously, is less often invoked than one might expect. It may be that it is too fundamental an assumption to need stating: in Philippe Lejeune's terms, veracity is part of the 'autobiographical pact' at the time, the contractual understanding between reader and writer that enables a text to appear as autobiography in the first place.[64] A notice of Edgeworth's memoirs in the *Quarterly* asserts that 'strict authenticity' is 'the whole charm ... of autobiography', and certainly any suspicion of actual falsehood, rather than partiality or misrepresentation, instantly condemns the whole work in all reviewers' eyes.[65] In autobiographical writing, though, 'strict authenticity' begs some questions, since the first-person stance presents individual opinions and perspectives as being subjectively, if not necessarily historically, authentic. As the same review notes: 'To speak of oneself with moral truth is difficult; with absolute truth perhaps impossible.'[66] Indeed, the criterion of truth more usually depends on factual content, on the principle that autobiography becomes useful or instructive if it is about true things. What this primarily means is that self-writing should suppress the self in favour of what the self observes (as in newspaper journalism, the reporter is supposed to function only as witness to the events). The model form of autobiography here would be travel writing. An article in the April 1806 *Edinburgh* explains the criterion very fully:

Life has often been compared to a journey; and the simile seems to hold better in nothing than in the identity of the rules by which those who write their travels, and those who write their lives, should be governed. When a man returns from visiting any celebrated region, we expect to hear much more of the things and persons he has seen, than of his own personal transactions ... In the same manner, when, at the close of a long life, spent in circles of literary and political celebrity, an author sits down to give the world an account of his retrospections, it is reasonable to stipulate that he shall talk less of himself than of his associates.[67]

Egotism is of course an offence against this rule, because it shows (as another review puts it) that 'the author was considerably more in the

---

[64] See Lejeune, *On Autobiography*, ch. 1. Lejeune's theory, however, loses much of its power in a situation like that of the early nineteenth-century British literary public sphere, where the concept of autobiography is still relatively new and under question.

[65] *Quarterly Review*, xxiii. 513.

[66] Ibid. 510.

[67] *Edinburgh Review*, viii. 108.

author's view than the subject'.[68] According to the analogy with travel literature, the 'subject' ideally detaches itself from the author: his or her personal experience ceases to be personal or private, since he or she is simply the medium for circulating it so that it can belong to others (readers) as well.

The criterion of objectivity works the same way, not surprisingly. If the egotistical narrator maintains an impersonal stance towards the 'subject' (content) of the work, there is no risk of private considerations interfering with reliably authentic and instructive narration. Another review of *The Spirit of the Age* worries that Hazlitt's 'pencil has been guided by personal feelings rather than by a regard to fidelity and likeness'.[69] When an autobiographer seems to possess the knowledge or the facts he or she records, those facts become private or personal; they cannot belong in (and to) an enlightened, Habermasian reading public which thinks of itself as forming opinions based on reliable evidence. In this view the perfection of self-writing would be to efface the self altogether, and some reviewers point out with evident relief that purely anecdotal memoirs achieve this by compiling reminiscences of other people. Theatrical memoirs in particular offer the chance to read autobiography as pure journalism. A rambling narrative like Tate Wilkinson's *Memoirs of His Own Life* (1790) can be praised for its 'becoming modesty' because the stories the author (famous as a mimic) tells about his own career have no less of a documentary quality than his recollections of Garrick and other luminaries.[70] Third-person autobiographical writing like that of William Beloe or William Hayley (Blake's patron, the biographer) also preserves the decorous illusion that the author has no personal investment in the narrative—as if, the *Quarterly*'s review of Hayley's *Memoirs* remarks, 'the author affected throughout not to appear his own biographer'.[71]

It is right to call this affectation, since in autobiography the stance of objectivity, like the pursuit of 'strict authenticity', is always an illusion. However much such texts aim to be pure reportage, they cannot escape being read to some extent as personal documents. Indeed, this is part of what contemporaries thought distinguished 'autobiography' from other first-person genres. The fact that 'the author was considerably more in the author's view than the subject', the fact that the first person does not simply function as a journalistic eye but becomes its own subject, is the

[68] *New Edinburgh Review*, i. 104.
[69] *Literary Gazette*, no. 438, p. 377.
[70] *Monthly Review*, NS vi. 172.
[71] *Quarterly Review*, xxxi. 264.

sign of 'egotistical biography'. The criteria of truth and objectivity thus inevitably come under pressure, and need to be modified somehow to make room for the idea that personal or private experience is instructive too. John Wilson's important (and thoroughly antagonistic) review of *Biographia Literaria* in *Blackwood's* of October 1817 is a representative reaction to the pressures. He opens with a lengthy rhetorical shudder at the mere idea of self-examination, before admitting that a ban on Rousseauan 'writing and publishing accounts of all our feelings' does not rule out the more neutrally biographical 'narration of our mere speculative opinions'. This effort to cordon off the domain of extreme privacy or interiority leaves him vulnerable, though; those are after all still 'our' opinions, singular and personal, and relating them is therefore tainted by the illicit procedure of acting as 'operators on our own shrinking spirits . . . probing the wounds of the soul'. Wilson therefore recommends that the individual life be objectified as far as possible:

It [the 'narration of . . . opinions'] requires, that we should stand aloof from ourselves, and look down, as from an eminence, on our souls toiling up the hill of knowledge . . . that we should mark the limit of our utmost ascent, and, without exaggeration, state the value of our acquisitions. When we consider how many temptations there are even here to delude ourselves, and by a seeming air of truth and candour to impose upon others, it will be allowed, that, instead of composing memoirs of himself, a man of genius and talent would be far better employed in generalizing the observations and experiences of his life, and giving them to the world in the form of philosophic reflections, applicable not to himself alone, but to the universal mind of Man.[72]

Wilson's metaphor tries to imagine the self-as-subject in a relation of detachment. One observes oneself, but from a distance, purged of autobiographical intimacy. It is a rather paradoxical effort, and leads logically to rejecting autobiography outright in favour of a 'generalizing' narrative which would distil instructiveness from a personal narrative and package it as a self-contained and separate sermon. Before reaching this point, however, the argument pictures an individual life in terms of a scientifically observable trajectory. The 'ascent' whose final 'value' can be calculated belongs in a scheme of Newtonian mechanics, where all movement and all forces are quantifiable and equally observable from all points of view. A person's story may be personal, but Wilson expects one to be able to observe oneself from a vantage point beyond the 'limit' of one's own knowledge or progress, and so construe the particular sequence of one's life as moving from position to position, from event to event. The scale measuring this individual progression, meanwhile, is in no sense personal. Actions and opinions have a fixed 'value', and the best autobiography can do is record the author's own track along the scale, as if tracing a line across a map whose contours are predetermined.

In general, then, prescriptive requirements of instructiveness depend on reading autobiography (in journalistic fashion) as the record of events whose significance comes not from their association with the author him- or herself but from some shared or public field of value. In Wilson's metaphor, everybody (or everybody worthwhile, at least) is toiling up the same hill, and in so far as self-writing is at all admissible it ought to leave a record of one route to the summit. (This is not the same as the more straightforward exemplary reading of the genre: Wilson is not imagining that it exists to show others the path to the top. He is recognizing the possibility of a unique record, while trying to place that uniqueness as firmly as possible within 'the universal mind of Man'.) Privacy is not an issue, because the life is understood as a legible, utilitarian, historical movement. Any event, interior or exterior, marks a stage in the overall journey, so nothing is actually located in any properly private sphere. Domestic circumstances and influences, eccentric opinions, or any other aspects of what might look like a personal life are turned into events in the communal plot.

As with all prescriptive positions, there are all sorts of ways in which Wilson's notions are contravened by autobiographical practice in the period. For our purposes, though, the important point is the vulnerability of his argument. His position boils down to a commonsensical assumption about what autobiography is about and what it is for (one very close to Johnson's in the *Idler* essay): an instructive record of objectively narrated fact whose value lies somewhere in the public domain. Narrative content is the key (hence the model of reportage or travel writing): autobiography is a way of telling us things. How, then, does one account for the pervasive intuition among reviewers and commentators that such texts are not reducible to their content, to events and facts, to the materials of the truth and objectivity criteria? The periodicals endlessly lament the numbing irrelevance or tedium of an individual's experience: 'the only question that remains is, whether the truth, the whole of the truth, which he offers us, is worth knowing by others?'[73] This is a particular problem with the memoirs of men and women of

---

[73] *Monthly Review*, NS vii. 207 (reviewing Lackington's *Memoirs*).

letters, apparently, because 'The life of a literary man is generally barren of events'; 'ordinary authors who "live in the world" are unlikely to produce anything worthwhile'.[74] From whatever lofty position one surveys such a life, it is always possible that the trajectory thus observed might look vanishingly trivial. The generalized, objectified course of a life can lack a certain distinctive value, and the *Quarterly*'s review of Hayley's third-person memoir finds an interesting phrase to suggest what is missing. Noting Hayley's effort to write his life as if it were someone else's (as Wilson's metaphor directs), the reviewer comments that 'by this useless artifice of style, one charm of auto-biography is destroyed. The truth remains; but the stamp which should authenticate it, is wanting'.[75] This 'stamp' is the same quality which in the *Monthly*'s review of James Lackington's *Memoirs* (1791) makes truth 'worth knowing by others'. It is something existing in excess of factual, public truth, some value not reducible to the narrative order Wilson takes as his standard. In the review of Hayley the pretence of objectivity is clearly blamed for the want of such a quality; Hayley's story fails as a biography as it would not if it confessed to being an autobiography. The author, that is, ought to admit his intimate relationship with the truth of his narrative. That is the peculiar 'charm' of the genre. Wilson wants all events to take place in the public domain, but many readers in the period seem to interpret the contents of an autobiographical record as being distinctively inflected by the person they (as it were) belong to. Otherwise, their documentary aspect reads as 'mere detail of the ordinary events of his life, dressed up so as to display his importance'.[76]

Truth and objectivity, then, can result in a barren, impersonal redaction of events which some readers see as a kind of falsification. The authenticating 'stamp' is marked only when the text's content testifies to the individual who authored it. For Wilson this shift of emphasis must be anathema, since it reinstitutes the person of the author as the subject of self-writing rather than the trajectory of a career. More enthusiastic commentators might defend the utility of this individualized subject of autobiographical writing by arguing (as D'Israeli, Foster, and Stanfield all do) that the genre is about 'human nature'. In this perspective the events mapping out the historical record of a life are only components of an overall understanding of that life: autobiography is less reportage than self-portraiture. Commenting on the publication of an eighteenth-

[74] *Monthly Review*, xiii. 57; *Edinburgh Review*, viii. 108.
[75] *Quarterly Review*, xxxi. 264.   [76] Ibid. 105.

century political memoir, the *Edinburgh* duly notes its importance as historical evidence, but adds that it is also valuable for the 'character which the author incidentally draws of himself'.[77] Self-portraiture, naturally, is instructive too. Foster imagines Rousseau as an exhibit in the 'moral museum of the world', on display for the edification of the curious, and this idea of autobiography's public function is widely held. The *London Magazine*'s review of the swindler James Hardy Vaux's 1819 *Memoirs* imagines a class of readers who, 'led by a sincere desire to improve mankind, first wish to know what man is'.[78] Each individual represents an opportunity to understand what people are like (very much corresponding with Foster's museum metaphor, since museums display single artefacts as instances of and therefore windows on to a culture, a civilization, a time, and place). This again contradicts Wilson's view that 'the universal mind of Man' can only be explored by refining away the personal dimension of experience. Slipping from one reading to the other, one sees how the notion of personality or human nature appears to be something separate from, or in excess of, the objective record of a life. Wilson looks like he is speaking for a basic consensus about autobiography's utility when he asserts that the genre is there to convey the truth about a person's experience, but his argument ignores an equally pervasive sense that the person is more likely to be the focus of reading than the experience. The *Edinburgh Magazine*'s 1822 article 'On Auto-Biography' rhetorically asks:

to what cause can we impute the insatiable appetite of the public for every species of Private Memoirs and Correspondence, except to that ceaseless curiosity with which we scrutinize all the varieties of human nature, in its minutest and most insignificant, as well as in its most important aspects?[79]

Historiography never gets a look-in here. The mention of 'curiosity' is, as I argued in Chapter 1, already a marker of the peculiar dangers attendant upon autobiography; in this case curiosity is just about converted into philosophical scrutiny of 'human nature', but it is at any rate nothing to do with documentary knowledge. Events are authorized only by the fact that they add up to a portrait, a whole necessarily more interesting than the sum of its parts, and not reducible to them.

It is telling that the writer in the *Edinburgh Magazine* speaks of an 'appetite' for the personal subject of autobiography, because in the kind

[77] *Edinburgh Review*, xxii. 476.
[78] *London Magazine*, NS viii. 55.
[79] *Edinburgh Magazine*, x. 742.

of reading he imagines instructiveness is always on the point of being submerged by amusement. Moving beyond an always implausible adherence to standards of history and reportage, interest in human nature can be interpreted as mere curiosity as well as enlightened study of 'what man is', and hence the object of an appetite rather than education or reflection. The image of the eavesdropping lackey slips back into the discourse. Readers find themselves wanting to know the 'nature' of the author, to gain intimate access to him or her, rather than surveying the author's achievements in the public domain. This necessarily involves opening doors, peering in corners, excavating those aspects of the self which are not (as in Wilson's scheme) straightforwardly observable and trackable. As the case of the *Confessions* illustrated, the result is a change in the reader's stance towards the text. One no longer reads autobiography the way one reads a historical record, or a newspaper. The book addresses itself instead to an 'insatiable' appetite or desire, obviously unpoliced by utilitarian functions. The *Critical Review* noted in 1807 that

Memoirs and anecdotes are alluring baits, and the prefixing of such a title to such a piece, is like a sign hung out to catch the eye of the traveller, to entice him to make trial of the entertainment the place affords.[80]

Reading moves into the sphere of advertising and consumption, the commodity realm where producing insatiable (and so continuous) appetite is an end in itself. (The simile strongly recalls Foster's loathing yet fascinated observation of courtesan autobiography, and his implicit analogy between reading such a text and entering into a contract with a prostitute.) Specifically, the desire is for insight into human nature— which, Lockhart would doubtless point out, is as good as saying a desire to see into private space.

Wilson is probably right to suspect that autobiographical writing cannot help producing (or at least inviting) readings of this sort. The criteria of truth and objectivity can only be maintained if (as he describes) self-writing becomes more or less a cartographic act, plotting out sequences from the viewpoint of omniscient detachment, and even then he remains suspicious of its individualized subject. Beyond those criteria lies a nebulous field of (in Coleridge's word) 'PERSONALITY', inhering in autobiographical performances however much the standards of utility are foregrounded. On one level commentators' relentless accusations of egotism are admissions of this situation. They indicate that the presence of the first person as the subject of writing acts as a risky excess or superfluity threatening to overwhelm the conversational exchange of information and opinions, as if autobiography only says 'I' and nothing else. No matter what he or she is saying the egotistical speaker becomes the centre of attention, the value of whose conversation is displaced from content to speaker. It turns out that this is at once a social (and therefore literary) offence against decorum and also a sign of how autobiography demands to be read. Autobiography is a performance, never quite reducible to its documentary function because the first person inevitably obtrudes its role as author and agent of the narrative. In Elizabeth Bruss's terms, egotism and the private sphere together signal the illocutionary value of an autobiographical act (or locution).[81] They cannot be admitted as the instructive content or 'subject' of such writing because they have no place in a rational, decorous public sphere. Instead, they locate the value or interest of the text behind a closed door, or in Foster's 'interior apartment'—where, as Foster says, 'none but [the author] and the Divinity can enter', and yet which is suddenly opened to the infinite appetite of a reading public.[82]

The *Analytical's* review of Wakefield—the one which speaks of managing the figure of egotism—demonstrates how quickly prescriptive criteria slip into the language of amusement and appetite, of a desire centred around the publication of privacy. 'The principal things requisite to ensure [an autobiography] a welcome reception', it says, are

that the subject of the piece be one, whose character and situation are sufficiently important to attract public notice, and that the narrative be accompanied with an honest exposure of his opinions and sentiments. Nothing gives such an irresistible charm to writings of this class, as when the author

> '—Pours out all himself as plain
> As downright Shipton, or as old Montaigne.'[83]

The 'irresistible' spell inevitably recalls Rousseauan fascination, a condition under which all critical criteria are hypnotically suspended, all prescriptive notions of genre held in abeyance, in the face of an expressiveness (a pouring out of oneself) that saturates writing with the aura of the first person divorced from questions of its right to speak or its public

[81] See Bruss, *Autobiographical Acts*, intro. and ch. 1.
[82] Foster, *Essays*, i. 113.
[83] *Analytical Review*, xiii. 394.

interest. This is a thoroughly 'Romantic' idea; and yet, significantly, it cohabits with regulatory Johnsonian assumptions, as in this review. There is no simple antagonism between prescription and practice, between Lockhart's reactionary defence of the public sphere and some Wertherish or Byronic autobiographical urge towards unfettered self-expression. Alternative readings of autobiography overlap, shade into each other. The literary public sphere accommodates them all; as Lockhart astutely observes, the genre's fascination with privacy is itself a reordering of 'literary decorum', not an escape from the public arena altogether. Faced with the 'charm' of the genre, it is as if the commentators are praying to be made chaste—but not yet. The management of egotism becomes a matter of continual negotiation, compromise, adaptation.

Rousseau and Wordsworth, once thought to define the essence of a Romantic autobiography, both take a defiant stand against the public: the former challenging readers to accept his singularity, the latter defying any public to read his manuscript at all. But self-expression is a matter of public interest, and these two autobiographers know it. When we turn to look at Romantic-period autobiographical writing itself it is evident that the fantasies of autonomy offered by egotism are always intensely aware of how they are situated in relation to a public that is both prescriptive and insatiable. Autobiography is forced to defend its territory, but neither by asserting (Romantically) its complete freedom from the constraints of public expectations and assumptions nor by acceding to those assumptions and following the rules of decorum. The slippages and contradictions apparent in the reviews are mirrored in the books—a fact which confirms most clearly the close relation between autobiographical writing and its contexts. Defiant individualism like Rousseau's may claim that authorship and self-expression have nothing to do with readers and decorums, but such gestures are part of the constitution of the genre; the literary public sphere recognizes them, absorbs them (even if anxiously), and incorporates them in its own discourse. The texts' sense of how they might be read, how their egotism positions itself in relation to a community, must occupy us next.

II

Prescription/Practice

4

Autobiography and publication

The issues of *Fraser's Magazine* for November and December 1833 introduced British readers to the effusive, rhetorically acrobatic mysticism of
an obscure German philosopher called Diogenes Teufelsdröckh. Broadly
inspired by the Idealism of a previous generation (Jacobi, Fichte, and
Schelling), and imbued with the most fantastical currents of German
Romanticism, his thinking poses as its first problem the issue of individual self-consciousness. As translated by the anonymous editorial figure
who imports Teufelsdröckh's work to the pages of *Fraser's*, the question
is put in quintessentially 'Romantic' terms:

'With many men of a speculative turn,' writes Teufelsdröckh, 'there come
seasons, meditative, sweet, yet awful hours, when in wonder and fear you ask
yourself that unanswerable question: Who am *I*; the thing that can say "I" (*das
Wesen das sich ICH nennt*)? The world, with its loud trafficking, retires into the
distance . . .—the sight reaches forth into the void Deep, and you are alone with
the Universe, and silently commune with it, as one mysterious Presence with
another.'[1]

Teufelsdröckh's sublime introversion carries an oddly specific echo of
the prevailing contemporary anxieties over egotism. By qualifying the
Idealist subject—'*I*'—as 'the thing that can say "I" ', he opens his rhapsody to the charge of licensing an indecorous use of the 'hateful
pronoun'. The passage is in every sense a manifestation of the 'egotistical sublime': socially and grammatically, as well as in the sense that
Keats's phrase means to apply to Wordsworth's poetry, the sense of raising the ego to the level of 'the Universe' and giving it power over the
world. Indeed, Teufelsdröckh's vocabulary swarms with what sound to
our ears like Wordsworthian buzzwords: 'meditative', 'sweet', 'wonder',
'fear', 'commune', 'mysterious', 'Presence'—not to mention the

---

[1] Thomas Carlyle, *Sartor Resartus*, ed. McSweeney and Sabor, 42. Hereafter cited in the
text by page number only.

pronoun itself. His description of a sudden access of self-consciousness, a moment of intense self-interrogation, recalls that aspect of Wordsworth which is (appropriately enough) worked out most fully in *The Prelude.* This is egotism transformed from a conversational vulgarity into the high Romantic quest described in M. H. Abrams's *Natural Supernaturalism.*[2] Prescriptive fussing about the impropriety of saying 'I' is swept aside. It retires with the rest of the noisy traffic of the 'world' (the public sphere, that is), leaving only a sublime privacy on one side and the 'Universe' on the other—a universe emptied of getting and spending and everything else, pictured instead (in aptly sublime terminology) as the 'void Deep'.

Self-questioning here takes place in hermetic isolation. There is a complicatedly autobiographical moment like this near the end of *The Prelude.* The poem's first-person voice is thinking back to its beginning, the search for appropriate poetic material narrated in book I. That originating impulse is retrospectively described as an asking of something like Teufelsdröckh's question ('Who am *I*; the thing that can say "I" '?):

> In that distraction and intense desire
> I said unto the life which I had lived,
> 'Where are thou? Hear I not a voice from thee
> Which 'tis reproach to hear?' Anon I rose
> As if on wings, and saw beneath me stretched
> Vast prospect of the world which I had been,
> And was; and hence this song
>
> (*Prelude*, XIII. 373–81)

As if to confirm Keats's judgement (made of course in ignorance of *The Prelude*), the poem envisages a magnificent system, where the 'I' and eye of the narrator are elevated only to find that everything he gazes on is himself. Teufelsdröckh proceeds from his own question to a position of poetic Idealism comparable to Wordsworth's metaphor (though Wordsworth himself could hardly have been further from Idealism):

So that this so solid-seeming World, after all, were but an air-image, our ME the only reality: and Nature, with its thousandfold production and destruction, but the reflex of our own inward Force. (p. 44)

---

[2] M. H. Abrams, *Natural Supernaturalism: Tradition and Revolution in Romantic Literature* (New York: W. W. Norton, 1971). The book is still the most cogent theorization of a 'Romantic' reading of Romanticism, its continued influence and vitality demonstrated in part by the number of critical histories which cite it as a starting point for more recent interpretative strategies (see e.g. Cynthia Chase (ed.), *Romanticism* (London: Longman, 1993), 2–4; Michael O'Neill, *Literature of the Romantic Period: A Bibliographical Guide* (Oxford: Clarendon, 1998), 7–9).

As Abrams argues, there is a straightforward link between this sort of answer to the question of self-consciousness and the corresponding autobiographical act.[3] Once the whole 'Vast prospect' on which the writer looks appears as a 'reflex' of the observer, it is obvious that all writing will tend to the condition of self-writing. Equally obviously, such a model of autobiography does not so much resolve the problematic border between the public and the private as ignore it. In Teufelsdröckh's phrase again, the sphere of publicity (in a recent discourse in Romantic-period studies its usual name is 'history') is made to retire into the distance, leaving the private 'I' meditating on a world constituted entirely by what 'I had been / And was'. Certainly *The Prelude* is the most monumental autobiographical achievement of the years this study is concerned with, or at least the one that most closely resembles the sustained and systematic exploration of the author's inner life and career which over the later course of the nineteenth century came to define our modern notion of what an achieved autobiography looks like.

Teufelsdröckh too turns out to be an autobiographer. In fact, according to a German commentator cited in the second *Fraser's* instalment, his life-writing is an essential conduit for his thought. Unlike abstract sciences, the commentator argues, 'no Life-Philosophy (*Lebensphilosophie*) . . . which originates equally in the Character (*Gemüth*), and equally speaks thereto, can attain its significance till the Character itself is known and seen' (p. 58). This is a logical enough deduction in the case of Teufelsdröckh (as of Wordsworth): a quest for the nature of 'the thing that can say "I" ' might well be conducted through the auto-biographical act, the saying of 'I'. However, unlike the situation in the lines from *Prelude* book XIII, where autobiography unfolds in the 'Vast prospect' of a landscape discovered effortlessly and spontaneously, the world that Teufelsdröckh had been and was appears in a form that offers no immediate panoptic revelation of the inner life and its 'significance'. The editorial author of the *Fraser's* articles describes himself opening the packet supposedly containing Teufelsdröckh's manuscript:

. . . now let the sympathising reader judge of our feeling when, in place of this . . . Autobiography with 'fullest insight,' we find—Six considerable PAPER-BAGS . . . in the midst of which sealed Bags, lie miscellaneous masses of Sheets,

---

[3] He writes of 'a familiar Romantic metaphysic and life history' (Abrams, *Natural Supernaturalism*, 130).

and oftener Shreds and Snips, written in Professor Teufelsdröckh's scarce-legible *cursiv-schrift*; and treating of all things under the Zodiac and above it. (p. 60)

In Chapter 1 I referred a number of times to the mention of 'these Autobiographical times of ours' (p. 73) in *Sartor Resartus*, the work in which Thomas Carlyle invents Teufelsdröckh along with his editor and commentators, first published as a serio-comic hoax in *Fraser's* between November 1833 and August 1834 (the first single-volume British edition was published in 1838). The enterprise adopts a conventional (though slyly Shandean) formula of the genre to describe itself: 'this our *Sartor Resartus*, which is properly a "Life and Opinions of Herr Teufelsdröckh" ' (p. 10). Yet from the moment the paper bags arrive it is evident that autobiography is very far from being taken for granted in *Sartor*. The effort to publish Teufelsdröckh's life is frustrated by the miscellany sealed in them: 'scraps of regular Memoir, College Exercises, Programs, Professional Testimoniums, Milkscores, torn Billets' (p. 84), and so on. Having nevertheless pieced together the outlines of Teufelsdröckh's journey through romantic despair and alienation to spiritual rebirth and heroic self-dedication—not entirely unlike the impaired and restored imagination of the latter books of *The Prelude*—the editor undermines his own labours by suddenly voicing a suspicion that 'these Autobiographical Documents are partly a Mystification!' (p. 153). *Sartor's* joke on the autobiographical act is based on inserting obstruction and uncertainty at the precise point where *The Prelude* takes its sublime leap into egotistical revelation. The poem's 'I' describes itself in search of itself—'Where art thou?'—only to find that the question spontaneously answers itself: 'and hence this song'. As against this beautifully fluent transition from self-interrogation to autobiographical writing, *Sartor* offers instead a comically exaggerated fissure between the raw material of Teufelsdröckh's life and its translation into 'printed Creation' (p. 62). By the early 1830s the passage from life to print was increasingly well worn; Lockhart's 1827 *Quarterly Review* article effectively admits that the road has already been opened to anyone who cares to take it, not just the 'great men' envisaged in eighteenth-century prescriptive formulae. Carlyle himself was to become a hugely influential advocate of what one study of autobiography calls 'the value of the individual'.[4] His earliest published writings are mostly biographies, and also include an article on 'Biography' for *Fraser's*, while his later interest in 'heroes'—a Victorian transformation of 'great men'—elevates life-

---

[4] Weintraub, *The Value of the Individual*.

writing above all other literary acts. For all its energetic irony and whimsy, *Sartor* undoubtedly takes just as high-minded a view of the significance of its 'Autobiographical times'. The work itself constitutes an obliquely sublime autobiography, since Teufelsdröckh's quest for personal and professional vocation encodes and enacts Carlyle's own progress towards the role of the 'sage of Chelsea'.[5] So the editor's efforts to expound 'the internal world of Teufelsdröckh' alongside his 'mysterious ideas' are certainly earnest and worthwhile; biography and philosophy lead equally towards the sublimely post-Kantian goal of 'victoriously penetrating into Things themselves' (p. 155). Yet the bizarre form in which that 'internal world' is conveyed to the editor indicates very clearly that autobiography cannot be straightforward. Even in 1830, when *Sartor* was begun, and even with an author completely unhindered by prevailing notions of literary decorum, the act of self-publication is attended by highly restrictive difficulties.

There are various ways of interpreting *Sartor*'s ironic treatment of autobiographical procedures and forms, and the work's method has in fact been more persuasively read as a didactic reinforcement of the sublime 'I' than any kind of ironic subversion of Teufelsdröckh's transcendentalism.[6] What concerns me here is the particular structure of *Sartor*'s joke. By openly splitting the autobiographical act into two separate elements—the data of Teufelsdröckh's experience and recollections, contained in the paper miscellany sealed in the six bags, and the editor's struggle to shape them into a published narrative—*Sartor* lays intense emphasis on the problems of textuality. The work brilliantly identifies the endemic uncertainty of autobiography as, literally, a difficulty in handling life on paper. Teufelsdröckh's experience is conveyed to the editor entirely in the form of writing, as autobiography demands. Yet the documentary quality of experience turns out only to reflect its chaotic, unedited heterogeneity. 'Close by a rather eloquent Oration "On receiving the Doctor's-Hat," lie washbills marked *bezahlt* (settled).

[5] On the autobiographical status of *Sartor* see Avrom Fleishman, *Figures of Autobiography* (Berkeley, Calif.: University of California Press, 1983), ch. 4; Linda H. Peterson, *Victorian Autobiography* (New Haven, Conn.: Yale University Press, 1986), ch. 2; and especially Paul Jay, *Being in the Text: Self-Representation from Wordsworth to Roland Barthes* (Ithaca, NY: Cornell University Press, 1984), 92–108.

[6] The best accounts are Janice L. Haney, ' "Shadow-Hunting": Romantic Irony, *Sartor Resartus* and Victorian Romanticism', *Studies in Romanticism*, 17 (1978), 307–33, and David Riede, 'Transgression, Authority, and the Church of Literature in Carlyle', in Jerome J. McGann (ed.), *Victorian Connections* (Charlottesville, Va.: University Press of Virginia, 1989).

[Teufelsdröckh's] travels are indicated by the Street-Advertisements of the various cities he has visited' (p. 61). The undifferentiated chaos of print and manuscript in the bags is a *reductio ad absurdum* of self-writing, a paper trail left by Teufelsdröckh's passage through time and space, submitted without further comment as his proper textual record. Autobiography in the conventional sense—according to the conventions of what could be seen as 'Autobiographical times', that is—thus becomes a matter of juggling paper, of selecting and translating and deciphering: not life-writing so much as life-*re*writing, or adapting life to the conditions of publication.

The contrast with *The Prelude* is instructive. In the light of *Sartor's* joke Wordsworth's leap into autobiography looks most of all like an entirely paperless exercise. The poem's continuous and sublime response to its own self-interrogation works by omitting the whole issue of publication which confronts *Sartor's* editor as a virtually insuperable obstacle.[7] Teufelsdröckh's egotistical self-consciousness may have equally sublime aims, but it involves itself with the problematic field of literary circulation. Simply by acknowledging its printedness, the autobiographical 'thing that can say "I" ' opens itself to contemporary debates over who can *write* 'I', and under what conditions. In the relative privacy of manuscript, *The Prelude* evolves a version of self-consciousness whose basis in representations of deep and dramatized interiority is recognizably modern. Its self-inscription, its writing 'I', is marked by psychological actions and effects ('My mind did at this spectacle turn round / As with the might of waters', VII. 616–17): memory, reflection, doubt, wonder, anxiety. *Sartor's* games and ironies, though, draw spectacular attention to the *textuality* of autobiographical self-consciousness. In close correspondence with the literary public sphere's habitual concerns (as described in the previous chapter), they play upon the fact that autobiography traverses the public–private border, and they comically express the discomfort of its transactions there. In Teufelsdröckh's case every historical or psychological aspect of his subjecthood stands in baffling relation to its equivalent printed form. (That is why his travels are recorded in sheaves of 'Street-

---

[7] This is not to say that *The Prelude* is not in fact troubled by the intervention of writing into moments of self-consciousness, nor that self-interrogation is not often blocked or blanked. See e.g. the incisive readings gathered in Mary Jacobus, *Romanticism, Writing and Sexual Difference* (Oxford: Clarendon, 1989). My contrast is meant only to illustrate the point at hand, not to deny *The Prelude's* availability for deconstructive or psychoanalytic readings.

Advertisements'.) *Sartor* insists that this mass of writing contains and adds up to the 'quite new human Individuality' (p. 8) of the autobiographical subject, the sublime ego of romantic Idealism; and yet at the same the book wittily but emphatically shows that publication is not a transparent window on to the 'Vast prospect' of the 'I' and its world. Autobiography may be the proper form of self-consciousness in the literary environment of the 1830s (and after), but, *Sartor* reminds us, it is still at least as much a public (published) situation as an articulation of the private self.

It would be misleading to imply that *Sartor* somehow represents the condition of Romantic-period autobiography better, or more characteristically, than *The Prelude*. Carlyle's strange quasi-novel is as utterly atypical of the general state of such writing as Wordsworth's poem, and was probably read with attention by not many more people, despite its circulation in a respectable literary monthly. However, it does (especially in juxtaposition with *The Prelude*) help to focus the best way of thinking about the point where autobiographical practice meets the prescriptive forces described so far. Just as prescription has to be understood in relation to practice, so the texts of Romantic-period autobiography are pressured and shaped by the conditions of their literary public sphere. This does not manifest itself as a direct repetition of the anxieties expressed by commentators like Foster and Wilson. Still less is autobiography visibly trying to contain itself in the various moulds prescriptive discourse suggests for it. The relation of practice to prescription is more indirect, though perhaps thereby stronger (since it operates at a more general level). We could put it like this: as the anxieties evident in the literary public sphere centre on the problematic transition from private to public, so autobiographical documents are characteristically inflected by a sense of complexity or uncertainty over the fact of publication. *Sartor* highlights this position by refusing to allow autobiography simply to appear, to arise spontaneously out of self-interrogation as it does in the grammar of *The Prelude*'s 'and hence this song'. To this extent at least, it reflects the situation in the prescriptive and critical discourse, where the whole idea of the genre seems to be automatically under question.

Carlyle is able to play sophisticated games with the idea of autobiography largely because he is writing at the end of the period we are concerned with. By the early 1830s the idea is there to be played with; indeed, one could argue that the appearance of a kind of parody of autobiography like *Sartor* confirms the emergence of a recognizable genre continuous with subsequent models. (The multi-volume anthology

Autobiography, published by Hunt and Clarke, had begun to appear in 1826, suggesting that a consensus about the discrete status of self-writing was forming among readers.) How, though, might one talk about the relation between prescription and practice in the terms I am suggesting here, if we look back to the later eighteenth century, when both practice and prescription were far less visible? Before the advent of the major review periodicals, it is even more unlikely that autobiographical writing would react directly to the strictures of literary commentators. Again, the more plausible approach is to chart the common ground shared by prescriptive criteria and autobiographical texts. The results are not so different from the situation in the 1830s, since the response to Rousseau's *Confessions* was very much focused on the inexplicable fact of publication, while the more theoretical strand of prescriptivism represented by Johnson's and D'Israeli's essays was concerned with the value of autobiography for readers (its currency in the circulation of print). The textuality of autobiographical acts, that is, remains a point of concern.

The 'Advertisement' to a short volume of travel memoirs published in 1796 begins by balancing the (private) impulse to write with a sense of obligation to the moment of publication. Its terms suggest that, in this case at least, the problems of putting the self into print are as prominent in the 1790s as they are in Carlyle's 'Autobiographical times':

The writing travels, or memoirs, has ever been a pleasant employment; for vanity or sensibility always renders it interesting. In writing these desultory letters, I found I could not avoid being continually the first person—'the little hero of each tale.' I tried to correct the fault, if it be one, for they were designed for publication.[8]

This introduction opens in a solitary scene of writing. The adjective 'interesting' clearly refers to no one's interest beyond the author's own, and nothing is implied by the word 'employment' beyond passing the time. Mentioning the epistolary format disturbs the solitude. Writing is now apparently addressed to someone. Accordingly, an apologetic note enters: the author becomes conscious of egotism (the problem of writing 'I') rather than experiencing selfhood in the acceptably introverted and heightened form of 'sensibility'. With the third sentence egotism

---

[8] Mary Wollstonecraft and William Godwin, *A Short Residence in Sweden and Memoirs of the Author of 'The Rights of Woman'*, ed. Richard Holmes (Harmondsworth: Penguin, 1987), 62. Hereafter cited in the text by page number only. Holmes's edition adopts *A Short Residence* as an abbreviated title for Wollstonecraft's volume, but I have preferred a closer approximation to the full title of the first edition, which is *Letters Written During a Short Residence in Sweden, Norway, and Denmark*.

becomes subject to an attempt at editorial correction, as if the author has now split in two, half transcribing the self with pleasure and interest and half censoring the resultant text with an eye on prescriptive pressures (the mock uncertainty over the word 'fault' nicely encapsulates the sense of a contestable critical environment). Publication is made explicitly responsible for this split. The more public writing becomes, the more it is aware of itself in ways not just to do with interest, pleasure, or purpose. Critical standards give way to a general sense of prescriptive pressure attached to the printed and circulated textuality of writing, a feeling that publication unsettles the enterprise. This is the kind of self-consciousness literalized in *Sartor*'s joke about making autobiography. The 1796 'Advertisement' goes on to demonstrate its effects. Defending the choice to publish 'remarks and reflections' in their original 'unrestrained' form, it claims that egotism is acceptable if the speaker 'can win on our attention by acquiring our affection'. Yet this defensive stance is quickly followed by a reference to the blandest standards of public instructiveness: 'My plan was simply to endeavour to give a just view of the present state of the countries I have passed through' (p. 62). Writing seems confident enough about its original impulses and uses; but as soon as it thinks of itself as a *book* it finds itself negotiating its way through different ideas of itself.

The author in this case is Mary Wollstonecraft, and the book her widely admired *Letters Written During a Short Residence in Sweden, Norway, and Denmark*. It has been observed before that the volume has a contentious relationship with the travel-memoir form. Both 'Romantic' and feminist readings have been used to explore the tensions: the former by tracing the reflex of melancholy sensibility that turns the narrator's eye inward, away from its duties as an observer, the latter by pointing out the gendered mobility which allows her to exploit different positions of observation and so offer conflicting interpretations of conventional travelogue material.[9] Immediacy and intensity of senti-

---

[9] For an exemplary reading of Wollstonecraft's Romantic stance see Mitzi Myers, 'Wollstonecraft's *Letters Written* ... *in Sweden*: Towards Romantic Autobiography', *Studies in Eighteenth-Century Culture*, 8 (1979), 165–85. See also Peter Swaab, 'Romantic Self-Representation: The Example of Mary Wollstonecraft's *Letters in Sweden*', in Vincent Newey and Philip Shaw (eds.), *Mortal Pages, Literary Lives: Studies in Nineteenth-Century Autobiography* (Aldershot: Scolar, 1996). A feminist reading of Wollstonecraft's descriptive rhetoric is Jeanne Moskal, 'The Picturesque and the Affectionate in Wollstonecraft's *Letters from Norway*', *Modern Language Quarterly*, 52 (1991), 263–94; the gendering of sublime space is discussed in Sara Mills, 'Written on the Landscape: Mary Wollstonecraft's *Letters Written During a Short Residence in Sweden, Norway and Denmark*', in Amanda Gilroy

ment—qualities which could be marked as both Romantic and feminine, especially in the discourse of sensibility—were noted as the *Letters'*
distinctions. The *Monthly Review* found Wollstonecraft's book unlike
ordinary travel writing because the reflections and meditations were
more interesting than the descriptions. Its notice reflects prevailing standards by admitting that 'fastidious delicacy' might judge the direct and
forcible transcriptions of personal impressions 'a defect', but it finds that
'the undistinguished disclosure of an enlightened and contemplative
mind' outweighs such scruples.[10] If the advertisement betrays some anxiety over the balance between egotism and its possible justifications, the
generally positive reception of the *Letters* suggests that their handling of
sensibility and sexual difference exploited the ambivalences in prescriptive discourse, rather than falling foul of them. It is more interesting, I
think, to associate the unease about publication enacted in
Wollstonecraft's prefatory remarks with the work's epistolary form—
following *Sartor'*s lead, which presents the physical form of self-writing
as a focus for specifically autobiographical difficulties.

A letter licenses first-person narrative and accommodates a reflective
and intimate tone. To that rather obvious extent, it presents itself as a
private, or at least personal, mode of writing, not necessarily concerned
with the decorums of the public sphere. One of the master-texts of sensibility, Goethe's *Werther*, casts itself is a series of letters in order to mime
a voice of exaggerated inwardness. A more direct influence on
Wollstonecraft's book, Rousseau's *Reveries of a Solitary Walker*, moves
further towards the illusion of fully private writing by doing away even
with the idea of an addressee, printing a series of quasi-epistolary meditations directed only to the author. An equivalent tone is often struck in
the *Letters*, as if writing directly inscribes moments of purely inward
experience: 'Now all my nerves keep time with the melody of nature. Ah!
let me be happy whilst I can. The tear starts as I think of it' (p. 128). Yet
the book presents its series of letters as more than a frame for combining narrative detail with lyrical subjectivity. Unlike Rousseau's *Reveries*,
a reader is present in the text: they are addressed *to* someone (even in
Werther this is rarely more than a convenient fiction). The identity of the
historical addressee, Wollstonecraft's lover Gilbert Imlay, is of course
withheld, but the text invokes a very specific second person ('You have

(ed.), *Romantic Geographies* (Manchester: Manchester University Press, 2000). On the
book's negotiation of gender positions see Janet Todd, 'Mary Wollstonecraft and
Enlightenment Desire', *Wordsworth Circle*, 29 (1998), 186–91.

[10] *Monthly Review*, NS XX. 251.

probably made similar reflections in America ... Even now I begin to long to hear what you are doing in England and France'; p. 122). Occasionally the effect is very startling. An angry exclamation at business fraud is cut off suddenly: 'But this, *entre nous*' (p. 195). The privacy conveyed at such moments is of a very different kind than that conjured by sentimental soliloquy. As with Hazlitt's *Liber Amoris*, the first person is not preoccupied with expressing and performing its subjectivity. It is busy instead with dialogue and negotiation, appealing to a specified (if ghostly) auditor.[11]

In published form, as Wollstonecraft's 1796 volume, this privacy becomes strangely displaced. Unlike the more theatrical effusions of sensibility, its concerns do not translate on to the printed page. Like the bizarre minutiae of Teufelsdröckh's documentary record, it preserves the printed outline of experiences that seem impossibly remote. We cannot be privy to the secrets shared between Wollstonecraft and Imlay, or between the text's first and second persons. Publication actually intensifies the aura of inwardness, because it positions us as eavesdroppers (just as Lockhart diagnosed), not fully occupying the subjective space the *Letters* evoke and so made aware of a further, more remote interiority. As a result the letters retain to an unusual degree the impression of being transcripts of actual, private manuscript documents. (Again compare *Liber Amoris*, where the oddness of this effect is more abrupt.) Their appearance in print seems less like a managed transition from private to public than an oscillating interpenetration of the two. Hence, the 'Advertisement' accurately prophesies what will follow: the documentary functions of travel writing coexist with the expression of subjectivity, because each letter appears simultaneously as a record of the journey and a manuscript document exchanged between individuals. Thus the text effectively advertises its transitions between public and private spheres by drawing attention to its textual forms (volume, letters). The autobiographical quality of the *Letters* is conveyed by something more than the stance of expressive interiority, powerfully though Wollstonecraft adopts that pose. More significant is the sense of the publication of intimate documents: the printing of autobiographical papers.

---

[11] The intersubjectivity of the *Letters* is very persuasively described in Nancy Yousef, 'Wollstonecraft, Rousseau and the Revision of Romantic Subjectivity', *Studies in Romanticism*, 38 (1999), 537–57. See also Mary Favret's study of the significance of their epistolary character: Mary A. Favret, *Romantic Correspondence* (Cambridge: Cambridge University Press, 1993), ch. 4.

Lyrical effusions were after all ubiquitous in the literary landscape of the 1790s. If we are searching published texts for signs of the peculiarly uneasy discourse of autobiography, these are not likely to be found in the domain of vocabulary or style. It would be going much too far to claim that the first person itself is marked by uncertainty. The huge majority of autobiographical texts throughout the Romantic period simply get on with the story, despite the steady flow of disapproving or doubting commentary from the periodical press. As *Sartor* comically points out, disturbances in the performance of autobiographical writing tend to come instead when such writing thinks of itself as an act of publication. In both Carlyle's book and Wollstonecraft's advertisement this is the point where the confidently subjective narrator is joined by an anxiously autobiographical editor/censor—and here I mean 'autobiographical' not in the sense of 'writing autobiography' but of 'producing or publishing an autobiographical document', a crucial shift of emphasis which we can now try and examine more carefully. This latter aspect of autobiographical practice is, I suggest, where the pressure of prescriptivism makes itself felt. (It is also the aspect that *The Prelude* dispenses with, at least until the more accommodating environment of 1850—though not entirely so, as we will see shortly.) In other words, prescriptivism does not affect Romantic-period autobiography as a set of implied standards (however contentious) which the texts variously accept or defy. It instead inhabits autobiographical practice as an idea about the process of making things public, about publication. The texts internalize the surrounding discourse by becoming self-conscious about their place in the literary public sphere. That is the most we can say in general terms about how the issues explored in preceding chapters impinge on our reading of the documents of Romantic autobiography.

As a general claim this might appear to be of limited interest, and perhaps not very surprising either. After all, a good deal of recent work in Romantic studies, notably books by Lucy Newlyn and Paul Keen, has emphasized the turbulence of the literary public sphere in an age of expanding reading and printing, and explored the damage done to inherited models of genre, writer–reader relations, the practice and profession of authorship, and so on.[12] In this environment it might seem to be no more than stating the obvious to say that one kind of writing

---

[12] Paul Keen, *The Crisis of Literature in the 1790s* (Cambridge: Cambridge University Press, 1999); Lucy Newlyn, *Reading, Writing, and Romanticism* (Oxford: Oxford University Press, 2000).

should be characterized by uncertainty over its transition into print. What is to be gained from drawing attention to autobiographical versions of the condition? Later chapters will look at versions of its operation in individual texts; but how do these general conclusions enable a more historically responsive and accurate account of Romantic autobiographical writing?

One straightforward but nevertheless important point is that we can no longer read autobiography as a mode of self-authentication. This contradicts a line of criticism which has posited the self as the genre's proper subject and argued that its Romantic manifestations assert (in the words of an introductory essay to a volume on nineteenth-century autobiography) 'the privilege accorded to Romantic notions of self-autonomy' by depicting subjectivity's triumphant productions of itself.[13] More pointedly for the present critical moment, it also contradicts the view that autobiographical writing represents a prop of a (or even 'the') Romantic ideology. By understanding self-writing as a fraught negotiation with the arena of publication and the fact of textuality, we need no longer assume that its main interest—overt or covert—is producing an interiority which is granted the transcendent status of the work of art.[14] In fact, the broad interpretation proposed here shifts attention away from subjectivity as the key term in Romantic autobiographical writing, replacing it with textuality (or at least the condition of print)—a move which certainly tallies with the historical evidence, since, as I have already remarked, most documents in the period have only the most perfunctory interest in the self. The relation between autobiographical practice and its prescriptive contexts allows us to relocate the whole theme of self-consciousness, in two related directions. First, the reflexive subject, the thing 'conscious' of its 'self', can be defined as the printed text rather than the authorial 'I' (we'll look in a moment at some forms of textual 'self-consciousness'). Second, the product of its reflections can be understood as uncertainty or anxiety rather than what *The Prelude* calls 'self-presence', the Romantic ideology of an autonomous and self-creating subject, 'our ME the only reality' in Teufelsdröckh's phrase (p. 44).

---

[13] Vincent Newey and Philip Shaw (eds.), *Mortal Pages, Literary Lives* (Aldershot: Scolar, 1996), 3.
[14] Both the critical history of autobiography as a literature of selfhood and a materialist, historicist critique of that history can be read in Nussbaum, *The Autobiographical Subject*, ch. 1. Her seminal book is essentially about 'identity' (see e.g. the summary of the argument on pp. 56–7); my concern here is with writing.

Since Wordsworth's poem (or poetic project) has so often been taken
as a central instance of Romantic autobiography, whether read as an
exemplary monument of self-authorship or a test case for exposing the
ideological structure of such a project, it might be helpful to illustrate the
altered perspective I am suggesting by taking a brief example from *The
Prelude*.[15] The earliest states of the poem recognizable as such—the accumulating manuscript fragments of 1798–9—begin, rather like the first
sentence of the 'Advertisement' to Wollstonecraft's *Letters*, in a scene of
writing occupied only with itself.[16] Unlike the advertisement, however,
the scene isn't being described for, or presented to, a reader. It appears
to be a fully private situation: a manuscript in which writing circles
around the subject of a reflexive creativity: 'a vital breeze that passes
gently on / Oer things which it has made'.[17] The appearance of the writing subject occurs as a self-interrogating intervention into the fragmentary descriptions of this 'redundant energy'. The first grammatically
complete sentence begins (reflexively) 'was it for this . . .?'; the question
introduces the questioning subject (someone has to be asking it), and the
autobiographical author, with his history, his memories, and his psychological relation to history and memories, is born. Wollstonecraft's advertisement speaks of the 'pleasant employment' of 'writing . . . memoirs',
and this very first *Prelude* draft ends by also dwelling on the pleasures of
memory: 'These hours that cannot die these lovely forms / And sweet
sensations which throw back our life'.[18] It is the introduction of an imagined reader, a second person to go with the first-person writer—in
Wollstonecraft's case, the addressee—which disturbs the idyll. The first
set of revisions to the initial *Prelude* fragments expel the manuscript
from its perfect privacy by referring to an anticipated reader.
Immediately the expression of self-writing's pleasures is incorporated

---

[15] I stress again that the aim here is to clarify the critical adjustment suggested in the
chapter overall; there is naturally much more that could be said about the particular case
of *The Prelude*. Among readings of the poem that place it at the centre of a fully developed
Romantic autobiography see especially William C. Spengemann, *The Forms of
Autobiography* (New Haven, Conn.: Yale University Press, 1980), 72–91, which interprets
the formal action of poetry as the authenticating ground of self-knowledge. Alan Liu,
Wordsworth: The Sense of History (Stanford, Calif.: Stanford University Press, 1989)
attempts a lengthy exposure of the strategic evasions and erasures involved in the production of self-consciousness.

[16] I am following the conjectural ordering of these fragments given in the introduction
to William Wordsworth, *The Prelude, 1798–1799*, ed. Stephen Parrish (Ithaca, NY: Cornell
University Press, 1977).

[17] Wordsworth, *The Prelude, 1798–1799*, ed. Parrish, 123.

[18] Ibid. 130.

into a defensive rhetoric, where writing self-consciously acknowledges
and justifies its own continuation:

> need I dread from thee
> Harsh judgments if I am so loth to quit
> Those recollected hours that have the charm
> Of visionary things, and lovely forms
> And sweet sensations, that throw back our life[19]

As soon as *The Prelude* thinks of itself as a legible text available to a
reader's eye, rather than a securely reflexive manuscript, it becomes 'self-
conscious' about its own status as autobiographical writing.

This, I suggest, is the fundamentally autobiographical moment, in so
far as the adjective refers to a form of writing entering the literary field
around the time of the beginning of Wordsworth's career. The pure play
of writing subjectivity in the initial fragments is as private as thought.
Despite the fact that it includes written first-person descriptions of past
events, it is autobiographical only in the sense that a memory (an event
of consciousness) is. Only when writing comes to think of its textuality—its material presence in a public sphere, even the extremely
restricted public sphere of a coterie audience as with *The Prelude*—does
it gain the form of self-consciousness relevant to the field of Romantic
autobiography. The 'recollected hours', that is, emerge from memory
and private history into the arena of textual circulation and consumption, and so become the objects of a kind of reflexiveness which focuses
on the legitimacy of writing and reading. That reference to being 'loth to
quit' them might sound as if it is talking about a preference for habitual
Rousseauan reverie, but in fact it clearly refers specifically to the conduct
of the text: what the sentence says is 'need I dread harsh critical judgements from you, my reader, if I continue to write autobiographically?'[20]
This bears witness to the first of the shifts in our critical paradigm
mentioned above, from psychological to textual self-consciousness. The
related shift from confident self-authorship to a more hesitant situation
is straightforwardly evident in Wordsworth's lines. Writing's autobiographical reflection on its existence is also a question about its propriety

---

[19] *Prelude* (1799), I. 458–62. These lines are quoted from the finished version of the two-
book *Prelude*. See Wordsworth, *The Prelude, 1798–1799*, ed. Parrish, p. 13, on how they
formed part of the second state of the poem as preserved in the 'Christabel' notebook.

[20] The biographical context—Coleridge's urging Wordsworth to make progress with a
grand philosophical poem (the *Recluse* project) and Wordsworth's apologetic focus on *The
Prelude* instead—is relevant here; but there is no need to refer to extraneous considerations
to illustrate the form of a specifically autobiographical self-consciousness.

(exactly as we would expect given the conditions in which the genre became visible). The 'dread' of 'Harsh judgments' may be rhetorically exaggerated, but the apologetic situation is unmistakable. It crops up a few more times in the final version of the two-book *Prelude*, always as the poem reflects on what it is saying or might say:

> not uselessly employed
> I might pursue this song . . .
> And to my friend who knows me I may add,
> Unapprehensive of reproof . . .
> It were a song
> Venial, and such as—if I rightly judge –
> I might protract unblamed . . .
>
> (*Prelude*, 1799, I. 198–9, II. 73–4, I. 248–50)

As it finally developed out of the draft versions, the conclusion to part I is an extensive apologia, casting the autobiographical project as a 'weakness' (I. 443) and a deviation from 'honourable toil' (I. 453), and unable to terminate these anxieties with anything beyond the unresolved question about the reader's judgement ('Need I dread from thee . . .?'; the question mark concludes part I). At the same time, then, that Wordsworth's monumental plan begins to conceive its possible course and purposes it also becomes conscious of its uncertain place in the literary sphere. The simultaneity is no coincidence. Numerous contemporary observations reveal what Carlyle's joke in *Sartor* points out: that autobiography discovers itself in crossing and recrossing the gap between its representations of 'self-presence' and its actual presence in the literary public sphere.

It bears repeating that *The Prelude* is not a Romantic-period autobiography, as far as this study is concerned. By avoiding publication it insulates itself from any significant relation to the environment I am describing. Nonetheless, the effect on the poem's progress of imagining just one reader suggests the possible consequences of placing the period's autobiographies in relation to prescriptive and descriptive discourses. We are tipping the balance in favour of what Newlyn calls an 'anxiety of reception', away from an aesthetics of autobiography or a categorical or taxonomic study of its forms. Newlyn's own account of this anxiety calibrates its pressure on authors' understanding of their own position and explores writers' strategic and rhetorical responses on both sides (writers reading as well as writers authoring). Her focus is on the intersections between a 'high' Romanticism, almost exclusively in the shape of poetry, and a developing literary-critical discourse (readers and reviewers making belletristic judgements about texts which they perceive to have the status of 'literature'): essentially, 'the relationship between poets and their critics'.[21] In the case of autobiography the anxiety of reception is rather differently organized. Rather than being an element in writer–reader relations, it centres around the idea of genre (of a particular mode of writing), and therefore operates in particular texts, not writers, with reference to the legitimacy of the genre itself (rather than to the variety of reading attitudes). It suggests that we read autobiography itself through the moments when the texts understand themselves to be legible as autobiographies. On these occasions the texts are effectively occupied by the pressure of prescriptive discourses. As Newlyn's model suggests, the apparent binary division between author and reader is collapsed, since the text articulates both the autobiographical subject and the conditions under which he or she expects to be read and judged.[22]

Temporarily at least, such an approach allows for a more inclusive approach to the enormous variety of autobiographical documents in the period. Whereas other kinds of criteria that have been used to define the field tend to fade away once one looks past the tiny proportion of canonical texts, the anxiety of reception is widespread. Anyone looking for the 'subjective impulse' (Jerome Buckley's phrase) or 'the dialectic between autonomy and community' (Martin Danahay) or 'a subtle and pervasive attentiveness to the inner rhythms and larger shapes of . . . subjects' lives' (Eugene Stelzig) or any such formal or thematic essence is likely to depend on a highly restricted set of readings.[23] The notion of textual self-consciousness brings a much more general autobiographical habit into view. (I describe the advantage as temporary because, as will be evident in this book, canonical documents still exert their centripetal pull. Even a condition as pervasive and vague as an anxiety of reception can sometimes have nothing but the most perfunctory effect, and such is the case in all but a few documents.) The place where it is usually most obvious is, not surprisingly, the place where published documents are encouraged by convention to reflect on their own purpose and place: the advertisements,

[21] Newlyn, *Reading, Writing, and Romanticism*, 223.
[22] Ibid. 3–23.
[23] Jerome H. Buckley, *The Turning Key* (Cambridge, Mass.: Harvard University Press, 1984), 3; Martin A. Danahay, *A Community of One* (Albany, NY: SUNY Press, 1993), 11; Eugene L. Stelzig, *The Romantic Subject in Autobiography* (Charlottesville, Va.: University Press of Virginia, 2000), 12.

prefaces, and introductions which are without doubt the single most characteristic feature of autobiographical writing in the period. In many cases, in fact, the prefatory front matter is the only place where these books offer later readers any sense at all of a literary event. So far removed from its original circumstantial contexts, the narrative content of many of them now reads like the most skeletal trace of lived experience, as entirely lost in forgotten historical particularity as the name and dates on a tombstone. There are very few Equianos or Hunts or Gooches or Wollstonecrafts whose accounts articulate the distinctness of historical and social conditions effectively enough to make those same conditions impinge on the reading process. Still rarer are the fully canonical De Quinceys or Wordsworths who invest narrative with the kind of expressive inwardness once taken for the goal of reading Romantic autobiography, if not assumed to be metonymic for the supposed genre itself. In the ubiquitous explanatory, apologetic, and/or defiant introductions to autobiographical narratives, however, we can still encounter the tensions and complexities of writing, no matter how much the subsequent account has ossified over time into mere information.

Needless to say, the front matter is as various as the books themselves. There are sentimental appeals to the generosity of the public, angry denials of published misrepresentations, expressions of pious or pragmatic desires to set a good example or warn readers away from a bad one. Explanations and justifications for the autobiographical act range in scale from brief and relatively casual remarks like Wollstonecraft's to J. H. Prince's first chapter 'On Writing Lives in general, and on writing my own Life in particular'. Editorial interventions (by writers other than the author, that is) can be used to give a moral context for publishing criminals' autobiographies, to guarantee the veracity of conversion narratives by uneducated writers, to explain the provenance of posthumous texts, to bridge the gap between obscure material and a cosmopolitan reading public, or to take over the role of apologist for autobiography if the text itself fails to open with this conventional gambit. Whatever the particular circumstances, the occasion is for our purposes always the same. The mere existence of the prefatory matter inflects our reading in two ways. First, it draws attention to the book's awareness of its own procedures; second, it presents those procedures as a problem which needs to be dealt with before the book can get under way. Here again is the characteristic pairing of self-consciousness with an anxiety of reception. Even in the most vestigial form, as a brief and entirely conventional one-paragraph declaration of modest intentions and strict veracity, the prefaces preserve the uncertainty of autobiographical acts.

Their most common ostensible function, reasonably enough, is to explain why the subsequent narrative is being published. This is what prefaces usually do anyway, and in the case of autobiographical writing, with its persisting air of transgression, an explanation might well seem more necessary than usual. Consequently, we often find ourselves reading a vocabulary of motivation and intent: a psychological language, a discourse of the self and its inner workings. An unusually clear example is the opening of the 'Preface' to the *Memoirs of Miss C. E. Cary* (1825):

THE following pages are the effusions of a mind agitated, and replete with the conflicting desire of promulgating truth, and of withholding an unnecessary exposure of persons and facts.[24]

Though the material is perfectly conventional (insisting on veracity, maintaining social decorums), the language draws us into the illusion of a Romantic first person. The author's 'mind' and its desires are made responsible for the text, which itself becomes (in a word strongly associated with the literature of sensibility) 'effusions', the visible form of a consciousness in the process of pouring itself outwards. Cary's language of agitated spontaneity is a concentrated and heightened version of a stance adopted by all sorts of writers. The ineffably complacent Percival Stockdale, who as the author of *Lectures on the Truly Eminent English Poets* (1807) would have despised Cary's melodramatic pose, claims in the 'Preface' to his 1809 *Memoirs* that his book 'proceeded from the absolute independence of my mind', and that 'therefore it would be the extreme of folly to relax in these memoirs, from my intellectual, and literary intrepidity'.[25] From vastly different imagined positions, both prefaces represent an author explaining the autobiographical act as an expression of an inward state ('and hence this song'). It is interesting, then, that the focus of attention turns out to be the appearance of the book, not the psychology (or character) that impels self-writing. Cary's conflicting desires should be immediately recognizable as a quandary over the legitimacy of publication. On the one hand is the truth criterion that licenses autobiography; on the other is the post-Rousseauan problem of 'exposure', the way that a published document disrupts the proper relation between privacy and the public sphere. What might at

---

[24] Catherine Cary, *Memoirs of Miss C. E. Cary*, 3 vols. (London: T. Traveller, 1825), vol. i, p. v. Hereafter cited in the text by page number only.
[25] Stockdale, *Memoirs*, i. x.

first sight seem to be a 'Romantic' self-consciousness is thus in fact a typical case of textual self-consciousness. The book may look as if it is accounting for itself psychologically, but the issues are precisely those which the prescriptive discourses bring into play. Like many of the more expressive and sensationalist autobiographers of the period, a mode particularly common in the decade after Rousseau's *Confessions* but (as here) still available in the 1820s, Cary defines her writing as the unmediated revelation of her inward being. 'My Memoirs', the preface goes on to say, 'contain a mere simple recital of the most secret instances of my life' (vol. i, p. vi).[26] Yet what the introductory remarks are really concerned with is the public status of this recital. 'Even in its imperfect state', Cary writes of her book, 'enough will be found to establish truth, which no efforts can destroy' (vol. i, p. viii). The secret life has here become a foundation for a verifiable document. Her experience has passed out of her 'mind' and into a realm where what matters about it is that it be read as truth. In this realm the text knows that its position has nothing to do with the thoughts and feelings with which it was written. Its integrity depends on how it is read: alluding to Harriette Wilson's notorious *Memoirs* (published the same year), Cary acknowledges that her book might be 'supposed to be prompted by motives of profit, like others of a recent date' (vol. i, p. x). Despite its initial vocabulary, the preface is concerned with the book's passage out of the private sphere into the public—just as Wollstonecraft's advertisement is.

Stockdale's pronouncements can be read the same way. By trumpeting the 'absolute independence' of his mind he is not really identifying the memoir as a transcription of his sublime egotism. The point of the gesture is to anticipate and defy any criticism of the project itself; the independence he declares is a freedom from prescriptive pressures. Their influence on the book thus simply becomes more palpable. In the act of claiming a purely inward and autonomous motive his preface exposes its deep concern with the propriety of publication (this is confirmed in the memoirs proper, whose first five pages are a defence of autobiography against all the standard charges). It is entirely characteristic that a language which looks as if it refers to authorial motivation should actually deal with

---

[26] For many women autobiographers the 'secret' or inward self can be equated with the eroticized body; the subgenre of courtesan autobiographies is only the most explicit indication of how the female body's passions and transactions can be synecdochic for the whole realm of private experience in which autobiography could be seen to be invested. The eroticism of Rousseau's narrative again represents the primary model of this equation for Romantic-period readers and writers.

accounting for the appearance of the text. The distinction might seem narrow, but it marks a fundamental redistribution of emphasis. It prevents the prefaces from being places where writers stake their claim to possess the autobiographical text (and there are few enough prefaces like Cary's or Stockdale's, even hinting that autobiography might be read as an effusion from the subject). Instead, they adopt front matter's conventional role: an opportunity to negotiate with readers over the status of the book in their hands. In the case of autobiography the need for some such negotiation is peculiarly acute. Only with the gradual normalizing of the genre in the 1830s and after does it become possible for the books to conduct themselves relatively unselfconsciously, or to concentrate their self-analysis on themes and content rather than the raw fact of publication. Sir Samuel Brydges's 1834 *Autobiography* merely states in its preface, 'I trust [these volumes] will be found to contain an unbroken stream of original thought and sentiment, expressed simply, frankly and clearly.'[27] If the hope is in both senses vain, it nevertheless bespeaks a straightforward confidence that no apology to the reader need be made.

The more usual form of preface in the years between Rousseau's *Confessions* and Brydges's dull effort to imitate them is precisely an apologetic one. Again, this is partly a convention of prefatory writing itself. The pose of humble submission to the reader's judgement was easily transferred from dedicatory prefaces over to the more general addresses to the reader appropriate to an age of mass audiences. Still, any instance of autobiographical writing immediately had something to defend itself against: the 'many reasons that might be advanced in favour of the suppression of these pages', as the editor of Mary Robinson's posthumous *Memoirs* puts it.[28] Over and over again the prefaces apologize for the mere existence of the book they are printed in. Often this takes the form of a direct admission of prescriptive accusations. De Quincey hopes that the public value of his *Confessions* as medical evidence excuses the egotistical first-person narrative; this appeal to documentary criteria has already been noted in the review literature, and it supplies another basic strategy for prefatory apologies. *A Narrative of the Sufferings of James Bristow* (1793), for example, tries to excuse

[27] Sir Samuel Egerton Brydges, *The Autobiography, Times, Opinions, and Contemporaries of Sir Egerton Brydges*, 2 vols. (London: Cochrane and McCrone, 1834), vol. i, p. vi.
[28] Mary Robinson, *Memoirs of the Late Mrs Robinson*, 2 vols. (London: Richard Phillips, 1803), i, 'Advertisement' (no pagination).

publishing the story of 'an obscure individual' by appealing to the author's first-hand description of the colonial campaigns in India, and any number of military or naval memoirs from the ranks begin similarly.[29] The manoeuvre is designed to inoculate the book against its own autobiographical form, insisting that the first person is only a side effect of the documentary subject matter. De Quincey's neat phrase is exemplary: 'Not the opium-eater, but the opium, is the true hero of the tale.'[30]

Just as often, though, straightforward apology slides into apologia: autobiography mounts a defence. Here we can watch the texts responding to prevailing attitudes by imagining justifications for their publication. The prefaces are very deliberately suggesting some possible uses for the book of the self. Because of their debatable place in the literary public sphere, they enter the debate themselves. In this mode the prefaces perform something more than the conventional role of placing the subsequent text in its proper corner of the world of letters. They hint at a more fluid and provisional negotiation, as if reader and book between them have to work out what kind of public use and value this particular volume will turn out to have. It is as if autobiographical writing reflects its environment by casting itself as a work in progress, a mobile element in the social and cultural transactions that define the purposes of reading.

As always, one has to be careful not to exaggerate the distinctiveness, or indeed the interest, of such effects. There is at least one bland, formulaic basis for any autobiographical apologia: the familiar criteria of utility and amusement, always ready to be presented to the reader as an obvious way of defining what the book is for. John Galt, for one, takes this line; 'my actual adventures', he writes, 'are as likely to amuse the reader as the incidents of any fiction', and as the author of novels conducted through realistic first-person voices he can tacitly claim authority for the judgement.[31] Still, we have already seen that amusement can be a shaky defence, inviting doubts about whether the pleasure involved in consuming autobiography is altogether innocent. At its extreme it can end up inviting the same sort of reading habits that so many Romantic-period commentators agonized over with respect to novels: a dissipating and enervated entertainment. So when the anony-

---

[29] James Bristow, *A Narrative of the Sufferings of James Bristow* (London: J. Murray, 1793), iii.
[30] Thomas De Quincey, *Confessions of an English Opium Eater and Other Writings*, ed. Grevel Lindop (Oxford: Oxford University Press, 1985), 78.
[31] Galt, *Autobiography*, i. 1.

mous author of the 1787 *Genuine and Authentic Memoirs of a Well-
Known Woman of Intrigue* coyly wonders 'how then can [my life] interest the public?', the answer is obvious as soon as she summarizes her
story with the confession that 'Inconstancy, caprice, levity, weakness and
sensuality are the sources of my elevation.'[32] The respectable Horatian
principle of amusement here slides easily into a voyeurism specifically
associated with autobiographical writing.

Instructiveness, too, can be a slippery justification. Its usual application to autobiography, as we have seen, comes through the idea of the
exemplary or counter-exemplary life. In the absence of the worthy documentary criteria—medical, military, geographical, biographical, and so
on—available to De Quincey and Bristow and others, this becomes the
most popular apologetic stance. So a picaresque miscellany like the 1795
Memoirs and Adventures of Mark Moore, which moves quickly but
aimlessly through stories of naval, theatrical, and criminal life, can preface itself with a typical piece of phrasing: '[I] shall feel amply repaid,
should any one of my readers, instructed by my misfortunes, be enabled
to avoid those shelves and rocks on which I have so often been thrown
by my imprudence.'[33] The formula is simply inverted in the case of
narratives that are equally unambitious but less racy. 'Should my
memoirs be attended with no other benefit to society,' writes the bookseller James Lackington in the preface to his popular 1791 volume, 'they
will at least tend to shew what may be effected by a persevering habit of
industry, and an upright conscientious demeanour in trade.'[34] Their
shared origin in Protestant conversion narratives shows how interchangeable these positions are. By describing the horrors of the unregenerate state as well as the process of remorse and renewal, conversion
autobiographies simultaneously and equally warn readers away from
one kind of model self and encourage them to emulate its opposite.
Secular versions of instructive testimony suggest that more or less any
narrative event can be read as either a negative or a positive model, thus
advertising a moral and purposeful reading. Outside the specific institutional situation of religious testimony, though, appeals to the criterion of
instructiveness waver slightly from the clarity of purpose they at first

[32] Anon., *Genuine and Authentic Memoirs of a Well-Known Woman of Intrigue*
(London: James Ridgway, 1787), 1, 3.

[33] Mark Moore, *Memoirs and Adventures of Mark Moore* (London: J. W. Myers, 1795),
p. iii.

[34] James Lackington, *Memoirs of the First Forty-Five Years of the Life of James Lackington*
(London, 1791), p. xvii.

supply. Where the religious context makes each individual life part of a pattern shared among a whole community, so that all the separate paths from sin to grace are effectively mapped on to each other, stories like Moore's and Lackington's inevitably draw attention to the circumstantial particularity of the model life. There is no prescribed form for either error or right action. So while Lackington's industry and Moore's imprudence are presented as universal ethical standards, available for copying or shunning by all readers, the details of their deeds and misdeeds (as well as the appropriate consequences) are highly specific. Both are narratives of *unusual* lives, unlike the demonstrations of grace in action which make Quaker or Methodist or Evangelical autobiographies testify to the single standard of value legitimized by whichever congregation they are addressed to.[35] Distinctiveness and difference set a limit on the instructive capacity of the book, however broadly the prefaces frame it. They draw attention instead to that aspect of the story which involves it most closely in the risky business of autobiographical writing: the narration of an individual life for its own sake. If readers are encouraged to think of the book as a repository of valuable instruction, it can nevertheless only be learned by pursuing the story through its particular twists and turns, and then drawing conclusions after the fact. The narrative as a whole is unlikely to be reducible to a governing moral framework.

It seems, then, that there might be a provisional quality to apologetic citations of the most conventional criteria. Even the most formulaic introductions cannot be certain of instructing readers about the proper nature of the book. Our sense of this uncertainty becomes much sharper when perfunctory formulae are replaced by more self-conscious reflections, when prefatory writing gives immediate and specific justifications for publication. The more explicitly a volume accounts for itself, that is, the more obvious its dependence on the contested and uncontrollable literary public sphere. Textual self-consciousness again proves itself to be nothing like the remote, withdrawn, autonomous, Romantic contemplativeness imaged by Teufelsdröckh's 'Who am *I*?' The question is instead argued out in full view of the public. Take, for example, the numerous memoirs claiming to be inspired by a need to set the record straight. Public figures, especially those whose standing is a matter of

---

[35] The fullest study of conversion autobiographies is Gerald Peters, *The Mutilating God: Authorship and Authority in the Narrative of Conversion* (Amherst, Mass.: University of Massachusetts Press, 1993).

significant controversy (anti-establishment politicians, say, or objects of society gossip), frequently preface their memoirs by describing the book as an authoritative riposte to misrepresentations circulated by their enemies. The *Account of the Arrest and Imprisonment of Samuel Bamford* (1817) presents itself as a vindication of Bamford's 'character as a Reformer'.[36] It is not just a first-person testimony relating to the circumstances mentioned in the title. It is about a character rather than a case; it aims to rewrite the idea of Bamford which is circulating in the public sphere. Similarly, the prefatory 'Dedication' that opens the extensive *Memoirs of Henry Hunt* describes the book as a demonstration through autobiography of the absolute consistency of the author's radicalism ('I have never deviated ... never shifted to the right or to the left').[37] A different kind of notoriety can prompt the same stance. Her reputation under attack, Catherine Jemmat apologizes for her 1772 *Memoirs* by explaining that silence might have been construed as submission to scandalous reports. She continues as if her character were on trial before the reading public: 'To arraign my words, thoughts, and actions, with the minutest truth, at the tribunal of publick justice, is one principal inducement to my resigning the needle for the pen.'[38] In all such situations the books are acknowledging their arrival in a sphere where writing of all kinds offers competing versions of the truth. There is no suggestion of autonomous self-determination: quite the opposite. Autobiography prepares itself to be a combatant in a paper war. Accordingly, the texts are intensely aware of their position, circulating in the chaotic arena of reading and writing.

In a significant number of instances the prefaces cite specific documents which they intend to refute. Our sense of autobiography as a kind of intertextual negotiation is here at its strongest. The *Confessions* of Julia Johnstone (1825) advertise themselves in their subtitle as being 'In contradiction to the fables of Harriette Wilson', whose highly readable *Memoirs* had been published the same year (and whose easily conversational bantering style Johnstone has no qualms about imitating as closely as possible). Lackington's 1804 *Confessions* actually set themselves the task of correcting his own *Memoirs* of the previous decade, earnestly embracing the Methodism that the earlier volume had treated so flippantly. Cobbett's *Life and Adventures of Peter Porcupine* (first published

---

[36] Samuel Bamford, *An Account of the Arrest and Imprisonment of Samuel Bamford* (Manchester: George Cave, 1817), 3.

[37] Hunt, *Memoirs*, vol. i, p. xi.

[38] Catherine Jemmat, *The Memoirs of Mrs Catherine Jemmat*, 2 vols. (London, 1772), i. 3.

in Britain in 1797) describes itself as an angry retort to a hostile newspaper article. Philip Thicknesse's 1790 *Memoirs* begin with an ironic dedication to James Makittrick Adair, author of (among others) *Medical Cautions* (1786), calling him a 'base defamer, a vindictive libeller, and a scurrilous, indecent, and vulgar scribbler'; needless to add, Thicknesse intends his own book as a response to a glancing accusation made in Adair's.[39] In such circumstances autobiography is quite clearly caught up in the disputatious literary public sphere, recognizing and reacting to its vagaries, forced to argue with readers for whatever claims it wants to make about itself. Its situation in fact comes to look very much akin to those later eighteenth-century memoirs which explicitly present themselves as commodities ('I must endeavour, by the sale of my book, to extricate myself from the labyrinth of difficulties I am engaged in'; 'To drive off this Fiend ['Want'], alas! [the author] has no other Hope, than from the Advantage she may derive from this faint Production of her Pen').[40] Either way, the book focuses on its availability for consumption, its participation in an economics of profit and loss (whether of reputation or of hard cash). This is of course a particularly uncomfortable situation. Not only can autobiography not be sure of how it will be read, it finds itself desperate for a sympathetic reading which it nevertheless knows is at best conditional. The pressure of the public sphere now conditions the texts' sense of their own existence; correspondingly, autobiography necessarily pictures itself as a fraught moment of publication. So far from imagining themselves as self-authorizing and self-confirming enterprises, the documents are most pervasively characterized by their tendency to reflect on the transition *out* of Wordsworthian or Teufelsdröckhian autonomy into the capricious sphere where print circulates and is consumed.

In this reading the relation between prescription and practice centres around that transition and the reflections attendant upon it. Genre, that is, emerges as the very form of a self-consciousness produced at the permeable border between public and private spheres. There is no mutually supporting set of critical definitions and corresponding master-texts. What autobiographers and commentators instead share is a sense of being unexpectedly preoccupied by one aspect of an extremely hetero-

---

[39] Philip Thicknesse, *Memoirs and Anecdotes of Philip Thicknesse* (Dublin: William Jones, 1790), iii.
[40] Elizabeth Sarah Gooch, *The Life of Mrs Gooch*, 3 vols. (London, 1792), i. 14; Margaret Coghlan, *Memoirs of Mrs Coghlan*, 2 vols. (London: G. Kearsley, 1794), vol i, p. xviii. Courtesan autobiographies will be considered in more detail in Chapter 6.

geneous and questionable kind of writing; that aspect being its way of intruding itself into the literary environment. For the commentators this becomes a matter of interrogating, prescribing, and policing the emergence of autobiography. With the texts the effect is to turn them outwards, as it were. They become works whose most important concern (viewed as autobiographies) is to do with their position and value in relation to the literary public sphere. In so far as we are interested in what we might call their 'autobiographicality' (as opposed to other themes or issues they raise), we can read Romantic autobiographical writing not as texts of the self, of privacy, consciousness, or inwardness, but as discourses on textuality, on publication, interaction, and legibility. As *Sartor* wittily suggests (before retracting the suggestion and embracing Carlyle's odd brand of pragmatic transcendentalism), autobiography is located not in the mysterious thought 'Who am *I*?' but in the chaos of paper fragments.

Another brief case study might be helpful, especially given that the enormous variety of autobiographical writing in the period means that even the broadest conclusions have very different critical implications depending on the text at hand. Thomas Scott (later known for his commentaries on the Bible) published the narrative of his conversion to a Calvinistic evangelicalism in 1779, under the title *The Force of Truth*. It is an unusually articulate and even-handed instance of such autobiographies, impressive enough to be in its fifth edition by 1798 and (outlasting the late eighteenth-century fad for Evangelical controversy) its eighth in 1808. Predictably, its themes are inward ones; as the preface to the 1798 edition acknowledges, the book 'seems to relate almost exclusively to [the author] and his own little concerns'.[41] It is a drama of conscience and intellect. At the end of the narrative Scott offers two possible descriptions of its content, interestingly taking sceptical readings into account alongside the more usual assumption of preaching to the converted; but both choices are equally centred on his inner life:

And now ... I have given, without one wilful misrepresentation, addition, or material omission, an history of the great things God hath done for my soul; or, if that suit not the reader's view of it, an history of that change which hath recently taken place in my religious sentiments and conduct. (p. 70)

The note of tolerant doubt is significant, because it immediately shows the book to be concerned with something more than dutifully producing

---

[41] Thomas Scott, *The Force of Truth* (1779; London: G. Keith and J. Johnson, 1808), 'Preface' (no pagination). Hereafter cited in the text by page number only.

a prescribed testimony (as many conversion narratives do). Rather than just bearing witness to doctrines already accepted by a known community of readers, *The Force of Truth* imagines itself entering a wider—and therefore unpredictable—literary public sphere. It thinks of itself as a *publication* not a testimony; and in doing so it loses a secure sense of its relation to readers, as so much autobiographical writing of the period does.

The result is that the text prolongs itself beyond the conclusion of the narrative. The completed 'history' is followed by a long postlude titled 'Observations on the preceding narrative'. This begins with exactly the kind of reflexive gesture usually found, in more or less perfunctory versions, at the front of autobiographical documents: 'MY design in writing this account of myself . . . was this' (p. 71). The usual explanations follow: Scott's story is supposed to be instructive in both exemplary and doctrinal senses. Here, however, the book plunges deeper into a complex reflection on its own documentary status. The particular significance of its title becomes clear as Scott wonders how his narrative actually manages to achieve his stated 'design'. Its veracity, he decides, is the key: if the story bears true witness to the intervention of divine grace into his inner life, then readers have to admit the reality and efficacy of God's work, and the rightness of the particular doctrines (especially the Calvinistic tenets of election and justification by faith) to which Scott has been led. But—and here the book is adopting what I have argued to be a characteristically autobiographical stance—how can truth be confirmed outside the domain of the private self? How, that is, can readers know it for truth? Scott realizes that the essential factor now becomes not the content of his narrative, the inward story of his soul's progress, but the state of his text and its transaction with its readers. He shifts his focus from himself to his book. For page after page he tries to explain how truthfulness can be proven to be an inherent quality of his text. The facts related in his narrative—the data of experience—must be interpreted, he believes, as decisive evidence of his 'earnest, hearty, sincere desire to *know the truth*' (p. 76). The long years of reading and contemplation described there, and the story of his discontent with an Anglican orthodoxy which it would clearly have been in his interest to leave unquestioned, are guarantors of intellectual and spiritual integrity. Thus the course of the narrative must surely (he argues) describe what happens when truth is sought with complete disinterested honesty; and so the position he achieves at the end of the narrative must be the position to which God and conscience finally bring the undeceived mind. It is a weirdly circular argument, and throughout its course one senses the frustrated earnestness of Scott's search for a way of making his text self-validating. Yet it shows very clearly how the autobiographical nature and purpose of the book is finally identified with its place in the literary environment. The inward self may depict itself filled with conviction and truth, but in the public sphere these qualities have to be negotiated with readers, and that negotiation is what *The Force of Truth* is ultimately about.

Scott's book is unusually eloquent on the transition from inwardness to outwardness, from privacy to publication. The process usually leaves a more vestigial mark on autobiographical texts; one might compare Scott's intricate 'Observations' to the glosses added by an educated and urbane editor to Mary Saxby's *Memoirs of a Female Vagrant* (1806), which temper Saxby's Evangelical enthusiasm with thoughtful comments clearly designed to mediate between her narrative and the reading public. Even the briefest and most conventional of prefaces is nonetheless a sign of the same shift. These gestures invite us to observe how autobiographical acts become embroiled with the conditions of their appearance in print; not just the specific conditions set out in the prescriptive discourse, but the fact of publication itself. Indeed, they suggest that we should not be thinking of them as autobiographical acts at all, but as *transactions* (with the implications of both crossing and negotiating). That, I think, is as far as a general theory of Romantic autobiography can go. Yet a general theory would be of limited interest anyway. Our conclusions carry more weight as ways of reading the situation of particular texts. Scott's book gives some idea of the possibilities; but the most striking case study in the period for exploring the resonances of autobiographical self-consciousness is certainly Coleridge's *Biographia Literaria* (1817). Perhaps because Coleridge was both a major theorist of Romantic ideologies and a prominent man of letters substantially invested in the transactions of the literary public sphere, his autobiographical work reveals with unmatched force what happens when the discourse of truth and inwardness meets the transactions of publication—when Teufelsdröckh's mysticism meets the 'Six considerable PAPER-BAGS'. There is an acute tension in *Biographia Literaria* between 'Romantic' self-consciousness and textual self-consciousness. By studying that tension it is possible to see what might be gained from reading autobiography at the intersection of private and public spheres.

5

Biographia Literaria

Even by Coleridge's standards *Biographia Literaria* turns a nervous and self-conscious face towards the public. Like the revised version of the 'Ancient Mariner', published the same year, or the *Statesman's Manual* (written later but appearing earlier) with its multiple appendices, it is a text which glosses itself. However, where the poem maintains a relatively stable dialogue between content and commentary, Coleridge's most influential prose work dramatically fails to organize its competing discourses into any discernible hierarchy. The apparent 'subject' of the text is variously autobiography, philosophy, or literary criticism; but these fragmentary and disjointed modes are interwoven with apologies, digressions, qualifications, and other peripheral discourses to the extent that the activity of glossing comes to seem almost the constitutive method of the book as a whole. Jerome Christensen has aptly described the *Biographia* as a 'marginal' text, punning on the central position it has occupied in many approaches to Romanticism.[1] It is assembled around other texts—the plagiarized sources drawn on so heavily in volume i, Wordsworth's poetry in volume ii, and other writings by Coleridge himself, some of them purely imaginary.

Most of all, it annotates its own content; so thoroughly, in fact, that the whole work feels like an extended preface. Apologetic gestures, editorial interventions, and self-justifying critical analyses are not confined to the front matter where by convention they belong. These and other manifestations of textual self-consciousness recur throughout the book. The state of the text—the physical condition of the published book, that is—seems always to be subject to negotiation and revision, writing itself as it goes along rather than being presented as a finished artefact. (The

---

[1] Jerome C. Christensen, 'Coleridge's Marginal Method in the *Biographia Literaria*', *PMLA*, 92 (1977), 928–40. For an analysis which aligns Coleridge's project with theoretical and methodological debates in Romantic studies see Stephen Bygrave, 'Land of the Giants: Gaps, Limits and Audiences in Coleridge's *Biographia Literaria*', in Stephen Copley and John Whale (eds.), *Beyond Romanticism* (London: Routledge, 1992).

Biographia was in fact dictated haphazardly and under difficult circumstances, but the relevant point is that the text visibly preserves this provisional quality in its published form.) In the preceding chapter I argued
that autobiographical texts are deeply invested in this kind of self-
consciousness. The intrusion of the authorial first person into the
discursive substance of the book, usually in introductory remarks, can in
fact be a more characteristic mark of autobiography than the first-person
retrospective account of the author's experience. For dedicated ironists
like Byron, Harriette Wilson, or Charles Lamb this opportunity to gloss
the narrative of identity or personality is a rich source of the autobiographical affect, the 'voicing' of subjectivity in writing. By contrast,
Biographia Literaria is embarrassed by its reflexiveness because its
tendency to comment on itself always marks the obstruction or evasion
of its proper subjects. The paradigmatic occasion is also the most familiar: the faculty of 'IMAGINATION', which is at least in theory the
central subject of the text (in so far as it provides the link between theol-
ogy, epistemology, and literature), fails to be educed in chapter 13
because of the interruption of the 'very judicious' but spurious letter
from a (fictional) friend, which glosses the *Biographia* as *'fragments of the
winding steps of an old ruined tower'*.[2] Nor need one penetrate so far into
the ruin to find such defensive commentaries on its architecture. The
first direct information the text gives about itself, halfway through its
first paragraph, is a version of the autobiographical apologetics familiar
from the preceding chapter: 'It will be found that the least of what I have
written concerns myself personally' (i. 5).

The question of how to interpret this innocent-looking hint is fundamental to a reading of *Biographia Literaria* as an autobiographical work.
A long tradition of criticism is founded on taking Coleridge's cue, ignor-
ing the personal material, and elevating the book into a magisterially
detached (if mysteriously obscure) didactic masterpiece.[3] More recently,
its autobiographical dimension has been resuscitated in some sophisticated interpretations.[4] Even so, the apparent suppression of personal

---

[2] Coleridge, *Biographia Literaria*, ed. Engell and Bate, i. 303, 304. Hereafter cited in the
text by volume and page number.

[3] The height of the *Biographia*'s reputation as a critical classic is well represented by
two extracts written in the early decades of the last century, provided in the introduction
to Engell and Bate's edition (vol. i. pp. xxviii–xxix). The two famous paragraphs from the
end of chapter 13, lifted from their surroundings, have entered the canon as a separate
gnomic pronouncement on 'the Romantic Imagination'; it is still common to find articles
that deal only with this part of the book.

[4] See in particular M. G. Cooke, *'Quisque Sui Faber*: Coleridge in the *Biographia*

material announced in the opening paragraph seems to be a problem for these readings. Sheila Kearns speaks of Coleridge 'in effect, figuring himself as textuality itself': exchanging, that is, the discourse of 'myself personally' for an abstracted figure of reading and writing that does the work of the autobiographical first person.[5] She finds a Coleridge who has been reabsorbed into his previous texts, existing autobiographically only as the author of *Lyrical Ballads, The Watchman, The Friend,* and various other documents cited, revised, or plundered in the *Biographia.* In readings of this sort 'what I have written' refers not so much to the autobiographical text itself as to the whole corpus of Coleridgiana.

The second chapter of Coleridge's book is a meditation on the nature of the man of letters, apparently treating literary character in the abstract as he discusses the cases of Shakespeare, Spenser, and Milton. Indeed, abstraction is offered as the defining feature of 'absolute *Genius*', whose power is 'self-sufficing' (i. 31). At this rarefied level issues of mere personality are banished; and this is presumably how we are supposed to read the earlier remark, with its implication that a *Biographia Literaria,* a 'literary life', transcends all that concerns 'myself personally'. Nevertheless, the gravitational pull of autobiography manifests itself through the reflexivity that seeps into chapter 2. Writing about literary character in general quickly becomes an effort to secure the identity of *this* author, who lays claim to the impartiality of genius for what quickly turn out to be the most obviously partisan purposes. The 'original sin of my character', Coleridge writes, 'consists in a careless indifference to public opinion, and to the attacks of those who influence it' (i. 44). He is implicitly recalling from a few pages earlier the incomparably 'august conception' (i. 37) of Milton after the Restoration, heroically aloof from an uncomprehending world. This claim of heroic indifference to the public does not hold good, though: the chapter ends with a remarkable outburst of mingled self-accusation and defensiveness. The essay refuting the '*Supposed irritability of men of Genius*' (i. 30) glosses itself as a highly personal, and extremely irritable, engagement with Coleridge's

Literaria', *Philological Quarterly,* 50 (1971), 208–29; Steven Vine, 'To "Make a Bull": Autobiography, Idealism and Writing in Coleridge's *Biographia Literaria*', in Peter J. Kitson and Thomas N. Corns (eds.), *Coleridge and the Armoury of the Human Mind* (London: Frank Cass, 1991); Susan Eilenberg, *Strange Power of Speech: Wordsworth, Coleridge, and Literary Possession* (New York: Oxford University Press, 1992), chs. 6–7; Sheila M. Kearns, *Coleridge, Wordsworth, and Romantic Autobiography* (Madison, Wis.: Fairleigh Dickinson University Press, 1995); H. J. Jackson, 'Coleridge's *Biographia*: When is an Autobiography not an Autobiography?', *Biography,* 20 (1997), 54–71.

5 Kearns, *Coleridge, Wordsworth, and Romantic Autobiography,* 107.

critics. So the chapter ends by personally appropriating the character of the man of letters, which here (as elsewhere in the book, especially in chapters 10 and 11 and throughout volume ii) forms the textual 'subject'. The fact that the autobiographical appropriation appears to contradict the theoretical argument about literary lives does not mean that the autobiographical moment is superfluous or incidental.

In fact, autobiographical writing in the *Biographia* tends to be associated with similar incidents of circumscription, where the text writes around itself, glossing, commenting, reflecting, transparently aware of itself as a printed publication. This reflexivity is a feature of self-writing, but at the same time it is a problem for autobiography. My intention here is to explore this ambiguity, with particular attention to how the book represents its own purposes and imagines itself being read. These are the constant concerns of autobiographical writing in the Romantic period, but the *Biographia* engages them at the most fundamental level, foregrounding questions of the authority of self-authorship, and vividly enacting autobiography's uncertainties about how it can proceed. While it is in no sense a typical (let alone exemplary) text, it offers what is effectively a theory of the 'literary life' (chapter 2 clearly contributes to this), and so allows us to read the indeterminacy of Romantic autobiographical identity at something like a theoretical level. The disjunction between the 'KNOW THYSELF' that is the 'postulate of philosophy' (i. 252) in chapter 12 and the anxious self-glossing which constitutes the book's autobiographical practice is a fissure that potentially accommodates the problematics of Romantic autobiography in general.

To understand the degree to which the *Biographia* wrestles with the problems of self-writing we have to recall the circumstances in which it was originally produced and read. The earliest reference to a 'Literary Life' in Coleridge's writings suggests the inseparability of life and opinions, of autobiography and philosophy:

Seem to have made up my mind to write my metaphysical works, as *my Life*, & *in* my Life—intermixed with all the other events/ or history of the mind & fortunes of S. T. Coleridge.[6]

The note dates from the autumn of 1803, when Coleridge was living in Keswick, and its immediate context is surely Wordsworth's renewed dedication to the task of producing the *Recluse*, also envisaged at that

---

[6] Kathleen Coburn (ed.), *The Notebooks of Samuel Taylor Coleridge*, 4 vols. (London: Routledge & Kegan Paul, 1957–90), no. 1515. (Subsequent notes also refer to entry numbers, not page numbers, in this edition.)

stage as a philosophical autobiography.[7] The most distinctive feature of the various reformulations of this project through to 1815 (when Coleridge began to dictate the *Biographia*) is that the work is always located as a conceptual or actual gloss on other writings. The 'intermixing' imagined in the original note becomes a series of attempts to make different kinds of text support and confirm each other. The idea of autobiography begins as a strength borrowed from Wordsworth, whose self-dedication and literary productivity both promised an achievement otherwise unattainable in Coleridge's unhappy and dilatory professional life. Autobiography conveys the intuition that selfhood can be contrived along with text: that an act of writing can be attended by an authorial commentary that will ground it in what the note calls 'the history of the mind'. Accordingly, the prehistory of the *Biographia* is the story of a series of prefaces, serving both as introductions to a volume of poems and retrospective revisions of the still controversial prefaces to *Lyrical Ballads*.

The plan is brought up in a letter of May 1811. Coleridge proposes a collection of poems introduced by 'a Preface of 30 pages, relative to the principles of Poetry, which I have ever held'.[8] Though the autobiographical intermixing appears to have been forgotten, the qualifying phrase indicates the desire to make the poems part of a consistent life-long theory. Coleridge wants 'the history of [his] mind' to be legible to his readers. The consistency of the principles of poetry—and of philosophy as well, for 'No man was ever yet a great poet, without being at the same time a profound philosopher' (ii. 25–6)—must be read through a literary life that has Wordsworthian continuity and assurance. This project is equally appropriate as an introduction to a different kind of volume. The '5 Treatises on the Logos' announced in September 1814 are to be preceded by 'a prefatory Essay on the Laws & Limits of Toleration & Liberality illustrated by fragments of *Auto*-biography'.[9] Here writing

---

[7] Coleridge's vicarious pleasure in his friend's activity is evidence of his own desire to produce a commensurate work. Cf. Coburn (ed.), *Notebooks*, 1546: 'now he is at the Helm of a noble Bark; now he sails right onward'. The allusion to Milton's sonnet *To Mr Cyriack Skinner* ('still bear up and steer / Right onward') reappears in the *Biographia* itself (i. 37), also as a vision of a productive literary life in implied contrast to Coleridge's own. On Coleridge's interest in Wordsworth's *Recluse* project and its relevance to *Biographia Literaria* see Paul Magnuson, *Coleridge and Wordsworth: A Lyrical Dialogue* (Princeton, NJ: Princeton University Press, 1988), 274.

[8] E. L. Griggs (ed.), *Collected Letters of Samuel Taylor Coleridge*, 6 vols. (Oxford: Clarendon, 1956–71), iii. 324.

[9] Griggs (ed.), *Letters of Coleridge*, iii. 533.

about the self runs in parallel with writing about writing. This confirms the intermixing of 1803, and suggests that its function is not merely a convenient yet arbitrary structuring of one discourse (philosophy) through the narrative form of another (autobiography), but an essential validation of the 'metaphysical works' by the 'history of the mind': an idea that already anticipates Schelling's philosophy of consciousness as it is incorporated into the *Biographia*. The next time the projected preface is mentioned in a letter its function of securing the right reading of the poems it now introduces is explicit: 'A general Preface will be pre-fixed, on the principles of philosophic and genial criticism relatively to the Fine Arts in general; but especially to Poetry'.[10] Less than a month after Coleridge wrote those words Wordsworth's *Poems* appeared in print along with their famous preface (mentioning among other things the distinction between fancy and imagination). Coleridge's project now becomes a gloss on this text as well as the others, restoring the original autobiographical dimension to the critical-metaphysical preface as the work approaches its extant form:

an Autobiographia literaria, or Sketches of my literary Life & opinions as far as Poetry and *poetical* Criticism is concerned.[11]

The *Biographia* slowly comes into being through various efforts to write a text that would properly position itself in relation to other discourses, making them correctly legible and interpretable.[12] In this sense its autobiographical aspect is far from incidental. Romantic-period autobiography easily accommodates the stance of recollection, revision, and justification. Coleridge's vacillations over his plan capture the ambivalence of contemporary autobiographical practice very clearly: on the one hand the 'history of the mind' provides the unique context in which other discourses become consistent and meaningful; on the other a personal narrative subordinates itself to the weightier matter it intro-duces. Either way, the writing of the self appears as the narrative which will fix other acts of writing. It is endowed with the same kind of literary function as the explanatory memoirs of Gibbon and Franklin, docu-ments which were prefixed to volumes of collected writings in order to

[10] Ibid. iv. 561 (March 1815).
[11] Ibid. iv. 578–9 (July 1815).
[12] Kearns sees this as the autobiographical strategy of the book as a whole. For her, this is a way of controlling acts of reading, a strategy of mastery. I would suggest that the gloss-ing text is not per se any more authoritative. Her analysis is very interesting, but it is less convincing when she allows the *Biographia* not just to reread already written texts, but to provide for correct readings of itself as well.

describe how an author's knowledge was achieved, how his opinions were made.

Contemporary readers had no difficulty understanding Coleridge's book as an autobiography. At no time since the moment of its publication has this reading been so obvious and natural. The brief notice in the *Monthly Magazine* went so far as to describe it as 'two volumes on his own dear self',[13] and we have already seen how John Wilson in *Blackwood's* treated it as the occasion for an extended essay on the perils of autobiographical writing. Even the generally sympathetic reviewer in the *British Critic* began with a warning about the immodesty of a writer who sets out 'to record the history of his own life and opinions'.[14] These reactions may now appear to betray a bewildering misapprehension of the *Biographia*, but in fact they demonstrate the same concerns apparent through the gestation of the work. What they query—with emphasis ranging from sarcasm to vituperation to confusion—is the proper purpose and value of the text, questions endemic to any occasion of autobiographical writing in the period. The reviews make it clear that the context of the *Biographia* is one in which the writing of a literary life belongs not to theoretical arguments about a textual figure of authorship but to immediate problems about what the 'I' is for. Autobiographical discourse is essentially implicated in the *Biographia*'s attempt to circumscribe the correct understanding of the other discourses it annotates, the philosophy and criticism which ostensibly constitute the material of Coleridge's life.

However, as the reviewers were quick to notice, the *Biographia* does not properly contain the risky practice of autobiography within the functions prescribed for it. Where the work's prehistory imagines mutually illuminating texts, the various discourses of the published version give the impression of being unreconciled, not 'intermixed'. Rather than contributing to the long-running debate about whether the *Biographia* is unified or not, I want to suggest that autobiography provides an organizing idea of the function of the book, but also exposes the impossibility of that intent: it simultaneously places and displaces other discourses.[15] Writing about the text and writing about the self occur

[13] *Monthly Magazine*, xliv. 154.   [14] *British Critic*, viii. 460.
[15] The terms of the argument over the book's unity (or otherwise) of purpose can be conveniently read in two books published in the same year: C. M. Wallace, *The Design of 'Biographia Literaria'* (London: Allen & Unwin, 1983), which (as its title implies) locates an overarching intent above the text's discontinuities, and Paul Hamilton, *Coleridge's Poetics* (Oxford: Blackwell, 1983), which attacks all such readings on theoretical grounds.

together (the first person conducts us through his literary life, as Coleridge and his reviewers expect). But, instead of defining and securing the content of the text/self, this relationship always reveals its anxiety, transgressing boundaries and exposing improper content. The book which ought to be a model of autobiography in the most valuable sense turns out to articulate contemporary concerns over the errors of writing the self.

I have already extracted a sentence from the first paragraph of the *Biographia* to illustrate the ambiguity of the autobiographical function. The point might be made still earlier in the text, where the book most openly refers to its intended purpose. The epigraph to the book is taken from Goethe's introduction to the first issue of the journal *Propyläen*:

TRANSLATION. Little call as he may have to instruct others, he wishes nevertheless to open out his heart to such as he either knows or hopes to be of like mind with himself, but who are widely scattered in the world: he wishes to knit anew his connections with his oldest friends, to continue those recently formed, and to win other friends among the rising generation for the remaining course of his life. He wishes to spare the young those circuitous paths, on which he himself had lost his way. (i. 3)[16]

The quotation locates the self in the text with explicit intent. Whether or not Goethe's words correspond to Coleridge's 1803 notebook entry, the writing of intellectual opinions 'as *my Life*' is formally endorsed here. The book invites others to read it as both a didactic document and a history of the first person: indeed, the two interpretations are interchangeable. As in the opening of Rousseau's *Confessions*, text and self are autobiographically equivalent. For Rousseau they share the property of singularity. For Coleridge the determining idea is purpose or method; like its near contemporaries the *Statesman's Manual*, the *Lay Sermon*, and the three-volume version of the *Friend*, the *Biographia* is being represented as doing something useful, and so incorporating its author into a lived community as well as a literary one. In contrast to mass readerships or anonymous critics, the 'widely scattered' readers of the epigraph do not simply relate to the book as a literary object, but correctly interpret it as an autobiographical vehicle of personal identity—the author's 'heart'—and so become Coleridge's friends.[17]

---

[16] See also Coburn (ed.), *Notebooks*, 3221.

[17] Cf. E. S. Shaffer, 'The Hermeneutic Community: Coleridge and Schleiermacher', in Richard Gravil and Molly Lefebure (eds.), *The Coleridge Connection* (London: Macmillan, 1990). Shaffer describes the *Biographia* as 'a search for a method' (p. 210) based on the

At the same time, though, the telling final sentence of the extract portrays the self (and thus the text also) as a counter-model.[18] Up to this point the epigraph seems to be describing the *Biographia* as the medium through which the author can identify and attach himself to those 'of like mind [*gleichgesinnt*] with himself', but this encouragingly positive equation of text and self mutates through the key image of 'circuitous paths' into a significantly different idea of the work's purpose. Now the utility of the narrative is said to lie in mapping out the errors of the past. Autobiography will trace Coleridge's wrong turns, as if the *Biographia* belonged among religious accounts witnessing the sins of the unregenerate self. In this interpretation an account of the past actually tells its readers what not to do; the first person ought to be avoided, not incorporated.

The image raises a problem about where error is to be placed, how it is to be read. Have the mistakes of the past been left behind by the autobiographer, or are they in fact the very content of the narrative in which the self is represented? As originally intimated in the 1803 note, the *Biographia*'s language constantly mixes life with opinions, arguing that intellectual history and personal history are the same thing. Real thinkers—men of genius, as chapter 2 calls them—internalize all their experience: the mind 'only then feels the requisite interest even for the most important events, and accidents, when by means of meditation they have passed into *thoughts*' (i. 31). Distinctions between truth and error are therefore processes of autobiographical narrative as well as parts of a didactic discourse. The sense of a mistaken past haunts the *Biographia*, vividly expressed in the ubiquitous rhetoric of escape or relief. This language is not confined to the narrative sections—'it was long ere my Ark touched on Ararat, and rested' (i. 200)—but pervades the various philosophical and critical projects, which often seem to be represented in terms of a Wordsworthian overcoming of delusion,

dialogic, communal interpretative methods of contemporary biblical higher criticism. However, the language of the epigraph appeals to activities beyond criticism and interpretation; the *Biographia* subsequently makes it clear that critical problems are personal as well as intellectual and methodological.

[18] The idea of a Coleridge caught in the alternations between opposed positions has been worked out across the whole range of Coleridge's writings in Seamus Perry, *Coleridge and the Uses of Division* (Oxford: Clarendon, 1999). Perry manages a superbly full reading of a 'self-opposing intelligence', demonstrating the productive energy generated by Coleridge's 'experience and exploration of division' (p. 17). My attention is confined to the attitude of one published text towards its own place and purposes; the divisions found here inhere in the *Biographia*'s public aspect, and so are not available to be put to use as part of Coleridge's overall career.

> Thenceforth calm and sure
> From the dread watch-tower of man's absolute self
>   to look
> Far on...[19]

By discovering its 'permanent principles' (i. 217), especially the fundamental principles of self-consciousness which Coleridge adopts from post-Kantian Idealism, the self assures itself of its final victory over the 'circuitous paths' of political, philosophical, or poetic contentiousness and inconsistency. Autobiographical recollection of the past becomes a prerequisite for demonstrating the necessary fixity of such principles. It prevents them from being arbitrary assertions, grounding them instead in a visible process, a progressive method (the same argument underpins the two lay sermons and the 1818 *Friend*, though without the autobiographical enactment of the method). The text is a guide through the pathways to truth. However, circuitousness is lodged in this narrative: the progressive autobiography manifests itself as digressive recollections, a series of erroneous counter-examples. The self is both the *result* of the text, emerging out of its processes, and the *content* of the text, enmeshed in what one review called an 'endless maze'.[20] Chapter 1 begins Coleridge's literary life in the appropriate place, discussing his first publications, only to confess in them 'a wrong choice of subjects' (i. 8). The chapter describes a model intellectual ambition, labouring 'permanently to ground my opinions, in the component faculties of the human mind itself' (i. 22). But the story of the growth of a poet's mind is deeply uncertain about its relationship to the past it narrates. As the epigraph has foretold, wrong choices are everywhere apparent, not just in matters of poetic diction but in the 'history of the mind' itself: 'At a very premature age ... I had bewildered myself in metaphysicks, and in theological controversy' (i. 15). This particular mistake soon discloses itself through one of literature's most emphatic accounts of circuitous error, as Coleridge quotes *Paradise Lost* to describe his 'favourite subjects'

> Of providence, fore-knowledge, will, and fate,
> Fix'd fate, free will, fore-knowledge absolute,
> And found no end in wandering mazes lost.   (i. 16)[21]

---

[19] Coleridge's description in 'To William Wordsworth' of Wordsworth's position as described in the final stages of *The Prelude* (Coleridge, *Poetical Works*, i. 405–6).
[20] *New Monthly Magazine*, viii. 50. The review goes on to compare the book to a lunatic's cell.
[21] Cf. *Paradise Lost*, II. 559–61.

More worryingly, the text cannot be sure that it has found the exit from this maze. The epigraph locates error in the past, but chapter 1 clearly hints that the self cannot be separated from its narratives. In this context autobiographical recollection seems to discover something equivalent to (in the phrase already quoted) the 'original sin of my character' (i. 44), an inescapable, compulsive selfhood:

Well were it for me perhaps, had I never relapsed into the same mental disease; if I had continued to pluck the flower and reap the harvest from the cultivated surface, instead of delving in the unwholesome quicksilver mines of metaphysic depths. (i. 17)

The remainder of volume i confirms that the disease is congenital. Instead of describing error as youthful folly—the kind of thing the 'young' addressed in the epigraph can avoid—the *Biographia* admits its probable repetitions of the same mistakes.

Moreover, it appears that recollection is itself digressive. Rather than constituting the progressive narrative of the self and its intellectual and literary history, which leads ultimately, as we shall see, to the 'great I AM' (i. 304; ii. 247), autobiography occasions disruption and evasion. Whenever the first person appears in the book it halts the argument, substituting anecdotalism or defensiveness for intellectual history or the deduction of the model self. Chapters 10 and 11 return as if compulsively to the wrong choices which the preceding refutations of materialism seem to have overcome. Chapter 10 even admits in its heading that it is to be '*A chapter of digressions and anecdotes, as an interlude preceding that on the nature and genesis of the imagination or plastic power*' (i. 168). This intention appears innocent enough, though the digressiveness recalls the epigraph's 'circuitous paths'; but the chapter goes on to present a dizzying series of circuits. There is the trip around the Midlands in order to raise subscriptions for the *Watchman*, a comic travelogue reminiscent of Smollett which Coleridge contrasts ironically with the journal's high-minded devotion to gospel truth. There is the tour of German universities; there is the *Morning Post* journalism, which only wins Coleridge censure for 'the length and laborious construction of my periods' (i. 220). Summarizing his literary life at the end of the chapter, he recognizes that it is a periphery which lacks a centre, a circuitousness embedded in the self as well as its writing:

I may perhaps have had sufficient reason to lament my deficiency in self-controul, and the neglect of concentering my powers to the realization of some permanent work. (i. 221)

Like the epigraph, chapter 10 appeals to communities: subscribers, students, like-minded readers and writers. But the narrative it tells repeatedly ejects the author from the community into which he seeks to be incorporated. The digressiveness of the text mirrors the erroneousness of the self.

When at the end of the book Coleridge returns to the theme of the epigraph, his hope to 'open out his heart' in a model autobiography has become displaced on to one of the *Biographia*'s numerous phantom texts. Recollecting his life, he interprets its significance in overtly moral terms, as a demonstration that we must love 'our neighbours', 'ourselves', and 'God above both'; 'no private feeling', therefore, 'that affected myself only, should prevent me from *publishing* the same, (for *write* it I assuredly shall, should life and leisure be granted me)' (ii. 237). An instructive autobiography remains to be written, but the *Biographia* is certainly not it. The narrative we actually have is mired in the mazes and circuits about which all the book's early readers complained; later investigation would discover plagiarism and mendaciousness as well as digression and obscurity.

Autobiography in the *Biographia* manifests itself in terms of problems of authority and truth. It fails to distinguish between the progressive unfolding of intellectual history and the byways of error. The self represented by and in the text consequently wavers between model and counter-model. It is entangled in the discourses it is supposed to gloss, unable to tell the difference between error and truth; the past (usually represented in this literary life by earlier writings, as Kearns observes) cannot securely be interpreted in the fashion required by the community of readers imagined in the epigraph and elsewhere. However, the *Biographia* also includes within itself a didactic purpose which (in theory at least) might restore the authority and accuracy of the self-affirming self. During the haphazard composition of the book the philosophical chapters—the bulk of volume i—probably emerged as a gigantic outgrowth of the narrative and critical material.[22] In these sections the subject of autobiography becomes the subject of metaphysics, with the advantage that the circuitous paths of the past and its disruptively anecdotal stories are bypassed. The *Biographia* here promises to reconstruct a self in absolute, essentialist terms, thereby securing all the prior material

---

[22] The best account is Daniel Mark Fogel, 'A Compositional History of the *Biographia Literaria*', *Studies in Bibliography*, 30 (1977), 219–34. See also Engell and Bate's summary (*BL* vol. i. pp. li–lviii).

(the critical and personal prefaces and revisions) to a set of principles whose authority would have the self-sufficiency of the 'absolute *Genius*' (i. 31), the authentic literary life. Self-authorship is refigured as post-Kantian transcendental theory through the 'primary self-knowing, which is for us the form of all our knowing' (i. 284).[23]

By grounding its autobiographical act on a pure intuition of consciousness rather than a recollection of the past, the *Biographia* reformulates the self-consciousness of autobiography as a metaphysical postulate rather than a problem of writing. (The fact that these sections of the book represent its most notorious problem of this kind, being extensively plagiarized from German sources, need not concern us at the moment.) Indeed, self-consciousness is described in a characteristically rueful footnote as *the* metaphysical postulate:

Poor unlucky Metaphysics! and what are they? A single sentence expresses the object and thereby the contents of this science. Γνῶθι σεαυτον: et Deum quantum licet et in Deo omnia scibis. Know thyself: and so shalt thou know God, as far as is permitted to a creature, and in God all things.   (ii. 240)[24]

Earlier the same assertion appears sandwiched between two long sections paraphrased from Schelling's *System of Transcendental Idealism*: 'The postulate of philosophy . . . is no other than the heaven-descended KNOW THYSELF!' (i. 252). Raised to this level, self-knowledge might abstract itself from the admissions of failure or (more alarmingly) 'mental disease' (i. 17) attendant on the narrative of the self. The mere act of introversion frees itself from its effects and becomes pure process, one that produces 'the philosophic imagination' (i. 241) rather than written text, or (in the terminology of the 'Genius' of chapter 2) '*thoughts*' instead of '*things*' (i. 31).

The ten theses of chapter 12 elaborate and ratify this position. In their search for a transcendental axiom from whose truth all other knowledge could be deduced, 'a truth self-grounded, unconditional and known by its own light' (i. 268), they fasten on a philosophical equivalent of an autobiographical fantasy of autonomy:

This principle, and so characterised manifests itself in the SUM or I AM; which I shall hereafter indiscriminately express by the words spirit, self, and self-consciousness. In this, and in this alone, object and subject, being and knowing, are identical, each involving and supposing the other   (i. 272–3)

---

[23] Coleridge here translates from Schelling (without attribution).

[24] The Greek motto *gnothi seauton* was inscribed over the portal of the oracular temple of Apollo at Delphi.

The injunction to 'KNOW THYSELF' reveals an autobiographical principle. 'I AM' is understood not as a mere fact of existence but as a dynamic apprehension: 'I am, because I affirm myself to be; I affirm myself to be, because I am' (i. 275).[25] The act of self-assertion constitutes the self, since it alone synthesizes being and knowing (the problematic poles of subject and object). Autobiography's characteristic doubleness—positioning the 'I' as both subject and object of discourse—is figured in Schelling's epistemological geometry, where 'I AM' is 'a subject which becomes a subject by the act of constructing itself objectively to itself' (i. 273). So Coleridge's remark on the *Biographia* in an explanatory letter from the month of its publication can be taken to refer (as the 1803 note intimated) to both its metaphysical content and its autobiographical dimension:

In my literary Life I have sketched out the *subjective* Pole of the Dynamic Philosophy, the rudiments of *Self*-construction.[26]

The link between Idealism and autobiography may seem to be little more than analogy, especially since I have already described the material of chapters 10 and 11 as a digression from the main philosophical project. However, as I suggested earlier, reflexivity (self-consciousness) is at once obstacle and resource. The transcendental deduction borrowed from Schelling operates through a characteristic series of metaphors and analogies: the capitalized 'I AM' belongs only to God, but self-consciousness—the 'sacred power of self-intuition' (i. 241)—pervades the created world, from the caterpillar and horned fly of one of the book's most striking metaphors (see i. 241–2) through to *Homo sapiens*. At the head of chapter 13 (which claims to supply the keystone of the metaphysical argument) Coleridge quotes Raphael's speech in *Paradise Lost* (V. 469–88) on the diffusion of the divine principle throughout nature. At the theoretical level there must be a meaningful relationship—in the *Statesman's Manual*'s terms, symbolic rather than allegorical—between God's 'I AM' and the finite 'I am' of the writer of an 'Auto-biography' (ii. 237). This relationship is boldly asserted in the *Biographia*'s most famous sentence:

---

[25] Coleridge here glosses Exodus 3: 14: 'And God said unto Moses, I AM THAT I AM'. Engell and Bate's note on thesis VI clarifies the degree to which Coleridge is adopting an explicitly theological model of self-consciousness, a position set aside by Schelling (from whom the theses are otherwise mostly derived).

[26] Griggs (ed.), *Letters of Coleridge*, iv. 767.

The primary IMAGINATION I hold to be the living Power and prime Agent of all human Perception, and as a repetition in the finite mind of the eternal act of creation in the infinite I AM. (i. 304)

The practice of autobiography may retrace the circuitous paths of an errant text, but this theoretical account redeems the process of self-consciousness as the first person's (Schelling's *Ich*'s) synecdochic identity with God. 'IMAGINATION' is what is supposed to weave together the various discourses of the *Biographia*, and so (in the language of the epigraph) to 'knit anew' the autobiographical self with its proper 'connections'.

As all readers of the book know, though, imagination is what is missing from the *Biographia*. The climactic chapter 13—'*On the imagination, or esemplastic power*' (i. 295)—leaves out the deductions it promises, substituting instead the altogether different self-consciousness of the book's most extensive gloss on itself. The 'letter from a friend' (i. 300) exemplifies a number of textual black holes throughout the *Biographia* (like the projected autobiography of chapter 24). References to a preface to the 'Ancient Mariner' (i. 306), to a work 'on the PRODUCTIVE LOGOS human and divine' (i. 136), or to 'a detailed prospectus . . . at the close of the second volume' (i. 304) relocate the discourse of the imagination into unwritten texts. Postponements of this sort inhere in the transcendental argument, which twice silences itself in order to preserve its holiness: first at the end of chapter 6 where 'it is profanation to speak of these mysteries' (i. 114) and then (in a quotation from Plotinus) as a reply to those who doubt the transition from transcendental intuition to philosophical certainty:

it behoves thee not to disquiet me with interrogatories, but to understand in silence, even as I am silent, and work without words. (i. 241)

At such moments the connection between 'I AM' and 'I am' itself becomes wordless. Like the faculty of imagination, it disappears from the text, leaving behind a self-consciousness that seems disturbingly akin to the recognitions of failure and error characteristic of the autobiographical discourse of the anecdotal chapters.

What the letter in chapter 13 supplies in place of the missing description of 'the powers of our own self-consciousness' (i. 299) is in fact a strikingly accurate and evocative assessment of the *Biographia* itself. The writer of the letter turns to the tropes of Gothic fiction to describe the bewilderment '*not without a chilly sensation of terror*' (i. 301) that afflicted the early readers of the metaphysical chapters. He points out the rupturing of the structures of analogy and connection on which both the argument and the ideal reading pictured in the epigraph depend:

You have been obliged to omit so many links . . . that what remains, looks (if I may recur to my former illustration) like the fragments of the winding steps of an old ruined tower.

Most pointedly, he complains of the book's betrayal of its ostensible autobiographical intent:

For who . . . could from your title-page, viz. "My Literary Life and Opinions," *published too as introductory to a volume of miscellaneous poems, have anticipated, or even conjectured, a long treatise on ideal Realism.* (i. 303)

The letter substitutes textual for theoretical self-consciousness. Autobiographical reflexiveness is thus figured equally in the unwritten account of the 'I AM' and the self-annotating text that describes this moment in the literary life, the writing of the self. As in the epigraph, ideal truth (the theory of the 'self-grounded, unconditional' principle of self-consciousness) and acknowledged error (the letter's consciousness of what the *Biographia* is really like) prove to be inseparable conditions of the work's autobiographical endeavour.

Autobiography's ambivalence is therefore enacted both in the book's textual practice (where self-writing is simultaneously digression and constitutive structure) and at the more theoretical level, where self-knowledge is at once ideal and guilty. Chapter 13 is paradigmatic of the many occasions when the *Biographia* refers to itself, because it centrally exemplifies the admission of failure that is perpetuated by these recurrent gestures. Rather than establishing the 'I am' as a finite but nevertheless parallel 'repetition' of God's self-authoring, the book's self-consciousness has almost the opposite effect: it produces a textual self that knows itself to be erring. This again makes it reminiscent of confessional autobiography, where the text's purpose is to acknowledge the author's separation from, not union with, the divine. The contrast with Coleridge's theory could hardly be more emphatic. The ninth thesis of chapter 12 affirms that

We begin with the I KNOW MYSELF, in order to end with the absolute I AM. We proceed from the SELF, in order to lose and find all self in GOD. (i. 283)

However, when the *Biographia* knows itself it finds itself admitting the circuitous deviations of both its author and its own discourse.

Chapter 11 is the most prominent instance of oblique confession. Following on from the at least partially humorous account of a literary life's disasters in chapter 10, it interrupts the autobiographical flow in order to moralize the narrative of the self in general terms: 'NEVER PURSUE LITERATURE AS A TRADE' (i. 223). The injunction recalls the double-edged instruction of the epigraph, in that Coleridge's experience is presented as a negative example to his readers. In other words, the narrative of chapter 10 is given a reflexive twist, so that the account of the life of a man of letters suddenly becomes able to gloss itself, to make itself instructive and functional. However, instead of producing the conventional apologias or justifications (as in any number of documents of the period which imagine how they might be read), chapter 11 transforms this characteristic autobiographical turn into an admission of guilt. Two alternatives to the life of a professional writer are offered: 'any honourable occupation' (i. 224), compounded of useful toil and a serene domestic life; or, more specifically, the model existence of a country parson. Both are described in the language of social and personal affection, suggesting the membership of a community which the epigraph proposes as the object of Coleridge's literary life. A professional literary man, however, loses 'sympathy with the world, in which he lives' (i. 228). Unlike the clearly defined social function of a doctor, lawyer, or clergyman, his only role is as a warning to those around him. The chapter imagines the temptations that a young man of the post-*Childe Harold* years, intent on becoming an author, might be confronted with, and comments:

Happy will it be for such a man, if among his contemporaries elder than himself he should meet with one, who [had chosen the literary life] . . . and who by after-research (when the step was, alas! irretrievable, but for that very reason his research undeniably disinterested) had discovered himself to have quarreled with received opinions only to embrace errors, to have left the direction tracked out for him on the high road of honorable exertion, only to deviate into a labyrinth, where when he had wandered, till his head was giddy, his best good fortune was finally to have found his way out again, too late for prudence though not too late for conscience or for truth! (i. 230)

It is not difficult to attach a real name to this imaginary elder author. Coleridge is clearly writing about himself: writing autobiography. Self-knowledge arrives in the passage suddenly and unexpectedly, through an imaginary encounter with an unidentified other. The 'self-duplication' (i. 281) spoken of in thesis IX of chapter 12 finds its textual equivalent in this confessional realization of the self figured as another. Chapter 10 had at least attempted to defend the author's consistency against misconceived or malicious accusations of tergiversation, employing autobiography's power to gloss the self for purposes similar (in kind if not degree) to Rousseau's energetic exculpations of his behaviour. Now, though, the book makes itself obliquely tell what is apparently the truth about the literary life. So far from leading to God, the 'I KNOW MYSELF' here tends in the opposite direction, as Coleridge enjoins his aspiring young author 'to ascertain with strict self-examination, whether . . . spirits, "*not of health*," and with whispers "*not from heaven*," may not be walking in the *twilight* of his consciousness' (i. 229–30).[27] As in the chapter 13 letter's Gothic imagery, a reflexive moment exposes something diabolical in place of the divine.

Similar instances of oblique self-revelation are scattered throughout the *Biographia*: the vicarious defence of the domestic and literary virtues of Southey in chapter 3, for example, or Coleridge's replication in chapter 23 of the anonymous criticism he elsewhere excoriates. What they suggest is that identity is not (as the theory maintains) achieved through acts of pure self-consciousness, but rather 'found' in the text, already supplied by autobiography (as the epigraph hints). Instead of affirming itself in dynamic '*Self*-construction', the literary life realizes that it is already circumscribed: by its past, with its labyrinthine errors, and by its writings, which are chaotically reassembled to form the present text.

It is important to recognize that the alternation between these opposing versions of autobiography (transcendental and confessional) is, like the ambiguity of the epigraph over whether the self is model or countermodel, not a simple polarity but what Christensen calls a 'chiasmus' that is 'Eddy rather than bridge'.[28] The *Biographia*'s opposites always threaten to turn into each other, to change places. The question of how, and to what effect, the book 'reads' the history of the literary life—articulates, that is, a series of reinterpretations of past writings (the 1800 *Lyrical Ballads* preface, the articles on Maturin's *Bertram* for the *Courier*, and so on)—is perhaps the most important instance of its characteristic double vision. The book is always writing about writing: conducting criticism, plagiarizing other works, or glossing itself. Critical activity merges into autobiographical practice, because criticism recollects and reinterprets existing writing in order to construct a literary life. The *Lyrical Ballads* project, for example, is both recounted and rewritten, so as to make it (along with all intervening works) part of a consistent poetic

---

[27] The allusion appears to be to *Hamlet*, I. iv. 40–1.
[28] Jerome C. Christensen, *Coleridge's Blessed Machine of Language* (Ithaca, NY: Cornell University Press, 1981), 27.

intent, and to demonstrate the correct way of reading texts, grounded in permanent truths about the nature of the mind. Both projects imagine an authoritatively truthful self constituted through its reflexive rewritings (narrations of the literary past) and rereadings (corrections of its texts).

This, however, is where the reversibility of the *Biographia* becomes most damaging. The autobiographical act has a double effect. Reflexivity—or, a more appropriately textual metaphor, circumscription—cuts both ways. Structurally, as we have seen, it appears both as the subject of the book and the digressive marginal method which effaces that subject. It is a similarly ambiguous principle in relation to the *Biographia*'s efforts to read itself. In theory, autobiographical recollection will unfold text and self together; to return to the words of the epigraph, the *Biographia* will 'open out' both the man of letters and the man. Hence, the situation of finding the self already given by the past or by past writing, which seemed so alarming in chapter 11 (and which is of course an orthodox deconstructive problem), does not per se disrupt the autobiographical project. On the contrary, the prescribed models of autobiography discussed in Part I of this book call for this purposeful reexamination of the narrated life, a process of useful reinterpretation or rereading which inheres in the representation of the past. So Coleridge plans to settle the 'long continued controversy' (i. 5) over *Lyrical Ballads* in chapters 4, 14, and 17–20, and to show the consistency of his philosophical and political principles in the intellectual biography of chapters 9, 10, and 'Satyrane's Letters'.[29] These rereadings correspond to the 'primary self-knowing' (i. 284) with which the science of metaphysics begins. In each case the purpose is organizing, structural. The reflexiveness of autobiographical writing is intended to fix and define, to 'ground' (a favourite verb in the *Biographia*) the self/text. Autobiography constructs an interpretative framework for reading the truth. 'KNOW THYSELF' is described as the one secure link to which

---

[29] Like the critique of Charles Maturin's Gothic melodrama *Bertram* in chapter 23, 'Satyrane's Letters' were inserted into the second volume of the *Biographia* at the last minute, when it became clear during the publication process that extra material would be required to pad volume ii out to the same dimensions as volume i. The letters are reprinted with minor revisions from three issues of the *Friend* (Nov.–Dec. 1809). Although they were clearly chosen in desperation at the urgent need to find extra material for the volume, both they and the articles on *Bertram* (reprinted from the *Courier*, Aug.–Sept. 1816) are certainly intended to be read as episodes in a literary autobiography. The letters are hurriedly introduced at the end of chapter 22 as illustrations of the author 'in the first dawn of my literary life' (ii. 159).

the chain of reason can be firmly attached; the self-knowledge that comes through reading one's past writings should manifest the Wordsworthian continuity of the self ('my heart was single', i. 180); critical activity reveals the true meaning of other texts, correctly interpreting Kant or Southey or Wordsworth. In this aspect circumscription is all about defining limits, finding proper connections, tracing true meanings.

Crossing Christensen's chiastic 'liminal traverse', circumscription becomes what is referred to in a telling phrase from chapter 12 as 'the anxiety of authorship' (I. 233).[30] Much as autobiographical identity is suddenly exposed at the end of chapter 11, self-consciousness now involves recognition of the otherness of selves and texts, both of which seem always to be saying the wrong thing. Efforts to set the proper limits of discourse end up confusing or dissolving the boundaries between one text and another, or between different interpretations. So Coleridge dismisses the literal Wordsworth—both what the 1800 *Lyrical Ballads* preface literally said, and the literalism or '*matter-of-factness*' (ii. 126) of the poetry—in order to achieve a proper alignment of Wordsworthian texts with the *Biographia*'s theoretical demands. Such discursive transgressions are also apparent in the metaphysical aspect of reflexivity. As Nigel Leask argues, the thrust of the latter parts of volume i is directed towards overcoming the boundaries marked so emphatically in the *Critique of Pure Reason*, allowing consciousness to have intuition of the kind of absolute truths forbidden by Kant's stern restrictions.[31] Rather than fixing their subject within a legible and purposeful structure, writing about writing and writing about the self reopen closed questions and reproduce interpretative uncertainty. What looks from one perspective like the authoritative settling of an issue is from another merely the repetition of metaphysical, critical, or personal controversy in a more acute form. The autobiographical effort to read the coherence and value of the literary life thus becomes entangled in its own glossings, unable to decide whether truth is really located in the written past or whether it is supposed to be supplied by alterations and redefinitions of the given text.

---

[30] Christensen, *Coleridge's Blessed Machine*, 27. Part of Lucy Newlyn's brilliant exploration of the anxiety attaching to writers being read—the sense of the reversibility of literary relations and hierarchies—is a case study of Coleridge (see Newlyn, *Reading, Writing, and Romanticism*, 49–90).

[31] Nigel Leask, *The Politics of Imagination in Coleridge's Critical Thought* (London: Macmillan, 1988), 124–34.

When the errors of the self are being confessed, therefore, the *Biographia* is instancing an autobiographical duplicity that pervades all its discourses. All such revelations of guilt—like the admissions of 'mental disease' (i. 17) or 'constitutional indolence' (i. 45)—serve as troubling rereadings of the contents of selfhood, inseparable from the ostensibly critical effort to determine the meanings of texts produced in the course of a literary life, or the metaphysical definitions of self-consciousness. The much-discussed contradictions of the *Biographia* can be traced back to the indeterminacy of its epigraph, where alternative possibilities for reading the autobiographical text are first proposed (and left unresolved). These alternatives condition the rewriting of the first person, whether as philosopher, poet, or anecdotalist. Not only is there ambiguity over whether these roles are exemplary or counter-exemplary (the confusion referred to in the chapter 13 letter, where the 'I AM' becomes an illegible fragment), but autobiography is itself ambiguous. It straddles Christensen's chiastic traverse, unable to locate itself either as transcendental self-construction or full confession. It cannot interpret itself; and so the contents of the literary life which it goes on to recollect are themselves pervaded by anxiety about how they can be read.

Coleridge's reference to the 'anxiety of authorship' specifically evokes the fear of misinterpretation which afflicts anyone who publishes their writing. This anxiety supplies the form of the *Biographia*'s most obsessive digression: attacks on the practice of reviewing. From the remarks attempting to ward off charges of plagiarism in chapter 9 (see i. 164) to the full-blown *ad hominem* assault of chapter 21, the book imagines itself being read with every degree of hostility. Its very legibility seems to be its most debilitating affliction. Of all the charges that have been levelled against it, the most familiar (and perhaps accurate) are all ones of which it prominently accuses itself: incoherence (it calls itself an 'immethodical . . . miscellany', i. 88), obscurity (chapter 13), plagiarism (chapter 9). If autobiographical writing is formally marked by its tendency to comment on itself, then the *Biographia* represents autobiography at its most acutely self-conscious. Unfolding the first person through its literary life, it surrounds that writing with legions of critical reviewers, real and imaginary (or, as with the author of the 'letter from a friend', both). Thus even as it highlights the first person's authoritative and purposeful ability to read itself, it raises the spectres of misreading and illegibility. Again, what is at stake in these alternatives is not so much the simple contrast of right and wrong critical practices as the difficulty of properly distinguishing them. When the procedures of criticism are incorporated into a literary life (as opposed to the more abstract discourses of the *Statesman's Manual* or the 1818 *Friend*), they become entangled with the author's own writings. Disinterested acts of reading overlap with the personal discourse of reviewing.

Coleridge's strictures on contemporary reviewers present themselves as part of the *Biographia*'s general effort 'to establish the principles' (ii. 107) of intellectual activity. He laments an age in which reading and misreading are not understood to be separate categories. Reviewers merely indulge their wit or their factionalism at the expense of the text before them; there is no attempt to establish criteria for correct judgement, no 'method'. In parallel with the first volume's search for a 'truth self-grounded, unconditional and known by its own light' (i. 268), volume ii looks to supplant the whims of the *Quarterly*'s or the *Edinburgh*'s reviewers with philosophical definitions of poetry and with the 'application of these principles to the purposes of practical criticism' (ii. 19). However, just as the deduction of the 'I AM' disappears into the anonymous review of chapter 13, the critical project keeps recollecting its own liability to being misread. Coleridge wishes to expunge 'unlicensed personality' (ii. 110) from the process of reading, but the *Biographia* is never capable of cordoning off readings of texts from readings of itself—of the literary life, that is, and the self that inhabits it. So far from being the guarantor of impartiality, the book's method veers into autobiography, rewriting the past as an apparently insurmountable series of misinterpretations and 'literary wrongs' (i. 45). Rather than serving simply as the negative image of the critical project, the hostile reviewers who inhabit the text of the *Biographia* represent its recollections of the risks of writing. Method cannot be impersonal because it too is given in text, a chapter in the life of a man of letters.

The significance of Wordsworth as a literary alter ego in volume ii is therefore crucial.[32] The unusual shared authorship of *Lyrical Ballads* offers Coleridge a valuable resource, in that it is a text which he can claim possession of while nevertheless being its critic. It is also a theoretical project which can be defined as incomplete (or at least incorrectly completed), but whose incompleteness can be attributed to Wordsworth. Coleridge can reclaim for himself an original 'plan' (ii. 6) which has not (yet) been betrayed by the inevitable failures of writing,

---

[32] For a penetrating reading of the critique of Wordsworth in the *Biographia* see Perry, *Coleridge and the Uses of Division*, 246–74. Perry explains in comprehensive detail how Coleridge's 'response to the contradictory loyalties of the Wordsworthian imagination' (p. 263) also articulates his own divided critical and philosophical self-definitions.

because it was superseded by the different, Wordsworthian intent
expressed in the controversial preface. 'With many parts of this preface',
he now explains, 'I never concurred' (ii. 9). *Lyrical Ballads* is thus refigured as a prototype for the *Biographia* itself, as the misreadable—and
aggressively misread—central document of Coleridge's literary life
which nevertheless contains a latent truth that can be extracted from its
patent errors. However, where the *Biographia* has to confess that the
errors belong to the self which authors it, the earlier volume appears to
provide the opportunity to distinguish criticism from autobiography by
substituting Wordsworth for the first person and so redeeming the
(unwritten, transcendental) original idea of *Lyrical Ballads* through the
application of an impartially discriminating search for true principles in
a text.

The extended analysis of Wordsworth in volume ii serves two functions, which are in fact aspects of the same purpose. Ostensibly, it is
supposed to exemplify the practice of right reading; more subtly, it
places this valid reading practice as the real story of Coleridge's literary
and intellectual history, by discovering the principles of criticism in the
very act of restoring the true meaning of the most contentious
Coleridgean text. Wordsworth is both scapegoat and substitute. He has
misread his own writing, and therefore been the cause of the reviewers'
hostility to Coleridge, who—thanks to the double authorship of *Lyrical
Ballads*—is interchangeable with his fellow poet in the eyes of malignant
readers. But this interchangeability can be exploited, so that the
Biographia's own imagined unity of poetry and philosophy through the
medium of 'IMAGINATION', missing from volume i, can be reclaimed
via a rereading of Wordsworth as the possessor of 'IMAGINATION in
the highest and strictest sense of the word' (ii. 151) and the potential
author of the 'FIRST GENUINE PHILOSOPHIC POEM' (ii. 156).
Though this is of course yet another of the *Biographia*'s phantom texts,
its non-appearance can be read as the consequence of a set of erroneous
Wordsworthian principles which the *Biographia*'s critical method has
overcome. The book is able to read its failure as someone else's digression from the autobiographer's model plan.

At the centre of this intricate act of rereading lies the discrimination
between truth and error which constitutes the book's fundamental article of faith. The value of *Lyrical Ballads* is that it seems to translate this
idea into 'practical criticism' (ii. 19): methodical reading can sort out
what the author did right from what he did wrong. As we have repeatedly seen, though, these discriminations tend to break down in the

Biographia, and the apparently clear-cut pragmatism of most of volume ii is no different. What Coleridge's review (literally, 're-seeing') of Wordsworth discovers is a split between theory and practice; but the proper interpretation of this disjunction keeps threatening to reverse itself. In chapters 14 and 17–20 the controversial theory of poetic diction apparently put forward in 1800 is said to bear no relation to how Wordsworth actually writes:

were there excluded from Mr. Wordsworth's poetic compositions all, that a literal adherence to the theory of his preface *would* exclude, two-thirds at least of the marked beauties of his poetry must be erased. (ii. 106)

When it comes to specific analysis of the poet's particular beauties and defects in chapter 22, however, Wordsworth's dogged literalism is seen as a feature of his *practice*, and his merits are relocated in distinctively Coleridgean theoretical terms. As before, he writes the opposite of what he means, but now it is the poems that are in error, rather than their supposed intellectual foundations. Reading the 'Immortality Ode', for example, Coleridge finds its literal content absurd, and instead describes its value and meaning in an extraordinary passage that returns us to the vocabulary of the first volume:

But the ode was intended for such readers only as had been accustomed to watch the flux and reflux of their inmost nature, to venture at times into the twilight realms of consciousness, and to feel a deep interest in modes of inmost being, to which they know that the attributes of time and space are inapplicable and alien, but which yet cannot be conveyed, save in symbols of time and space. (ii. 147)

Objecting to 'an apparent minute adherence to *matter-of-fact* in character and incidents' (ii. 129), Coleridge replaces actual content with such transcendental values as 'impressing modes of intellectual energy' (ii. 143–4), 'meditative observation' (ii. 144–5), 'sympathy' (ii. 150), and 'the gift of IMAGINATION' (ii. 151).

The reversible opposition of theory and practice necessarily turns the reading of Wordsworth into a reading of the *Biographia*. Truth and error change places with each other across the divide opened up by the split between the actual text and its theoretical content. The danger of using Wordsworth as an alter ego is that his exemplary failure to align his writing with his secret purpose becomes readable as Coleridge's own. Even here, seemingly distant from the autobiographical ambivalence of the epigraph, the relation between intended function and actual effect is again the site of crippling indeterminacy. Rereading *Lyrical Ballads* is supposed to rescue the authority and truth of an unwritten intention, but instead it confirms the *Biographia*'s anxiety about the inevitability of misreading, because it is unable to match text to idea. An authoritative literary history remains as elusive as an authoritative literary life. The victory of the hostile reviewers is conceded in the *Biographia*'s last chapter. Coleridge summarizes his life as a litany of misrepresentation and unmerited abuse. He is still the victim of acts of reading, not the author of a corrective and authoritative act of writing; the *Biographia* has been a re-inscription of his failures rather than the theorized '*Self-construction*'.[33] The reason lies in its strange inability to read its own discourses, or—more accurately—the failure of its self-glossings to provide an interpretation of the self/text they refer to. Intelligibility (legibility) itself is the book's most pressing problem, as Coleridge hints at the beginning of his final chapter:

It is within the experience of many medical practitioners, that a patient, with strange and unusual symptoms of disease, has been more distressed in mind, more wretched, from the fact of being unintelligible to himself and others, than from the pain or danger of the disease. (ii. 234)

This condition is the apparently inevitable corollary of autobiographical self-knowledge as practised by the *Biographia*. The work's notion of method raises process over content: what matter are the principles of knowledge, the grounds of judgement, rather than the otherwise arbitrary judgements themselves. Philosophy begins with a metaquestion: '*Is philosophy possible as a science, and what are its conditions?*' (i. 140). The literary critic 'announces and endeavors to establish the principles, which he holds for the foundations of poetry in general' (ii. 107). But the result of perpetual reflexiveness is to force the text to read itself, and so (autobiographically) to discover the deviations and wrong choices of self-consciousness or literary history. Recollecting the history of the self paradoxically makes the author 'unintelligible to himself', since he cannot decide between his authority and his error.

The nature of autobiographical writing in the Romantic period is such that the mere act of autobiography becomes more significant than the text produced. As the *New Monthly Magazine*'s review of the *Biographia* put it, 'Self biography is a very delicate undertaking, and few instances can be mentioned wherein it has yielded satisfaction.'[34] The work's epigraph (the passage translated from Goethe) is accurate in its

---

[33] Griggs (ed.), *Letters of Coleridge*, iv. 767.
[34] *New Monthly Magazine*, viii. 50.

intimation that self-reference will prove an insuperable problem for the *Biographia*; its inability to discriminate the valuable purpose of autobiography from the 'circuitous paths' traced by the text prophetically anticipates the book's inability to locate truth in either its subjects or the glosses that surround them. But because (in theory at least) Coleridge's work elevates autobiography into a method, its failures are coterminous with its aims. Reflexiveness obscures or effaces content (paradigmatically in chapter 13), but we can read this process as autobiography's reflection on itself: its possibility, its purposefulness, its legibility. If autobiography of the period tends to make its own processes more prominent than the narratives it contains, the *Biographia* marks the extreme point of this tendency. It is a book about self-authorship in which the very structure of self-consciousness, the act of rereading a literary life, makes the past indeterminate or unintelligible. What it discovers is that autobiography's self-consciousness itself constitutes the 'circuitous paths' that it hopes to evade. Writing about the self—writing around the texts of a literary life—enacts the mazy reflexivity of autobiographical discourse, the purpose and value of which cannot therefore be secured.

III

Practice

6

Autobiographical transactions

Biographia Literaria's epigraph sets up a kind of reflexiveness which turns out to be peculiarly debilitating for the subsequent book. Apologetic to the point of guiltiness, self-deprecating to the point of prostration, its idea of the place and purpose of autobiographical writing leaves the whole project unsure of itself. Yet (to use a distinction Coleridge was fond of) in this respect the *Biographia* is different in degree but not in kind from the general practice of autobiography in the Romantic period. As the ubiquitous preface-writing discussed in Chapter 4 shows, autobiographers almost always begin with some sort of negotiation with the public. There is an effort to place the narrative properly, or at least acceptably. It follows that the narratives themselves are at least in part continuations of the negotiating process. Exhibiting a mild form of the condition that the *Biographia* suffers from so acutely, the stories they tell are to some degree (however small) about what they are for, about what this particular fragment of a written life might be imagined to have to offer its readers. Coleridge, typically, tries to answer the question at a transcendental level. By refiguring the reflexive situation of autobiographical writing as the self-authorizing reflexive principle 'I AM'—'I am, because I affirm myself to be; I affirm myself to be, because I am'—the *Biographia* elevates the principle of self-knowledge far above the messy, confused, error-strewn details of his self-narrated literary life.[1] The narrative may be fatally defaced by its erring 'circuitous paths', but fortunately the higher reflexiveness of imagination and self-consciousness stands as an a priori condition impervious to admissions of defeat. So the theory goes: and, if true, it would salvage the *Biographia* as a master-text of Romantic self-fashioning, a story of the mind or soul triumphant over the apparent failings of a literary career. However, as I have argued, this is not how Coleridge's book works. Instead, the supposedly autonomous and transcendental principle of selfhood is lost

---

[1] Coleridge, *Biographia Literaria*, i. 275.

in the uncertain transactions of writing. Rather than being 'self-grounded, unconditional and known by its own light' (Coleridge's description of the 'I AM'), the *Biographia*'s sense of purpose is sucked into the circuitousness and instability of authorship, the story of writing going wrong.[2]

I resume the argument in these terms here because the *Biographia*'s brilliant failures suggest a starting point for pursuing readings of some other autobiographical efforts. For Coleridge writing's transactions with the public sphere are always where it goes wrong (hence the injunction 'NEVER PURSUE LITERATURE AS A TRADE').[3] Genius and imagination are fixed and inward principles; the poetic self is only betrayed once it begins negotiations over its place in the world. Yet the failure to sustain this theory invites us to reverse it. What if we start with the business of writing, and think about how other autobiographical effects—in particular, the idea of the 'self'—are produced out of it? Our reading of the situation of Romantic autobiography so far certainly indicates that the likeliest candidate for its first principle would be represented by the transactions of publication. Formed out of an unstable dialogue between prescription and transgression, and maintained in a state of anxious self-consciousness, 'autobiography' begins as a proposition within the literary public sphere. It follows that our readings of autobiographical texts should begin by looking at how they imagine their public situation.

In a straightforward sense almost all Romantic-period autobiographical writing comprises narratives of transactions. Transactions between individuals and God, between individuals and governments, between business partners, between employers and employees, between travellers and natives of other countries, between parents and children, between wives, husbands, and lovers, between actors, their colleagues, and their audiences: autobiography almost always tells one side of such systems of social and economic interaction. Nowadays we tend to think of the genre more as a narrative of actions: the doings of one single person, that is, linked into a coherent portrait of the self by the continuity of those deeds and their basis in the inward personality that performed them.[4] But the

---

[2] Coleridge, *Biographia Literaria*, i. 268.

[3] Ibid. 223.

[4] This generalization glosses over a number of pertinent issues, especially those to do with the kinds of action and transaction available to different kinds of autobiographical subjects (for example, women and working-class writers) within social and cultural orders. It is however a broadly accurate way of distinguishing nineteenth-century instances of published self-writing from generic contemporary autobiography (the kind of book that regularly appears nowadays with that word in the title).

vast majority of late eighteenth- and early nineteenth-century autobiographical publications are occupied with detailing the author's position in relation to various external factors, not to his or her overall nature and development. This could take the form of a discontinuous, breezily anecdotal memoir of some eminent figures with whom the author happens to have come into contact, like Tate Wilkinson's green-room tales of 1790, or the volumes published by peripheral literati such as William Beloe (1817) or Joseph Cradock (1828). Or there can be a relation to more specific kinds of transaction, a narrative of a given career—Lackington the bookseller's (1791), for example, or James Hardy Vaux the swindler's (1819), or John Shipp the soldier's (1829). Or the narrative can be focused on a single occasion or issue, one transaction which the writer wishes to recount: conversion stories, Bristow on his imprisonment and escape (1793), the radical cobbler Thomas Preston on his arrest (1817), De Quincey on opium and its effects. Romantic-period autobiography is unsystematic; its variety resists pigeon-holing. The point is that the books are involved in one way or another with the events and situations they relate. *The Prelude*'s intensely reflexive self-regard is absolutely the exception rather than the rule. This involvement or engagement becomes the basis of what I am calling the autobiographical transaction: the way each text tries to establish its purpose as a publication and to position itself in relation to readers. In the simplest version the history of the transactions *in* the book is itself the ostensible purpose *of* the book: the autobiography tells us that it is published for the purpose of making these particular doings public. The Johnson of the *Rambler* and *Idler* essays on self-writing would have immediately recognized this conception of the genre. Unlike actions, however, transactions are provisional and debatable. I want to start exploring the problem by looking at the slippage between autobiography's recording of events and its self-presentation as a record, between the transactions it relates and its own transactions with readers.

A pair of examples clarify the issue, sharing as they do a curious textual history. The two works are *The Life of Mrs. Gooch* (1792) and *The Confessions of William Henry Ireland* (1805), and they are both expanded, recognizably autobiographical versions of prior pamphlets which, although autobiographical in the sense of being first-person testimonies, were published (as their titles indicate) quite specifically and explicitly to perform a single public function: respectively *An Appeal to the Public on the Conduct of Mrs. Gooch* (1788) and *An Authentic Account of the Shaksperian Manuscripts* (1796). In both cases the pamphlet is the author's direct contribution to matters of public notoriety. The subsequent autobiographical volumes cover largely the same material, but with significant changes in detail, style, and deployment of the first-person stance. These differences add up to a revealing shift in the documents' implied purposes. Effectively, they allow us to watch what happens when a narrative record becomes autobiography.

Elizabeth Gooch (née Villa-Real) was the only child of a wealthy Portuguese father, who died in her childhood, and an English mother, who seems to have spread exaggerated rumours of her daughter's inheritance as she entered her in the marriage market. Elizabeth was duly snapped up by a family of titled and landed gentry. The marriage was unhappy from the start, and in her account her in-laws immediately began to plot a separation: 'As soon as my fortune was seized, it was time to dispose of my person.'[5] Whether engineered or not, the discovery of an indiscreetly worded note sent to her from her Italian music teacher provided the occasion. William Gooch's family made the episode public, destroying Elizabeth's reputation and forcing her to leave the country, separated from her children, her mother, and all her fortune except a settlement of £200 a year. Abandoned in France at the age of twenty, she attracted the attention of various adventurers, and was quickly initiated into the demi-monde, 'a life of expensive dissipation among worthless acquaintance' (*Life*, ii. 139–40). She was eventually confined to a debtor's prison, where she wrote her 1788 *Appeal to the Public*. The pamphlet attracted enough attention to go into a second printing the same year, and enough sympathy that she soon found her most pressing debts settled, enabling her release. The publication of the three-volume *Life* in 1792 was still more successful in securing public approval and patronage. Encouraged by its reception, she went on to publish a small quarto of poems in the conventional style of mournful sensibility, a volume of informal Rousseauan reveries, and four novels.

As the perpetrator of the notorious Shakespearean forgeries of 1795–6, William Henry Ireland's story is better known.[6] He published his *Authentic Account* in order to settle the increasingly acrimonious controversy over the documents he had been supplying to his father, the engraver and collector Samuel Ireland, who was beginning to be widely accused of perpetrating the forgeries himself. Like Gooch's *Appeal*, the

[5] Gooch, *The Life of Mrs. Gooch*, i. 142. Hereafter cited in the text as *Life*.

[6] See e.g. Bernard Grebanier, *The Great Shakespearean Forgery* (London: Heinemann, 1966).

pamphlet is intended as sworn testimony in the court of public opinion. It ends with three 'declarations' to which he says he is 'willing to make affidavit': acknowledging sole authorship of the fakes, vindicating his father from the accusation of being party to them, and—apparently by analogy with a legal document—insisting on the truth of the preceding account. The emphasis is on a straightforward relation of the facts, punctuated by brief and apologetic explanations of his motives. Gooch's pamphlet is likewise mainly concerned to publicize factual details relative to the stories circulating about her and the specific legal and financial oppressions imposed on her—although the stance of injured womanhood inevitably makes her dwell more indulgently on the rhetoric of self-justification than does Ireland. Both pamphlets are clear about their purpose. The authors have been driven to publication by an identifiable requirement, as the opening sentences declare. Ireland publishes 'IN Justice to the world, and to remove the odium under which my father labours'.[7] Gooch also stresses external compulsions:

I have lived long in hopes that I should not be forced thus publickly to lay open to the world the many injuries I have endured; after having borne them in silence for ten years, I would still be satisfied to do so, did not my situation and my embarrassments force me to complain, and to appeal to the laws of my country, and before the tribunal of Justice.[8]

The legal language is not merely rhetorical. Gooch ends her appeal openly wondering whether her husband is 'answerable for my debts if I have no regular settlement' (*Appeal*, 66). Her prior attempt to obtain a divorce, which would have made financial independence possible, had been rejected by the House of Lords (her father-in-law was a baronet) on a technicality, and the *Appeal* also alludes to this injustice. Gooch's 'injuries', like Ireland's impostures, need to be made known; the pamphlets supply the medium. That is the extent of their ambitions. Since both publications involve a confession of misdeeds, there are inevitably some appeals for sympathy and pardon, but these are not prominent enough to become ends in themselves. Both writers subordinate apologetic rhetoric to the primary purpose of conveying information 'to the world'.

[7] William Henry Ireland, *An Authentic Account of the Shaksperian Manuscripts* (London: J. Debrett, 1796), 1. Hereafter cited in the text as *Authentic Account*.
[8] Elizabeth Sarah Gooch, *An Appeal to the Public on the Conduct of Mrs. Gooch* (London: G. Kearsley, 1788), 1. Hereafter cited in the text as *Appeal*.

When Gooch's seventy-page *Appeal* mutates into a three-volume *Life*, and Ireland's briefer pamphlet expands into the more than three hundred pages of the *Confessions*, it is immediately clear that the proposed attitude towards the literary public sphere has changed. Where the two pamphlets open with relatively uncomplicated assertions of the need to make certain transactions public, the autobiographical volumes find themselves—characteristically—casting around more self-consciously for ways to describe their purpose. Both note in their first paragraph the interest aroused by the earlier publications. They reinterpret the quasi-legal testimonies as literary performances; a standard which measures the readability of the publications rather than their veracity and informativeness, and so makes Gooch and Ireland authors instead of witnesses. The new texts thus offer themselves as objects of interest in their own right. Ireland's preface speaks of the 'amusement' to be derived from the full story of his forgeries, and expresses some concern about how reviving the tale will affect him 'as a literary character'.[9] The narrative transactions are now (1805) old news; instead, the book is proposing a literary relationship with readers which (as we will see) should transform the theme of Ireland as a maker of texts. Gooch's preface also draws attention to the qualities of the text itself. 'This work is the offspring of solitude and reflection', she tells us, and it is written in 'the language of the heart' (*Life*, 6, 7). No longer a matter of simply hearing the facts, reading has become a test of sensibility: 'Let those, then, on whose callous minds sensibility has ceased to make its impressions, save themselves the trouble of reading a book recording the misfortunes and errors of the last Villa-Real!' (*Life*, 8–9). A transaction between author and reader, a contract of literary sympathy, has here quite explicitly replaced the actual 'misfortunes' and 'errors'—the *Appeal*'s 'injuries'— as the book's proper subject.

The pamphlets imply a relationship between the reader and the narrated facts (Ireland's forgeries, Gooch's injuries). Autobiography puts the consumption of the text at the centre of its transactions with the reader. The difference is literalized in Gooch's respective financial ambitions for each publication. Part of both texts' function is to raise money, but whereas her *Appeal* hopes to inspire public benevolence by disclosing the oppressions she has suffered, the *Life* recognizes *itself* as a literary commodity. I have already mentioned the passage where Gooch writes

---

[9] William Henry Ireland, *The Confessions of William Henry Ireland* (London: Thomas Goddard, 1805), 'Preface' (no pagination). Hereafter cited in the text as *Confessions*.

of her hopes for 'the sale of my book' (*Life*, 14) as a transparent example of autobiography's sense of purpose. In context, it images the contract of sensibility with the imagined reader. Autobiographical writing offers itself—the book—as a point of transaction; hence the heightened self-consciousness attaching to the expanded volumes, compared with the pamphlets. In Ireland's *Confessions* the negotiation is about 'literary character'. His 1796 *Authentic Account* is concerned only to acknowledge responsibility for the imposition. The later book retrospectively views his forgeries as authorial, literary acts. It is the difference between executing imitations of Shakespeare's writing and writing like Shakespeare. The pamphlet confesses to the former; the autobiography bears its own witness to the latter, giving lengthy extracts from Ireland's compositions and recalling the praises they won. Indeed, the whole notion of reading is completely reconfigured. The *Authentic Account* instructs readers to devalue the supposed Shakespearean documents, and teaches them the technical secrets of their fabrication. Reading them as Ireland's creations confirms their worthlessness, since it authoritatively settles the controversy over their provenance.[10] In the *Confessions* reading the forgeries is a revelation of Ireland's literary capital. The convergence between him and Shakespeare has become a matter of poetic relations, not mechanical forgery. His autobiography turns into a kind of anthology of Ireland's work, in a context which conflates it not only with Shakespeare's but also—more significantly—with Chatterton's, mentioned as an inspiration in the early autobiographical passages. Effectively, the book tries to change a narrative admission of fakery into a textual demonstration of real poetic writing, much as Gooch's *Life* changes an appeal for justice based on the facts into an appeal for sympathy based on 'the language of the heart'.

Narrative testimony is still important to the autobiographies, of course. Though the essential matters of public interest are already known, thanks to the earlier publications and the general notoriety of both stories, the later volumes repeat the facts. There is however a noticeably greater stress on vindication. (Again, this indicates a shift from emphasizing the facts to negotiating a relationship between the text and the public.) Ireland's pamphlet ended with a three-point 'affidavit' concerning its veracity; his *Confessions* closes with a seven-point *defence* of his conduct, asking 'whether I may not be acquitted of every thing

---

[10] Although, sadly, Ireland's father refused to credit his son's confession, and died still trying to convince the public that the documents were genuine.

except boyish folly' (*Confessions*, 315). Publication has gained a more complex rhetorical purpose, acknowledging and shaping the fluidity of the narrative's status, rather than insisting on its use as evidence. The same fluidity always inheres in Gooch's story; unlike Ireland's *Authentic Account*, where guilt is not really an issue, her *Appeal* recognizes at least some need to defend her position, given that in the social morality of the day her 'injuries' do not absolve her from the stigma of being a fallen woman. Nevertheless, there is a difference between the kinds of defence offered in the *Appeal* and the *Life*. In keeping with its function as testimony, the pamphlet makes Gooch's sins the consequence of her situation. She is (it claims) the victim of the circumstances the narrative discloses. So the apologia takes the form of an appeal to objective judgement:

To a mind unprejudiced against me—a mind that will attentively reflect on the situation in which I then was, it must evidently appear, that it was almost impossible for me to avoid that impending ruin which had been long suspended over my head! What *could* I do?—with these ideas, and my natural levity of disposition, I could not avoid plunging deeper into destruction   (*Appeal*, 49–50)

An interestingly different rhetorical stance directs the *Life*'s version of the same moment in the story: 'Put yourselves in idea, for a few moments, in *my* situation! . . . do you, can you wonder that now indeed I fell?' (*Life*, i. 153). The direct appeal to the reader's sympathetic identification is not at all the same kind of manoeuvre as the pamphlet's idea of a disinterestedly analytical jury. Strikingly, it evokes the moment of reading itself. It makes the book the site of an intimate interchange between reader and author (as the tear-spotted pages of the literature of sensibility so often do). The pamphlet's line of defence involves Gooch surrendering her agency ('What *could* I do?'); the autobiography re-establishes it at the level of writing, so that the victim of the story mutates into the author whose book makes the reader feel as she felt. This difference accounts for the simultaneously mournful and defiant tone of Gooch's vindications of her conduct in the *Life*. Rhetorical self-presentation transcends the mere record of events, so that instead of listening to the story and then judging the protagonist the reader is invited into a system of grief, repentance, and heroic self-righteousness. 'I had not a prospect nor a hope of deliverance'; 'I am not a proper person to combat the artifices of mankind, or to be prepared against them'; 'Affliction and confidence are arms against which I cannot make resistance; but I have a soul that will never bend under the yokes of tyranny and oppression'

(*Life*, iii. 43, 137, 72).[11] With this language, blame is no longer a matter of who did what. Instead, it depends on whether the contract of sensibility between author and reader will be broken or maintained. If we concede the force of sentimental rhetoric, the autobiographer's mode of self-representation itself vindicates her position.

Ireland's autobiography also wants to move judgements from the sphere of ethics to somewhere more literary or aesthetic. After all, he frequently points out, no one has been materially harmed by his forgeries and no gain has accrued to him from them. (These are arguable points, which is presumably why they are not brought up in the *Authentic Account*, with its single-minded testimonial function.) His vindication rests on the idea that the fakes were really acts of poetic homage. The earlier pamphlet, recounting Ireland's actions without defending them, gives a less noble picture: he recalls thinking that 'if some old writing could be produced, and passed for *Shakspear's*, it might occasion a little mirth, and show how far *credulity* would go in the search for antiquities' (*Authentic Account*, 3). He also declares that 'my object was only to give my father pleasure' (*Authentic Account*, 9), a claim repeated in the *Confessions*. Explanations are not, however, the autobiography's concern. The expanded narrative places the forgeries as part of a larger story of devotion to England's literary inheritance. Ireland relates his youthful obsessions with Walpole's *Castle of Otranto* (whose preface passes the novel off as a transcription of a medieval manuscript) and with Chatterton, of whom he writes 'I used frequently to envy his fate, and desire nothing so ardently as the termination of my existence in a similar cause' (*Confessions*, 11). Implicitly, the volume hopes to compare Ireland's documents to Walpole's and (especially) Chatterton's: *literary* creations, the products of Romantic inspiration rather than of criminal or self-interested motives. Even when describing specific forged documents, the *Confessions* ask us to refer to the criteria of literary criticism, which might conclude that Ireland has in fact added to the nation's poetic treasury. Take for example his account of producing the supposedly authentic manuscript of *King Lear*:

As I scrupulously avoided, in copying the play of Lear, the insertion of that ribaldry which is so frequently found in the compositions of our bard, it was generally conceived that my manuscript proved beyond doubt that Shakspeare was a much more finished writer than had ever before been imagined. (*Confessions*, 118)

---

[11] For 'confidence' in the sense of 'impudent and overbearing behaviour', see *OED* s.v. 'confidence' (*n.*) 4a.

Quoting at length from Ireland's productions, the autobiography invites the public to judge whether he is Chatterton's equal as a prodigy (Ireland stresses how young he was at the time) and as a poet in his own right, inspired by the genius of an earlier age.

In both cases autobiographical writing treats narrated events as an occasion to explore complex alternative transactions with the imagined reader. Whereas the pamphlets essentially rely on identifying the text with the narrative it publishes ('this is what happened'), these mechanical, financial, social, or sexual transactions are embellished in the subsequent volumes with a rhetoric that stresses writing's power to pursue its own purposes and to lend the author an agency and a position that are not entirely defined by their recorded actions. In Ireland's *Confessions* we can name this alternative position 'genius': the fabricator of poetry metamorphoses into a 'literary character'. For Gooch sensibility provides the new meaning of the text. Writing her story becomes a rhetorical drama of its own, as in the account of the day of her marriage:

Why cannot I write this page with composure?—Why, at the recollection of these *past times*, cannot I partake of that easy indifference, that stoic apathy, which cheers the path of other mortals throughout life?—Why, at this long, this distant period, do my eyes swim in tears, and blot what I am writing?—But I must not, I dare not revert to my own feeling. (*Life*, i. 75)

Sensibility and genius seem to mark those aspects of autobiographical writing which evade straightforward evaluation. If the governing purpose of the pamphlets is to establish facts and settle doubts, these new propositions raise an entirely different set of questions, focused on the issue of how the book is going to be read. I have already argued at length that this issue defines the condition of Romantic autobiography. Gooch's and Ireland's pairs of texts helpfully suggest that it might be a specifically autobiographical transaction—one, that is, which draws the distinction between autobiographical writing and some more explicit narrative mode.

To be sure, the distinction cannot possibly be maintained categorically: as usual, it will not supply us with any sort of working definition. It is not hard to come up with examples of self-writing in which the record of transacted events is indistinguishable from the text's sense of its purpose and place. The obvious instances are historical and political memoirs, and travelogues. Publications of these kinds by and large represent themselves as vehicles for the information the author possesses, much as Ireland's *Authentic Account* does. The startling effect of Wollstonecraft's *Letters Written During a Short Residence* comes from the book's unexpected, abrupt insertions of expressive commentary and intimate reflection into the more conventional records of foreign topographies, customs, and manners. The first person's sense of being out of place is largely the result of these textual disruptions. By establishing a range of complex and often contentious attitudes to various implied readers, she contravenes—and so highlights—a more conventional transaction: placing her experience in the hands of the polite reading public ('the world', as Gooch and Ireland both call it). The purposes of descriptive or historical autobiographical writing are supposed to be self-evident. Wollstonecraft's language of secrecy and confusion is a negative demonstration of this requirement. When Henry 'Orator' Hunt announces his care 'not to gloss over or slight any one political or public act of my life', he is recognizing the political autobiographer's contract with the public: the narrative substance of his story is what the book is *for*.[12] Although one can always unearth some degree of deviation from this contract in any given text, there is still a large body of autobiographical writing in the period which depends on maintaining the relationship that Wollstonecraft disturbs.

Nevertheless, the terms of that relationship—the way autobiography is placed in relation to the literary public sphere—themselves suggest how we might approach the complications arising within individual texts. Suppose that we think of the commonsensical, Johnsonian view of autobiography's purposes, the view identifying the act of publication with the events narrated, as a way of securing the status of an autobiographical transaction. (This is how prescriptive attitudes treat the genre as a whole: they want to make sense of the decision to publish.) In effect, this makes the published text a knowable commodity. It can be used and valued in appropriate ways. We might then think of alternatives to this relationship—Wollstonecraft's abrupt reflections, say, or Gooch's sensibility, or Ireland's 'literary character'—as transactions operating at a level different from commodity exchange. Their uses, their values, are unclear, or indefinite, or at least inherently open to question. I have already proposed this argument in relation to the general situation of autobiographical writing; but as an approach to particular texts it encourages us to look closely at what is left out of the transactions of narrative, or what is placed beyond the domain of such transactions. We would however do so without endorsing the *Biographia*'s (or indeed *The*

Prelude's) view that autobiography is properly occupied with transcendental concerns like imagination or the poet's mind. As with the shift from Gooch and Ireland's pamphlets to their larger volumes, the aim is to pay attention to something that emerges around the knowable commodity of the text, something that does not fit into the surrounding conditions of publication—but not something that claims to abolish them entirely.

Initially at least we can pursue this aim without privileging texts like Wollstonecraft's, which obviously—and, for later readers, compellingly—exceed the conventional positions of autobiographical writing. We are moving towards the study of more canonical (and therefore more exceptional) documents. By the time we reach them, though, I hope to have put their exceptional qualities in the context of a wider field of autobiographical practice. A good set of examples for exploring the slippage out of secure autobiographical transactions is the courtesan memoirs. Commodification is here an explicit theme. Obviously enough, the courtesan is herself a commodity, passed from procuress to procuress or from 'keeper' to keeper in a series of more or less regulated transactions. Her book, too, is almost always explicitly commodified.[13] Especially in the eighteenth century, before a more developed publishing industry fully realized the commercial potential of scandalous confessions, such memoirs were usually privately printed. The authors risked the costs in the hope of raising income from sales, and also advertised themselves to potential patrons. In Harriette Wilson's ingenious blackmail scheme, the contents of the book were in fact largely determined by a set of negotiations: those who paid had their names suppressed, while those who refused—most notoriously the Duke of Wellington—became part of the story. This is an extreme case, though, and also a late one (1825); more usually, the courtesan appears only as the object of transactions, submitting to the laws of her market place.

According to the literary public sphere's prevailing attitudes, needless to say, courtesan autobiographies were the prime examples of the genre's dubious status. Our concern now, though, is with the conduct of the texts themselves. Their narratives consist largely of recorded transac-

---

[13] Sonia Hofkosh discusses how 'Prostitution serves in this period as a general metaphor for the debasement of literary practice into a promiscuous professionalism that renders authorship meaningful only by disempowering the author *as such*' (Hofkosh, 'A Woman's Profession: Sexual Difference and the Romance of Authorship', *Studies in Romanticism*, 32 (1993), 245–72, at 257. The article does not however read any writing *by* prostitutes.

tions, governed by sexual and economic pragmatism. Autobiography thus records an implacable commodification. The laws of desire turn the female body into an object of consumption; the laws of the market make it an object of ownership. These processes are usually encoded in narrative as stories of generalized 'oppression', thematically reminiscent of Richardson's novelistic touchstones of eroticized female innocence.[14] Margaret Coghlan's description of her noble clientele matches Lovelace or Mr B., or indeed the more extravagant villains of Radcliffe's Gothic romances, and so casts herself and those like her as victims of sexual and financial privilege: 'they conceive that *Men* and *Women* are made merely for *them*; to be the passive instruments of their voluptuousness'.[15] Like Gooch's protest 'What *could* I do?', such rhetoric invokes a stance of helplessness. Despite the ubiquitous admissions of folly and levity, the authors are acquitting themselves of any collusion in their own downfall, any role in the story except that of the object on which other forces work—a fact acidly noted by one courtesan reflecting in her memoirs on the conventions of the genre:

Let the mere comman-place [*sic*] scribblers, who borrow from the frippery of stale sentiment those memoirs which they retail to the public, let them . . . blame the villainies of the world, and the deceits, cruelties, and many *et ceteras* . . . I was merely miserable by misconduct. Vanity and self-gratification first ruined me.[16]

Phebe Phillips's frank acknowledgement of her moral ('vanity') and sexual ('self-gratification') agency is the exception, though. The narrative pattern is more usually like that of Gooch's *Life*. A series of oppressions leaves the protagonist in a position where it is impossible to resist the moment of ruin, and from then on she is literally a known quantity, traded among consumers. The texts depict a ruled and ordered environment which determines the story's progress. Virtue and morality, being in essence matters of choice, are written out of the equation. They do not define the state or the being of the first person (naturally this evasion is strategically desirable for courtesan writers). The 'I' is figured instead as the sum of its commercial history.

---

[14] Writing in 1765, Catherine Jemmat (née Yeo) asks 'why may not the true story of Catherine Yeo, who absolutely does exist, divert as much, allowing for the different abilities of the authors, as those of Miss Pamela Andrews, or Miss Clarissa Harlowe . . . ?' (Jemmat, *Memoirs*, i. 115). Her autobiography was issued five times in seven years.

[15] Coghlan, *Memoirs*, i. 142–3. Hereafter cited in the text by volume and page number.

[16] Phebe Phillips, *The Woman of the Town* (London: J. Roe, 1801), 8.

Take for example the *Authentic and Interesting Memoirs* (1787) of Ann Archer (née Sheldon). The introduction avoids sentimental euphemism: 'I have known the highest splendour of elegant prostitution.'[17] If this reads like a teaser, inviting the reader to consume the narrative as eagerly as if they had purchased the author, the subsequent narrative begins with an extraordinary tale of abductions, imprisonments, escapes, recaptures, and a rape. The equation between the 'extravagant gaiety' (i. 186) of prostitution and a form of relentless, often violent compulsion is very clear. As the narrative meanders on into disjointed tales of further nego- tiations and liaisons—'this pantomime of my life' (ii. 101)—the author dissolves into a cipher of those compulsions. The text becomes a repeti- tive catalogue of the names of successive 'keepers' (the word is Phebe Phillips's), with their various demands and failings; Archer is simply the thread along which the texts string these lists. 'I was destined', she writes, 'to be the slave of variety' (ii. 170). It sounds like the kind of titillating suggestion to the reader that so alarmed John Foster, but in fact the vari- ety is only that of anecdotal narration, and the slavery is not an erotic compulsion inscribed in the body but an abjection to the sequence of contracts and purchases the narrative records. The book can find no sustainable rhetorical alternative to the inevitability of the sequence. Gooch's language of nostalgia, melancholy, and defiance never makes an appearance; nor do the terminologies of pleasure and guilt which might signal the erotic dimension of the text's relation to readers (as in many of the responses generated by Rousseau's *Confessions*). Archer's complete helplessness as told in the story translates into the narrative's subservience to its other agents. In effect, it becomes a record of her owners. Writing ends up reproducing the commodification of its narra- tive subject, functioning as a receipt, a documentation of completed transactions.

By comparison, Gooch's rhetoric of sensibility looks like the textual mark of a superfluity or an excess: something specifically not contained within the oppressions of the narrative order. Staining the page with her tears is at the thematic level an obvious enough resistance to the constraints of a courtesan's life, meant to assert an inward innocence against the loss of bodily virtue, and to claim suffering (not pleasure) as the fallen woman's proper mode of experience. But 'the language of the heart' also asserts an aspect of writing which is not reducible to a system

---

[17] Ann Archer, *Authentic and Interesting Memoirs of Miss Ann Sheldon*, 4 vols. (London, 1787), i. 3. Hereafter cited in the text by volume and page number.

of transactions.[18] In specific relation to courtesan autobiography it speaks of something which is literally not for sale.

Coghlan's interesting *Memoirs* find a language that functions similarly, although now the terms are political rather than literary. She was the illegitimate daughter of Colonel James Moncrieff of the British army, but her early experiences in America at the time of the War of Independence were all among the 'Citizens struggling for Freedom' (ii. 91), and she writes in London in 1793—a moment when this sort of language was peculiarly loaded—as an open enemy of 'that Inequality of Condition which now prevails' (ii. 169). The political discourse that surfaces occasionally in her narrative is not at all systematic (her hymns to freedom are usually occasioned by her indignation at being imprisoned for debt, and her assaults on the moral debasement of the upper classes sit oddly with her direct appeal for a wealthy patron). The effect of her vaguely republican interjections is rather to articulate a resistance to the narrative order of her story. They interpret the familiar sequence of events—parental oppression, a forced marriage, a '*brutish unfeeling tyrant*' (i. 79) for a husband, escape to a series of protectors, the courtesan career—in Paineite terms, as an exposure of arbitrary power and abused privilege, so casting her as their victim, and making her subjection to the transactions of the sexual market place an occasion for voicing a faith in liberty. Apologizing for her revolutionary outbursts, she calls them 'the spontaneous emanations of a soul . . . flowing with zeal' (ii. 40). Writing here presents itself as the medium for something standing in direct opposition to the courtesan's story. Against the 'horrid chains of matrimony and SLAVERY' (ii. 74) binding her to her condition, it expresses at least the idea of uprooting the political order that is accused of incarcerating her within her career, her narrative. Like Gooch's sensibility, Coghlan's 'zeal' is rhetoric operating both outside and against the realm of commodification.

One might compare the sentimental and political rhetoric of *The Interesting Narrative of the Life of Olaudah Equiano* (1789). As the autobiography of a West African former slave its narrative is also subject to the transactions of the market, here in their most violent and implacable form. By the time of publication Equiano had been active in the abolitionist

---

[18] The discourse of sensibility often sets up a binary opposition between feeling and economics. This is a kind of economy in itself, a way of setting relative values against each other according to a system with known laws; but that does not nullify the rhetorical force of the contrast. The best survey of the discourse of sensibility and its basic rules is Todd, *Sensibility: An Introduction.*

movement for a number of years, so his account of his abduction and enslavement powerfully emphasizes the miseries and cruelties he encountered (by contrast with, say, the brief 1772 *Narrative* of James Albert Ukawsaw Gronniosaw, which records the state of slavery in a rhetorically neutral register, reserving its literary energies for the Evangelical drama of conversion that is its main theme). Equiano invests his narrative voice with the power of imagining alternatives to the compulsions it records. Recalling his first experience on a slave ship, at the age of about eleven, he describes a rather poetic longing:

Often did I think many of the inhabitants of the deep much more happy than myself. I envied them the freedom they enjoyed, and as often wished I could change my condition for theirs.[19]

Such language is embedded in the narrative: it is presented as the recorded thought of the narrator at the time, the result of what he calls 'my love of liberty, ever great' (i. 53). Thus the story itself contains the conflict between the institutions of slavery, which treat him as a commodity, and what Equiano and other abolitionists considered the universal and natural condition of human individuality. As the narrative develops, the stark one-sidedness of this conflict becomes obvious, and the extreme disjunction between the laws of commodification and the individual subject becomes the occasion for rhetorically intensified passages. This is particularly striking at the point in the story when Equiano is sold to a new owner just as he is expecting the freedom his previous master had promised. Writing now overloads its narrative with an urgency of expression that barely pretends to represent the narrator's past thoughts (as does the recollected language of the eleven-year-old). Its force is instead aimed at dramatizing the hideousness of enslavement itself:

THUS, at the moment I expected all my toils to end, was I plunged, as I supposed, in a new slavery . . . whose horrors, always present to my mind, now rushed on it with tenfold aggravation . . .

what tumultuous emotions agitated my soul when the convoy got under sail, and I a prisoner on board, now without hope! . . . I was ready to curse the tide that bore us, the gale that wafted my prison, and even the ship that conducted us . . .

My former slavery now rose in dreadful review to my mind, and displayed nothing but misery, stripes, and chains; and, in the first paroxysm of my grief, I called

---

[19] Olaudah Equiano, *The Interesting Narrative of the Life of Olaudah Equiano*, 2 vols. (London, 1789), i. 80. Hereafter cited in the text by volume and page number.

upon God's thunder, and his avenging power, to direct the stroke of death to me, rather than permit me to become a slave, and be sold from lord to lord. (i. 180–1, 187, 190)

The rhetorical register, like the appeal itself, is melodramatic. There is in fact no alternative to the serial transactions Equiano predicts.[20] *The Interesting Narrative* is the most relentlessly commercial of books, not just in its account of the reduction of human beings to commodities, but throughout the subsequent story of Equiano's own mercantile progress, which culminates in the accumulation of enough capital to buy him his freedom—a transaction that casts some doubt on his pious faith that 'The worth of a soul cannot be told' (ii. 150). All his outburst can do is pose an alternative language. Like the eleven-year-old's poignant wish, but with 'tenfold aggravation', it expresses an entirely visionary opposition to the rigid laws governing Equiano's worlds.

Politically, of course, this way of using language is immensely significant. In the face of entrenched economic interests, the abolitionist movement often turned to an anti-commercial rhetoric in its effort to force a change in the law. Characteristically, though, Equiano bases his final appeal on the late eighteenth-century's dream of an imperium of free trade: 'Supposing the Africans, collectively and individually, to expend 5 l. a head on raiment and furniture yearly when civilized, &c. an immensity beyond the reach of imagination!' (ii. 253). Mercantile fantasies also dovetail tidily with his Methodist language, according to which the endeavours of the faithful are blessed with profit ('Providence was more favourable to us than we could have expected, for we sold our fruits uncommonly well', i. 239–40). When Equiano invests his text with grandiloquent evocations of humanity and sensibility, then, we need to read the new register as the sign of something apart from both history and future progress, something outside both the narrative of enslavement and the prospects of religious and political reform. Commodification is only opposed at what we might again call a literary level, where the text curses the winds and calls upon God's thunders. In

[20] The particular complexity of voices and rhetorical positions in slave autobiographies has been much studied. With specific reference to Equiano see William L. Andrews, *To Tell a Free Story: The First Century of Afro-American Autobiography, 1760–1865* (Urbana, Ill.: University of Illinois Press, 1986); Paul Edwards, *Unreconciled Strivings and Ironic Strategies* (Edinburgh: Centre of African Studies, Edinburgh University, 1992); Robin Sabino and Jennifer Hall, 'The Path Not Taken: Cultural Identity in the *Interesting Life* of Olaudah Equiano', *MELUS*, 24 (1999), 5–19; William Mottolese, ' "Almost an Englishman": Olaudah Equiano and the Colonial Gift of Language', in Greg Clingham (ed.), *Questioning History* (Lewisburg, Pa.: Bucknell University Press, 1998), 160–71.

the course of an impassioned attack on the slave trade at the end of his fifth chapter Equiano writes: 'it is the fatality of this mistaken avarice, that it corrupts the milk of human kindness and turns it into gall' (i. 233). Elsewhere in the book 'avarice' might be harder to distinguish from the ordinary striving for increased capital he will later pursue so efficiently. Here, though, the Shakespearean language endorses a simple contrast between familial humanity and the evils of commodification. 'Surely', he goes on, 'this traffic cannot be good, which spreads like a pestilence, and taints what it touches!' (i. 233). According to the book's narrative order Equiano must be doubly infected by this plague, first as a victim of the traffic and then later as his owner's agent on board the slave ships. The comment, though, rises out of the surrounding story and appeals more vividly to something which cannot be transacted. The text has named it a little earlier: 'is not the slave trade entirely a war with the heart of man?' (i. 220). Much as in Coghlan or Gooch's autobiographies, rhetorical intensification associates itself with an inward, impassioned, and literary discourse—'the language of the heart'—that emerges in absolute opposition to the governing transactions of the story as a whole.

Inwardness, passion, and literariness have become standards for distinguishing the master-texts of Romantic autobiography from the non-canonical mass of the period's self-writing. Courtesan and slave memoirs help to restore at least part of the context for these quintessentially 'Romantic' criteria. We should not think of them as qualities bequeathed from Rousseau to a select group of subsequent autobiographers. They have a close relationship with the transactions that more widely determine autobiography's sense of itself; but the relationship, I suggest, is one of deflection, evasion, separation. In the above examples it is at its most straightforwardly antagonistic. Where the transactions of narrative are at their most oppressively binding 'the language of the heart' most strongly asserts its textual independence, its articulation of a different stance. What this tells us is that the language of inwardness— the *Biographia*'s 'infinite I AM'—can be produced around, and out of, the ordinary writing of experience.

The most inward, passionate, and literary of all British Romantic autobiographical documents (and so after *The Prelude* the most canonical) is, interestingly, one whose haphazard formal character and restricted scope make it less unrepresentative of the period's autobiographies than its exceptional qualities might lead us to assume. In its original form, as published in the *London Magazine* in September and October 1821, De Quincey's *Confessions of an English Opium Eater* is a fairly short, discontinuous, often anecdotal memoir, very far from the coherent narrative of an unfolding identity which the word 'autobiography' has come to denote.[21] The work's canonical eminence derives instead from its representation of a visionary inwardness, conveyed in bursts of sublime rhetorical intensification and theatrical self-dramatization. Where does this inwardness come from, though? The canonically based view of Romantic autobiography would answer either that it is innate to the author's genius and imagination (a *Biographia*-like reading) or that it grows organically, *Prelude*-style, in the secret chambers of the self. We could however approach the question by reading the *Confessions* beside Equiano and the courtesans of the age of sensibility. De Quincey's work, after all, also narrates violent compulsions attached to a commodity.[22] Its distinctive rhetoric is woven into the narrative of opium's 'fascinating enthralment'.[23]

De Quincey announces his text's purpose very much in the conventional manner, establishing a transaction between the act of confession and its readers controlled by classical standards:

TO THE READER.—I here present you, courteous reader, with the record of a remarkable period in my life: according to my application of it, I trust that it will prove, not merely an interesting record, but, in considerable degree, useful and instructive. In *that* hope it is, that I have drawn it up: and *that* must be my apology for breaking through that delicate and honourable reserve, which, for the most part, restrains us from the public exposure of our own errors and infirmities. (p. 1)

The vocabulary of unveiling and 'exposure' inevitably recalls the eroticized fascination of reading Rousseau, as of course does De Quincey's title. It therefore becomes a pressing concern to distinguish these *Confessions* from the 'acts of gratuitous self-humiliation' (p. 1) which he diagnoses as a contagion in the literary public sphere. He does so by

[21] A very useful survey of immediate reactions to the articles, giving a sense of how unlike autobiography in the modern sense they seemed to many of their first readers, is John O. Hayden, 'De Quincey's *Confessions* and the Reviewers', *Wordsworth Circle*, 6 (1975), 273–9.

[22] Opium is treated as a medication rather than a tradeable commodity in the *Confessions*. As much recent scholarship has shown, however, the work is heavily inflected by opium's role as the major component of the imperial economy in south-east Asia (see esp. Josephine McDonagh, 'Opium and the Imperial Imagination', in Philip W. Martin and Robin Jarvis (eds.), *Reviewing Romanticism* (New York: St Martin's Press, 1992)). De Quincey's addicted and diseased habituation to Orientalist and imperialist discourses is vividly described in John Barrell, *The Infection of Thomas De Quincey* (New Haven, Conn.: Yale University Press, 1991).

[23] De Quincey, *Confessions*, 2. Hereafter cited in the text by page number only.

calculating the text's value for its readers, weighing the decorums of autobiographical publication against the usefulness of evidence:

> on the one hand, as my self-accusation does not amount to a confession of guilt, so, on the other, it is possible that if it *did*, the benefit resulting to others, from the record of an experience purchased at so heavy a price, might compensate, by a vast overbalance, for any violence done to the feelings [of 'natural' literary decorum] I have noticed, and justify a breach of the general rule.   (p. 2)

He goes on to reaffirm that 'the present act of confession' is accountable to 'the service I may thereby render to the whole class of opium-eaters'— 'a very numerous class indeed', he adds, widening the range of his transaction and legitimizing it by alluding to eminent politicians, divines, and writers who are included among the publication's beneficiaries (p. 2). A specific autobiographical contract is established in the introductory pages. It depends on identifying the author exclusively as the 'English Opium-Eater' (the *London Magazine* articles were anonymous as always). His narrative is there to testify to the experience of consuming the drug, like a report of a medical experiment; later De Quincey will joke that he has 'for the general benefit of the world, inoculated myself, as it were, with the poison of 8000 drops of laudanum per day' (p. 58). The contract also specifies that the confession's proper readers are opium eaters too ('The moral of the narrative is addressed to the opium-eater', p. 79). Opium, then, is the commodity which secures the status of the autobiographical transaction. It is shared between writer and readers as a matter of common interest, and it defines both medical and moral functions of publication. The passage I have cited in preceding chapters is essential to the text's idea of its own legibility, its place in print: 'Not the opium-eater, but the opium, is the true hero of the tale; and the legitimate centre on which the interest revolves. The object was to display the marvellous agency of opium' (p. 78).

As with Archer or Equiano, the first-person narrator of the *Confessions* is (in narrative terms at least) more the vehicle of an external 'agency' than an agent in his own right.[24] The concept of addiction is

---

[24] For a full reading of opium as an endorsement of 'the aesthetic of lost agency' in De Quincey's autobiographical writings see Josephine McDonagh, *De Quincey's Disciplines* (Oxford: Clarendon, 1994), ch. 6. Edmund Baxter's detailed study of the situation of De Quincey's autobiographical writing also sees his 'self' as the victim of material processes, especially the economics of authorship: the autobiographical self 'can never be given by writing, but can only give writing instead' (Baxter, *De Quincey's Art of Autobiography* (Edinburgh: Edinburgh University Press, 1990), 110). See also Matthew Schneider, *Original Ambivalence: Autobiography and Violence in Thomas De Quincey* (New York: Peter Lang, 1995).

not available in 1821, but De Quincey apostrophizes the drug as 'dread agent!' (p. 37), and devotes much of the text to describing how it acts on him and his consciousness.[25] The usual mode is compulsion. Opium has the Burkean sublimity of irresistible power, whether for good—'opium . . . can overrule all feelings into a compliance with the master key' (p. 47)—or ill: 'the opium-eater . . . lies under the weight of incubus and night-mare . . .—he would lay down his life if he might but get up and walk; but he is powerless as an infant, and cannot even attempt to rise' (p. 67). Even in the substantial autobiographical narrative that precedes the first accounts of the drug's effects the *Confessions* thematizes compulsion and victimization. The story is held together by 'subtle links of suffering derived from a common root' (p. 35), a kind of physiological experience of perpetual privation which will later metamorphose into the specific bodily and mental torments of opium. In the story the first person is effectively commodified. His body may not be subject to economic transaction, as are the courtesan's and the slave's, but his role as author is so completely identified with his subjection to the 'sevenfold chain' (p. 4) of a material substance that the transactions of writing are indistinguishable from the story of opium's pains and pleasures, its gains and losses, its quantities, its proper uses, its impulses, restrictions, and tyrannies. After the section describing incidents from the narrator's childhood and youth, nothing actually happens in the *Confessions* apart from the changing actions of the drug; and even the autobiographical incidents are partly explained 'as furnishing a key to some parts of that tremendous scenery which afterwards peopled the dreams of the Opium-eater' (p. 4), as if conventional narrative self-writing is also in thrall to the demands of the drug's story.

Much of the effect of the *Confessions* does not however operate at the level of narrative. In fact, narrative progressively disintegrates as opium's mastery becomes more complete. 'I could not', the narrator confesses in the latter stages, 'without effort, constrain myself to the task of either recalling, or constructing into a regular narrative, the whole burthen of horrors which lies upon my brain' (p. 62). The story's tendency to fragment is consummated in the final 'Pains of Opium' section, where diary entries and lists of dreams overlap with autobiographical recollection. But as narration dissolves into discontinuous expressions of the drug's effects, the surface of the text is increasingly dominated by those remarkable

[25] On the early nineteenth-century understanding of opium's effects see Alethea Hayter, *Opium and the Romantic Imagination*, rev. edn. (London: Crucible, 1988).

extravagances of rhetorical prose which give this autobiographical document its distinctive literary colouring. These rhapsodies are on the one hand offered as evidence of the nature of opium, and therefore contributions to the 'moral of the narrative' (p. 79), the autobiographical purpose explicitly set out in De Quincey's introduction. On the other hand they clearly extend writing's ambitions beyond that stated purpose. If it is opium that apparently produces the extravagance of rhetoric— 'thou buildest . . . out of the fantastic imagery of the brain, cities and temples, beyond the art of Phidias and Praxiteles' (p. 49)—it is nevertheless clear that prose in this register presents itself as an aesthetic performance and so casts the narrator as a literary author rather than just a figure for the commodity which rules his experience. Reading Gooch, Coghlan, and Equiano I suggested that rhetorical intensification marks an excess, a dimension of writing not contained within narrative and commodity transactions. No rhetoric could be more excessive than the artfully compounded sublimities of the *Confessions'* set pieces. Their effect is as it were to transmute the raw substance of opium and its tyrannical agency into the sphere of aesthetics, of genius—much as Ireland's *Confessions* turn the mechanics of forgery into Chattertonian achievements.[26] Such writing happens outside the negotiated balancing of decorum, utility, apologetics, and guilt performed in the introduction. And although the paean at the climax of the 'Pleasures of Opium' section refers to the 'potent rhetoric' of 'eloquent opium', it also exceeds and evades the compelling commodity itself. Writing at this pitch suggests that it cannot be transacted (in the same way that the Burkean sublime abolishes quantitative judgements). It appropriates any narrative functions for a sublime *effect*; not the effect of the 'dread agent' on the story, but the effect of writing itself in an aesthetic domain (comparable to the field of sensibility in which Gooch's and Equiano's interjected appeals presume to operate). If there is a transaction with the reader here, it is a literary one, based around the consumption of highly wrought prose— precisely the kind of dangerous Rousseauan indulgence denigrated in De Quincey's opening remarks. Rhetoric deflects, and perhaps ultimately effaces, the record of opium which supposedly organizes the *Confessions*.

Consider, for example, a description of one of the drug's baleful effects:

---

[26] An immensely suggestive study by Robert Maniquis has demonstrated De Quincey's lifelong investment in transforming material relations into aesthetic ones (Robert M. Maniquis, 'Lonely Empire: Personal and Public Visions of Thomas De Quincey', in Eric Rothstein and J. A. Wittreich (eds.), *Literary Monographs*, *viii* (Madison, Wis.: University of Wisconsin Press, 1976)).

whatsoever things capable of being visually represented I did but think of in the darkness, immediately shaped themselves into phantoms of the eye; and, by a process apparently no less inevitable, when thus once traced in faint and visionary colours, like writings in sympathetic ink, they were drawn out by the fierce chemistry of my dreams, into insufferable splendour that fretted my heart.   (68)

This recounts a typical form of subjection to the alien power. The narrator's own thoughts are instantly possessed and reified as external events, which of their own accord then accumulate a suffocating magnitude within his consciousness. The elaboration of the sentence, though, progressively submerges the account of intolerable victimization beneath a vocabulary and a register of magnificence. Opium's 'phantoms' are made to blaze brighter and more vividly, but both brightness and vividness become properties of the text's own language, rather than narrated recollections of sensory torment. The phrase 'insufferable splendour' is more splendid than insufferable; its contradictoriness generates a sublime excess of representation. The climactic verb 'fretted', strikingly unexpected and rather exotic in prose of this period, denotes a slow, gnawing consumption, but inevitably resonates with its other main meaning, the process of decorative interlacing. Vocabularies of suffering and ornamentation overlap. As in so many of the impassioned passages of the *Confessions*, rhetoric evokes an experience of splendour. De Quincey's artifice thrusts itself into the foreground. This is prose striving to approximate the effect of music, whose rhythms and harmonies strike the ear independent of any referential or narrative function.

The overall effect of the *Confessions*' self-consciously literary rhapsodies is to construct a completely different version of the narrator from the one established in the apologetic introduction, the one that identifies him exclusively as the 'English Opium-Eater' (the man who lived this narrative). Rhetorical excess produces instead the figure we know as Thomas De Quincey: the professional author, the man of letters, the purveyor of a unique brand of eloquence.[27] Here is the answer to the question we began with: Where does this text's 'Romantic' inwardness come from? It is an effect produced at the point where writing exceeds

[27] The production of De Quinceyan subjectivity is traced at length in Alina Clej, *A Genealogy of the Modern Self: Thomas De Quincey and the Intoxication of Writing* (Stanford, Calif.: Stanford University Press, 1995). Clej reads De Quincey as an originating instance of a modernist self, perhaps too quick to attach a literary-historical chronology to 'the anguishing sense that the subject is nothing more than his words' (p. 256). Her study of the relation between rhetoric and narcosis is very stimulating. The economic and political values of De Quinceyan subjectivity are discussed in McDonagh, *De Quincey's Disciplines* chs. 5 and 6.

the negotiated transactions of autobiographical publication. (To grasp the point schematically, think of *The Prelude*: the extreme of inwardness, the full denial of publication.) A rhetorical presence which cannot be included among those transactions takes on the appearance of what we would now call the autobiographical 'self'. Thus De Quincey's work seems to modern eyes somehow 'more' autobiographical (and so has become more canonical) than most other Romantic-period autobiographies because it indulges in rhetorical excess far more freely and powerfully than most—and not, one must stress, because it is a superior expression of the author's inner life. The *Confessions* illustrates with exemplary brilliance the inseparable relation between the self and literariness. If *Biographia Literaria*'s autobiographical project is an effort to isolate the 'I AM' from the 'circuitous paths' of writing and publication, then De Quincey's book has indeed correctly diagnosed Coleridge's disability, as its teasing reference to 'one celebrated man of the present day' (p. 2) among the class of opium eaters claims to be doing.[28] Addiction is not the issue. The flaw in the transcendental project does not lie in the author's self. What De Quincey shows is that the 'I AM'— the autobiographical assertion of the self's presence—is a literary event.

Looking back over the (admittedly limited) collection of documents in this chapter, we might now attempt a more general interpretation of those tendencies which evade or resist autobiography's sense of its published purpose and place. They appear as a rhetorical or literary presence in the text whose relationship with the public involves transactions that take place at the level of aesthetics rather than commodity; and we can name this textual presence 'self', 'subjectivity', or—the most appropriately contemporary word—'personality'. Gooch's 'language of the heart', Ireland's Chattertonian genius, Coghlan's Paineite interventions, Equiano's imaginary imprecations, De Quincey's sublime or beautiful prose exhibitions: all are occasions when autobiographical writing does more than the literary public sphere expects from it, and—by doing so, I argue—produces at least an outline of what we have come to think of as the 'Romantic' self: inward, expressive, autonomous. The critical point is the sequence of this process. A different kind of argument would interpret all those moments in the texts as expressions of a self, transcriptions of psychological depth, momentarily (or in De Quincey's case

[28] For a detailed analysis of the relation between the *Confessions* and the *Biographia* see Nigel Leask, ' "Murdering One's Double": De Quincey's *Confessions* and Coleridge's *Biographia*', in Peter J. Kitson and Thomas N. Corns (eds.), *Coleridge and the Armoury of the Human Mind* (London: Frank Cass, 1991).

lengthily) allowed to break the autobiographical conventions of the age and inject some subjectivity into the narrative. This approach would let the monuments of Romantic self-expression—Rousseau, Wordsworth, De Quincey—throw the less distinguished mass of the period's autobiographical writing into deep shade. If, though, we start by thinking about autobiography's problematic place in the world of readers and writers, then questions of writing come *before* questions of selfhood. Autobiography looks less like an effort to write the self, and more like a mode of writing which (sometimes) produces a sense of literary personality. This is certainly a more accurate picture of self-writing in the fifty years after Rousseau's death. It is also, I believe, a more promising approach to reading individual texts as autobiographies.

Our inherited assumptions about autobiography do, after all, describe precisely how the huge majority of autobiographical documents in the period did *not* want to be read (this despite the fact that those assumptions are sometimes held to be Romantic in origin). The texts' self-conscious negotiations with the reading public stress the narrative's instructive and/or amusing qualities; the first-person subject is only to be mentioned apologetically, if at all. Choosing to approach such works as autobiographies therefore means tracing the circuitous paths of writing, in much the same way that thinking about the supposed genre of Romantic self-writing involves studying uncertainties in the literary public sphere. It is clear that there is no such thing as a Romantic self, or even a Romantic mode of self-consciousness or self-fashioning—or, if there is, that autobiographical writing is not the place to go looking for it. The period's documents are not going to add up to some overall portrait of Romantic self-representation. What we have instead are individual texts which negotiate with the conditions of autobiography, and produce something close to our modern idea of self-writing as those negotiations fail. Indeed, the more spectacular the failure, the closer one is brought to the autobiographical 'great tradition' that has established itself over the last hundred or so years. Rousseau's book struck many of its first readers as an inexplicable phenomenon; until 1850 Wordsworth's great poem did not strike the public at all. The point about these canonical works is not that they are central, as one instinctively assumes the canon to be. They do not anchor a tradition of Romantic autobiography. It is their extreme quality that makes them significant. They tell us that coherent, continuous self-representation—'autobiography' as it has come to be understood—is dislocated writing, writing that knows itself to be out of place. The discourse of the self, like Gooch's 'language of the heart', is a disturbance in a text's legibility.

One last brief illustration: one of the most self-expressive documents of the period, Hazlitt's anonymous *Liber Amoris* (1823), has proven itself (then and since) to be among those whose place and purpose are hardest to pin down. In fact, judging by its critical history, the absence of any governing transaction with the public sphere is the book's most distinctive feature. Almost all commentary on *Liber Amoris* tries to define what kind of relationship its content has to the implied reader. So Jonathan Wordsworth writes in his introduction to the Woodstock facsimile edition that here 'life and art are in abnormally close relation', while Jonathan Gross recognizes the temptation to read this narrative as 'an event in [Hazlitt's] life which seems to have no place in his literary career'.[29] This pattern of antithetical reference to 'life and art' goes back to the book's earliest reviewers. The *Blackwood's* notice, for example, clearly sees what is at stake when it asserts 'this work is not a novel, but a history'.[30] Literariness offers *Liber Amoris* a safe haven, a way of reading which would allow it to be aestheticized and so made sense of; but the book itself seems intent on expelling itself from this refuge into the domain of history, where it speaks all too explicitly (and inexplicably) of the real circumstances under which it was written. The problem is that it deals so directly with tawdry details of Hazlitt's infatuation with Sarah Walker, daughter to his landlord. It has all the unapologetic erotic intensity of the earlier parts of Rousseau's *Confessions* with none of the idealizing atmosphere. There is an uncomfortably abrupt disparity between the frantic, often eloquent energy the first-person narrator ('H.') invests in his obsessive love and the grotesquely banal unfolding of the story. The published text of *Liber Amoris* is very closely related to Hazlitt's own letters sent to friends during the course of the affair. No obvious literary act has intervened between these personal details and the public version of the story.

As with Rousseau, the most common reaction to *Liber Amoris* was a shocked bewilderment at its mere existence. Henry Crabb Robinson recognized the book's literary kinship with the two most obvious parallels, Goethe's *Werther* and Rousseau's *Julie*, only to note that Hazlitt's narrative of overwrought erotic passion seems not literary but embarrassingly personal: 'such a story as this is nauseous and revolting'.[31]

---

[29] William Hazlitt, *Liber Amoris* (Oxford: Woodstock, 1992), 'Introduction' (no pagination); Jonathan Gross, 'Hazlitt's Worshiping Practice in *Liber Amoris*', *Studies in English Literature 1500–1900*, 35 (1995), 707–21, at 707.

[30] *Blackwood's*, xiii. 641.

[31] Edith J. Morley (ed.), *Henry Crabb Robinson on Books and their Writers*, 3 vols. (London: J. M. Dent, 1938), i. 296.

Twentieth-century judgements include, among other terms, 'disgusting', 'silly', a 'tragic piece of futility'; some nineteenth-century ones are predictably more virulent: 'this wretched compound of folly and nauseous sensuality', 'mixed filth and utter despicableness', 'beastly trash'.[32] There is a faint effort to disguise the autobiographical quality of *Liber Amoris*, via a short 'Advertisement' that throws the flimsiest of veils over the actual authorship of the book. The tale of Hazlitt's infatuation was, however, widely known in London literary circles by 1823, thanks largely to Hazlitt himself (he is recorded as having berated virtual strangers with all the details). In effect, *Liber Amoris* seems to be nothing but the open circulation of the most humiliating particulars of its author's private experience.[33] Critics have thus been forced to make it into something other than an autobiography: an imaginative portrait of a mode of Romantic sensibility (Robert Ready), 'a satire on autobiographical self-expression' (Marilyn Butler), an ironic critique of its age (James Mulvihill), a complex study of the interdependent relation between private and public identities (Kurt Koenigsberger).[34] Read simply as an autobiographical act it seems inevitably to become a pathological document, exposing the murk of the author's inwardness, as the gleefully vituperative *Blackwood's* review claimed ('a *veritable* transcript

---

[32] See Gross, 'Hazlitt's Worshiping Practice', 707; *Literary Chronicle*, 28 June 1823, 409; *Literary Gazette*, xxxi. 339–40; *John Bull*, 9 June 1823, 180.

[33] An article on *Liber Amoris* summarizes and considers the options which appear to have been available to critics of Hazlitt's book: Kurt M. Koenigsberger, 'Liberty, Libel, and *Liber Amoris*: Hazlitt on Sovereignty and Death', *Studies in Romanticism*, 38 (1999), 281–309. He observes that attempts to read the subject of the work—the figure of 'H.' and his story—tend 'to reinforce the distinction between biography and fiction' (p. 286). As in the case of the *Blackwood's* reviewer, these alternatives are systematically exclusive. If 'H.' is read as 'an autonomous aesthetic object' (p. 286), then the book becomes an artefact of confessional literature, situated at a distance from the messy details of Hazlitt's embarrassing infatuation with Sarah Walker. Otherwise, he is identified with the historical circumstances of Hazlitt's abortive affair, and *Liber Amoris* becomes a documentary record. The choice seems to be: art or life? Acutely, Koenigsberger notices how the particular strangeness of this text is recorded 'within an interpretative economy characterized by a logic of the excluded middle' (p. 286). Critics seek the 'something between' literature and history, and yet find themselves forced into polarized alternatives which debar them from that hinterland.

[34] Robert Ready, 'The Logic of Passion: Hazlitt's *Liber Amoris*', *Studies in Romanticism*, 14 (1975), 41–57; Marilyn Butler, 'Satire and the Images of Self in the Romantic Period: The Long Tradition of Hazlitt's *Liber Amoris*', in G. A. Rosso and Daniel P. Watkins (eds.), *Spirits of Fire: English Romantic Writers and Contemporary Historical Methods* (London: Associated University Presses, 1990); James Mulvihill, 'The Anatomy of Idolatry: Hazlitt's *Liber Amoris*', *Charles Lamb Bulletin*, NS 70 (1990), 195–203; Koenigsberger, 'Liberty, Libel, and *Liber Amoris*'. See also James Treadwell, 'The Legibility of *Liber Amoris*', *Romanticism on the Net*, 17 (2000), <http://www.ron.umontreal.ca/>.

of the feelings and doings of an individual living LIBERAL').[35] It is a paradigmatic case of how the effect of expressive self-writing appears in conjunction with the collapse of proper autobiographical transactions. *Liber Amoris* appears to speak straight out of the author's private experience because the text offers no other mode of address. In the absence of any clear instructive or amusing purposes, self-writing looks like the limit of legibility, a last resort.

Reading the practice of Romantic autobiography, then, is a matter of exploring the space which self-writing creates for itself within the text, and registering its presence in excess of the text's sense of purpose. Or, in the absence of self-writing in anything beyond a straightforwardly narrative mode, it is a matter of tracing autobiography's transactions with the literary public sphere. Over the course of Parts I and II I have outlined the latter alternative, as a way of describing what most Romantic-period autobiographical writing actually looks like. Talking about the practice of self-representation, however, requires that we move past general discussion of the situation of autobiography in the world of letters, the sense of purpose and place that governs the very idea of 'autobiography' as it emerged in the period. This is because self-representation occurs as some kind of evasion of those governing conditions. The task is instead to analyse the particular shape of the evasions in specific instances, as this chapter has begun to do. We can now approach some more detailed readings of autobiographical conditions and effects.

[35] *Blackwood's*, xiii. 641.

7

Childe Harold canto III

Over the course of the year 1816 the whole question of autobiography's illicit but fascinating commingling of private experience with the literary public sphere became concentrated in the figure of Lord Byron. Not since 1783 had the British world of letters encountered so iconic a case of a personality and its published texts in a relationship with each other which threw the whole structure of such relationships into evident confusion. For all sorts of reasons the Byron affair registered an even greater turbulence in the autobiographical arena than had the British publication of Rousseau's *Confessions* and *Reveries*. The machinery of literary publicity had enlarged itself hugely in the intervening decades. In 1816 there were far more newspapers and periodicals to mediate the conjunction of Byron, his domestic circumstances, his publications, and the reading public. By that year there was also a firmly established 'Byronism' in wide circulation, a cultural phenomenon which already treated published texts and the figure of the author as simultaneous, permeable, interchangeable fields. Rousseau, by contrast, had at the time of his death two rather separate reputations: his eccentric and misanthropic personal character was thought of more or less separately from his achievements as writer and philosopher. The *Confessions* could thus be categorized as a symptom of a genius's peculiarities, somehow distinct from the proper legacy of printed works. Following the 1812 arrival of the first two cantos of *Childe Harold's Pilgrimage* the figure of Byron had developed in the form of an inextricable union of published writings with a distinctive personality's self-expression. Byronism incarnated, and (by virtue of its completely unprecedented popularity) legitimized, the idea that writing needed no purpose other than manifesting a highly charged inwardness. Not that Byron's poems published between March 1812 (*Childe Harold* I and II) and November 1816 (canto III) were in any recognizable sense autobiographical. But, as Francis Jeffrey observed in a brilliantly perceptive review of *The Bride of Abydos* (1813) and *The Corsair* (1814), the moody, exotic melodrama of these and the other oriental tales quintessentially manifested the fact that 'It is chiefly by . . . portraitures of the interior of human nature that the poetry of the present day is distinguished.'[1] Unlike Rousseau, Byron had effectively prepared the public for an autobiographical turn in his published work.

Furthermore, Rousseau had at least observed the basic decorum of dying before startling the world with his *Confessions*. Exile—Byron's substitute—was in no way comparable. His continuing involvement in the nexus of texts and events which came to a crisis in 1816 further complicated the issue; indeed, the explicitly autobiographical stance of canto III of *Childe Harold* orients itself as much towards futurity as reflection. The canto begins with a direct reference to the controversial past, recalling in dangerously sentimental terms Byron's separation from his wife and infant daughter, and its concluding effort to imagine his future relationship to that daughter is a still more transparently competitive engagement with his domestic catastrophe, drawing defiant attention to unresolved questions of blame, of rights and wrongs, which were still very much the currency of public discourse. Rousseau was criticized for introducing the names of people still living into his scandalously frank narrative. In Byron's case, though, the scandal, as well as the persons, was still alive. *Childe Harold* III is pervaded by a striking grammatical immediacy of tense, from its first stanza, which purports to be written at exactly the same moment as the thoughts it transcribes occur, through to the iterated 'Now's, 'Here's, and 'It is's of its loco-descriptive meditations. It positively advertises the instantaneous, unimpeded transformation of intimate experience into writing, beyond even the 'burning periods' of Rousseau's narrative (which is after all a retrospective, and so at least partially detached, account).[2]

Moreover, just as Rousseau's book was still an object of occasionally horrified fascination well into the second decade of the nineteenth century, so the thirty-odd years between its publication and the advent of Byronism had seen little change in the general status of autobiographical writing, despite the increasingly coherent formation of a genre under that name in the world of reading and writing. Though the number of published autobiographies was increasing steadily (along with the numbers of virtually every other sort of publication), and the popularity of such books was becoming more and more obvious to the

---

[1] *Edinburgh Review*, xxiii. 203.
[2] D'Israeli, *Miscellanies*, 103.

spokesmen of the literary public sphere, there is no reason to believe that enough time had passed since 1783 for the events of 1816 to have seemed less startling. As the evidence studied above suggests, there is no gradual accommodation of autobiography to its environment over the course of the Romantic period. If Byron was given rather more temperate treatment in the mainstream literary press (as opposed to the newspapers) than another writer guilty of similar autobiographical offences might have expected—Hazlitt's *Liber Amoris* attracted much stronger language for publishing somewhat similar erotic-domestic material, for example—that is certainly because his rank and connections precluded commentators from indulging in the enthusiastic rhetoric of contempt and disgust with which the periodicals assaulted those who contravened their ideas of propriety in publication. A clear sign of this deference appears among the reviews of *Childe Harold* I and II. Byron's preface to the 1812 cantos, like so many other prefaces to instances of published self-writing, seeks to deflect the anticipated charge of writing autobiographically by insisting that Harold is 'the child of imagination'.[3] However we now choose to read the relationships between Harold, the narrator of the poem, and Byron himself, contemporary readers found it easy to ignore the preface and treat author and hero as interchangeable figures.[4] Yet the reviews shared a supine readiness to at least pretend to take the 'Noble Author' at his word. Jeffrey's review of *Childe Harold* III recalls Byron's complaints 'of those who identified him with his hero' at the time of the first two cantos, and acknowledges the general cooperation evident in 1812: 'in noticing the former portions of the work, we thought it unbecoming to give any countenance to such a supposition'.[5] The *Quarterly*'s notice of cantos I and II, whose author had been to the same Cambridge college as Byron and was a member of the same club, performs extraordinary contortions as it tries to raise the issue of Harold's questionable character while accepting, 'in consequence of the author's positive assurance', that Byron has shown an appropriately gentlemanly 'unwillingness to appear as the hero of his own tale'.[6] The review in the monthly *Satirist* is typical in its reluctance to go beyond hinting that the obviously autobiographical transaction has taken place:

[3] *Lord Byron: The Complete Poetical Works*, ed. Jerome J. McGann, 7 vols. (Oxford: Clarendon, 1980–93), ii. 4. Subsequent citations of Byron's poetry by line number refer to the texts printed in this edition.

[4] See Reiman, *The Romantics Reviewed*, pt. B, for an exhaustive compilation of early reviews of all Byron's work. A more manageable selection is Andrew Rutherford (ed.), *Byron: The Critical Heritage* (London: Routledge, 1970).

[5] *Edinburgh Review*, xxvii. 293.   [6] *Quarterly Review*, vii. 192.

Childe Harold is a fictitious character; for the noble Lord in his preface disclaims any intention of painting from a real personage, with an earnestness which would lead one to believe that he was apprehensive it might be suspected he had sat to himself for his own portrait![7]

It is easy to imagine how differently the suggestion of disingenuousness would have been handled in the case of a less privileged author.

In what sense, though, does one speak of *Childe Harold* as an autobiographical text at all? What justification is there for reading the unfolding crisis of 1816 under the sign of autobiography, as one obviously can in the case of the reception of Rousseau's *Confessions*? It should be clear, I hope, that no reference is meant to what one might call the traditional formal definition of an autobiographical text. None of Byron's works is a sustained narrative of events in the author's life. *Childe Harold* comes closest, in that its motion is sequentially structured by the historical circumstances of Byron's own life. Still, its first readers placed cantos I and II within a genre of loco-descriptive poetry, and even the more explicitly personal first-person stance of the later cantos conforms more closely to models of lyric rather than narrative subjectivity: poetic effusions and meditations rather than autobiographical documents in a familiar sense. Nevertheless, this sort of taxonomy is not relevant to the situation of Romantic-period texts. That is, there is little use in talking about autobiographical writing of the time in generic or formalist terms. As regards the events of 1816, I use the word in the sense developed in this book. 'Autobiography' stands for an act of publication situated problematically at the border between private experience and the literary public sphere, and self-consciously engaged in transactions with the public concerning its place. The word is not meant to define a particular text that finds itself in such a situation; it should refer to the situation itself, the nexus of negotiable questions about the authority, legitimacy, and autonomy of self-writing, and the transactions between a text and its readers as those questions come into play.

By any account, the sequence of events from the very public collapse of the Byrons' marriage in January 1816 through to the publication of *Childe Harold* III on 18 November provides an unusually intense example of that situation. The figure of Byron had existed at the convergence of private, public, and literary spheres ever since the first two cantos had created their sensation in 1812.[8] Its 'privacy' was defined in sexual and

---

[7] Reiman, *The Romantics Reviewed*, pt. B, 2111.

[8] The nature of what I call 'the figure of Byron' is well summarized by Frances Wilson:

emotional arenas, the spheres of intimacy and inwardness with which Byron became peculiarly associated; its publicity belonged to the social environment which found the figure so fascinating, and kept its fascination in circulation; while the steady flow of new poems supplied virtually unprecedented numbers of readers with published versions of the same figure over Byron's signature, the Harolds and Giaours and Conrads and Selims invested with auras of mysteriously inaccessible inwardness and yet presented to the public with melodramatic immediacy, so that they are simultaneously remote and vividly present:

> On—on he hastened—and he drew
> My gaze of wonder as he flew:
> Though like a Demon of the night
> He passed and vanished from my sight;
> His aspect and his air impressed
> A troubled memory on my breast
>
> (*The Giaour*, 200–5)

Initially the crisis of 1816 involved a clash between public and private spheres in a purely social setting. That is, the circulation of Byron's domestic crisis was a matter of gossip and scandal. As the sphere of privacy began to contain more private matters (as it were)—rumours of incest and homosexuality rather than just profligacy—so the public sphere became 'more' public, as Lady Byron's formal request for a separation gave the whole drama an official currency. The irreversible intrusion of the literary sphere into this redrawing of the figure of Byron came with an article in the weekly literary miscellany *The Champion* on 14 April headed 'Lord Byron's Poems On His Own Domestic Circumstances'. The title maliciously presents the two poems 'Fare Thee Well!' and 'A Sketch from Private Life' as autobiographical reflections. Byron had written both the strategically sentimental address to his wife and the vicious satire on her maid in March, and had them printed in

'Byron now belonged to his readers, as if by being read the writer were literally purchased. The "Byronic" became public property and Byron found that his identity was no longer synonymous with his image, that there was a severance between the self he experienced himself as being and the self returned to him in the eyes of his audience' (Wilson (ed.), *Byronism* (London: Macmillan, 1999), 4). A portrait of the figure of Byron is drawn in Peter L. Thorslev, Jr., *The Byronic Hero* (Minneapolis, Minn.: University of Minnesota Press, 1962). An important recent account, much more attuned to the machinery of cultural commodification, is Nicholas Mason, 'Building Brand Byron', *Modern Language Quarterly*, 63 (2002), 411–40. Drawing on a fascinating range of references, Mason suggests very persuasively that *Childe Harold* marks 'the instance when branding extended from the industrial to the cultural sector of the British economy' (p. 414).

small private editions in early April. In that state they uneasily straddled domestic and wider environments. The private edition was large enough—fifty copies—to spread throughout Byron's circle, allowing the poems to operate as propaganda. But 'Fare Thee Well!' was also sent directly to his wife, becoming precisely the personal appeal its printed form simulates, while 'A Sketch' dispenses with all the formal standards of classical or Augustan satire to indulge in invective so brutally personal that it demands to be read as a fully private document. *The Champion*'s unauthorized republication of the poems effectively makes Byron an autobiographer of the most transgressive sort, using the medium of print to open the most intimate recesses of domesticity to the public. The fact that Byron was not himself responsible for the act of publication is irrelevant; he appears in the *Champion* as first-person author, the verses his literary revelation of the affair. Their appearance before a mass readership—they were immediately republished in a number of other newspapers—completes the transformation of Byronic literary intimacy into unacceptably personal autobiography. In the period's characteristic autobiographical paradox, the poems bear their own witness, in print, to the fact that they should not be in print.[9] Their legibility itself constitutes their impropriety. Byron left England for good only eleven days later.

In this context the opening gesture of *Childe Harold* III is an astonishing piece of bravado:

> Is thy face like thy mother's, my fair child!
> Ada! sole daughter of my house and heart?
> When last I saw thy young blue eyes they smiled,
> And when we parted,—not as now we part,
> But with a hope.—
> > Awaking with a start,
> The waters heave around me   (1–6)

The appearance of a new canto of Harold's pilgrimage ought to signal the resumption of the Byron figure's most effective and popular literary incarnation.[10] It might have presented itself as a return to the moment of his most glorious public success, bridging the intervening disaster. Yet,

---

[9] In the face of numerous pirated editions Byron's publisher John Murray finally decided to issue his own small volume of Byron's *Poems* (including 'Fare Thee Well!' and 'A Sketch') in September 1816. His 'Advertisement' treads carefully around the issue, claiming (by proxy) the poet's own authority for this edition while still implying that Byron is not really responsible for circulating these texts at all.

[10] On the poem's public standing see Peter J. Manning, '*Childe Harold* in the Market Place', *Modern Language Quarterly*, 52 (1991), 170–90.

instead of resurrecting Harold, that icon of Byronism at its most eagerly circulated and consumed, the canto opens in nakedly autobiographical mode. Its illusion is of unmediated access to the interiority of the figure of Byron at its most scandalous, the exiled husband still writing poetry 'On His Own Domestic Circumstances' with exactly the same combination of sentimental self-pity and half-concealed accusation that informed 'Fare Thee Well.' Byron's infant daughter was an important thematic presence in both that poem and 'A Sketch'; the latter demonizes Lady Byron's maid by imagining her supplanting the husband and father's station in the household: 'Though all her former functions are no more, / She rules the circle which she served before' (ll. 39–40). Ada was a central element in the private–public discourse of the 1816 crisis, so her appearance in the first line of the new publication, alongside her mother, draws the clearest possible attention to the scandalous circumstances that Byron's departure from England might have been supposed to have put behind him. In essence, the opening lines repossess the autobiographical aspect of the scandal which had been instigated by the *Champion*'s article. Byron (the figure of Byron, that is; the first-person author of *Childe Harold*) takes over responsibility for writing publicly about his private life. Indeed, the improper conjunction of publication with extreme privacy could not be accented more strongly, because of the lines' uncanny way of merging the printed text into the author's first-person consciousness. Even the moment of writing, the hand holding the pen, seems to have been dispensed with. The sequence of events leaves no room for it: the caesura in line 5 turns the prior four and a half lines into a purely mental reverie, from which consciousness awakes to take in its physical surroundings. These, it seems, are not so much lines on domestic circumstances—both 'Fare Thee Well!' and 'A Sketch' have an air of strategic calculation, of being written and addressed with deliberation—as *thoughts* on those circumstances. The 'now' of line 4 floats in a strangely unspecifiable chronology. It cannot be made to refer to the moment of writing, since no writing seems to be happening. It cannot refer to an actual narratable event, since the first half of the line tells us that the parting from Ada has already occurred in time past. It can only be explained by reference to a supposed thought or feeling inside the first person, a sense that some new and irreversible (without 'a hope') parting is happening 'now', as the thought forms itself. The next line's abrupt caesura has the same quality; it seems to stand for some break in thought itself (the 'start'), an invisible event in a temporal sequence defined only by the time it takes for the lines to happen—what would later be called a 'stream of consciousness'. Only with the present-tense narrative verbs and predicates of line 6 ('The waters heave around me') do the narrating voice and its surroundings achieve a stable location and a definite relation to each other. Before that it is impossible to read what is happening. We have only an illusion of 'pure' autobiography, the published text apparently identical with an inward consciousness (the rather unstructured syntax adds to the effect: the question coming out of nowhere, the disorganized accumulation of clauses in lines 4–5).

By the second stanza this remarkable effect has mutated into the more familiar mode of overt Byronic self-dramatization. A theatrical first person establishes itself as the focus of the text's rhetorical energy:

> Still must I on; for I am as a weed,
> Flung from the rock, on Ocean's foam, to sail
> Where'er the surge may sweep, or tempest's breath prevail.   (16–18)[11]

Sublime self-pity offers an obvious avenue for self-writing in the aftermath of exile. It is unmistakably the language of Byronism, so it gives the authorial figure the chance to reappropriate the established rhetorical vehicle of 'his' inwardness, its habitual gloom given added autobiographical pertinence by recent events (known of course to all readers). Again, a return to Harold, and to 1812, becomes a possibility. Stanza II as a whole clearly echoes 'Childe Harold's Good Night', the first lyric interjected into canto I:

> With thee, my bark, I'll swiftly go
>   Athwart the foaming brine;
> Nor care what land thou bear'st me to,
>   So not again to mine.
> Welcome, welcome, ye dark-blue waves!   (I. 190–4)[12]

The new canto seems ready to offer Byronism once again as the vehicle for writing inwardness, forgetting the more disconcerting autobiographical mode of the opening lines in favour of a known literary effect. This would be an apt strategy, since the all-too-public events of 1816 had brought the figure of Byron into much closer convergence with the

---

[11] On this stanza see Thomas Fotherington, 'Utterly Wet and a Weed: Saturation in Canto III of *Childe Harold's Pilgrimage*', *Journal of European Romantic Studies*, 9 (1984), 111–29.

[12] Cf. III. 10–12: 'Once more upon the waters! yet once more! / And the waves bound beneath me as a steed / That knows his rider. Welcome to their roar!' The allusion to the familiarity of the setting makes for another connection with the extant cantos, and with the already circulated Harold.

figure of Harold, with his satanic aura of past crimes, blasted youth, and misanthropic contempt for social virtues. At the close of stanza II, canto III gives every sign of being ready to exploit that convergence, casting the first person as Harold, and thereby as 'Byron' in the established public–private (inward-but-circulated) sense.

Instead, the poem performs a visible reconfiguration of the relation between Harold—icon of Byron's extant personality and texts—and his author. Rather than affirming the vitality of Harold as an autobiographical figure, the narrating first person discovers in his literary persona traces of the death of subjectivity, of inwardness:

> In my youth's summer I did sing of One,
> The wandering outlaw of his own dark mind;
> Again I seize the theme then but begun,
> And bear it with me, as the rushing wind
> Bears the cloud onwards: in that Tale I find
> The furrows of long thought, and dried-up tears,
> Which, ebbing, leave a sterile track behind,
> O'er which all heavily the journeying years
> Plod the last sands of life,—where not a flower appears.   (19–27)

The Byronic persona is now revealed to be (or to have been) a text, a 'Tale', its rich simulation of sublime inwardness merely the 'sterile' trace of the thoughts and feelings it expressed. The stanza's closing metaphor is hard to decipher, partly because of this self-conscious insertion of difference between 'I' and 'the theme'. In the earlier cantos 'long thought', 'tears', and 'the journeying years' would all have been aspects of the consciousness (its feelings and experiences) which all readers recognized as the poem's centre of interest, and which could be named 'Harold' or 'Byron' without the choice making much difference. Now, however, there is a clear sense of an intervening chronology at work, which relegates Harold to the past—'my youth's summer'—and sets him against the narrator ('in that Tale I find . . .'), who exists in the absolutely immediate present established in the canto's abrupt opening lines.[13] There is a doubly autobiographical effect. First, the narrator is reviewing and reflecting on his past; second, the text is apparently transcribing his

---

[13] The relationship between Harold and Byron, and its reconfiguration in canto III, is discussed at length in Jerome J. McGann, *Fiery Dust: Byron's Poetic Development* (Chicago, Ill.: University of Chicago Press, 1968), 67–94, and Frederick Garber, *Self, Text, and Romantic Irony* (Princeton, NJ: Princeton University Press, 1988), 3–31 and 102–16. Both treatments understand Harold as a correlative to Byron's 'self', rather than to the (public) figure of Byron.

private thoughts, producing the kind of intense 'self-presence' we tend to think of as Wordsworthian. Together these generate a strongly felt disjunction between the Haroldian inwardness of 'thought' and 'tears' and the narrator's vision of himself retracing the faded marks of that past inwardness in a present desert. The theme of the stanza, then, is separation, as it was—in a different but related autobiographical mode, alluding openly to the public events of the preceding months—in stanza I. But this separation works to disentangle the convergences between public, private, and literary identities which previously sustained the figure of Byron. Prior to 1816 'Byron' was a mysteriously exaggerated privacy circulating itself through the continuous publication of eagerly consumed poems.[14] Here, though, the private aspect of the self appears in the guise of consciousness meditating on its emptiness; the literary aspect appears as no more than a defunct phantom of interiority (thoughts and feelings); while the public aspect is defined by the crisis of 1816, signified so openly by Ada and Lady Byron, which reduces Byron's pilgrimage to aimless plodding over the faded landscape of Harold's prior success, now turned sterile.

This last feature of the altered situation occupies the next stanza. 'Byron' now speaks in his role as purveyor of Byronism to the public:

> Since my young days of passion—joy, or pain,
> Perchance my heart and harp have lost a string,
> And both may jar: it may be, that in vain
> I would essay as I have sung to sing.
> Yet, though a dreary strain, to this I cling   (28–32)

Again, the gesture is brilliantly intricate. The stance of passion wasted and outlived, of growing old before one's time, is quintessentially Haroldian or Byronic. Yet it is now appropriated for the newly autobiographical consciousness, which sharply separates itself from the effort of reproducing Byronic texts. To sing as the narrator has sung before, to reconnect the nexus that binds him to Harold (and to *Childe Harold* and other poems), would be to restore the public configuration of Byronism. However, the artificiality of any such performance is now openly exposed. Harold's old cynicism and detachment are brought to bear on

[14] My argument here is partly indebted to Jerome Christensen, *Lord Byron's Strength* (Baltimore, Md: Johns Hopkins University Press, 1993), whose treatment of 'Byron' is exemplary in recognizing that the discourse of subjectivity and personality cannot be thought of separately from the textuality and commercial history of the Byron phenomenon. ' "Byron" is identical with its medium' (p. 172). Christensen's elaborations of this insight are often obscure in their relation to analysis of Byronic texts.

Harold himself, and so also on the very figure of Byronism. In effect, the stanza catches Byron in the act of extricating himself from his prior figure. We are justified in naming the author-narrator, the one who does the extricating, as Byron, because the whole force of the opening stanzas is to create a newly authentic autobiographical subjectivity; one which gives the aura of authenticity by making intimate reference to the public events connected with the name of Byron, and also by distinguishing itself from its outworn prior form. Byronic melancholy is now (the stanzas imply) 'real'. Instead of expressing and propagating a sublime inwardness, as in the earlier cantos and the oriental tales, subjectivity produces itself as that which reflects on its personal history and its published texts. Indeed, the narrator stresses in these early stanzas the absence of any kind of profound inwardness underpinning his consciousness: appealing for 'Forgetfulness' (l. 35), calling himself 'Nothing' (l. 50), referring to his 'crush'd feeling's dearth' (l. 54). The events of 1816 have destroyed 'feeling' and ruined the figure of Byron. In their place comes an autobiographical presence conjured in the act of remembering that ruin (the speaker of ll. 1–5 can only be the historical Byron, the father of Ada).

The resumption of *Childe Harold's Pilgrimage*, then, renews the figure of the author in the form of Byron reflecting on his own figure. Instead of the implicit equation of Harold with Byron, we encounter an explicit disjunction between the two, which allows an intensely autobiographical first person to come into being in the very process of deconstructing the relation between texts and selves.[15] Hence the famous lines in stanza VI, answering the question of why the narrator has chosen to revisit the outworn persona of Harold:

> 'Tis to create, and in creating live
> A being more intense, that we endow
> With form our fancy, gaining as we give
> The life we image, even as I do now   (46–9)

Again the peculiarly abrupt 'now' surfaces, evoking the presence of consciousness by its very elusiveness (for readers that 'now' is always an indeterminate 'then'). The clause 'even as I do now' turns the lines from some sort of theory or programme into an autobiographical event, as do the present participles, 'creating', 'gaining'. As the narrator grasps the

---

[15] Garber finds a 'dialectic of making and unmaking' to be central to *Childe Harold* from its beginnings; see his discussion of cantos I and II in Garber, *Self, Text, and Romantic Irony*, esp. pp. 20–31.

difference between himself and Harold—'What am I? Nothing; but not
so art thou' (l. 50)—he endows himself with a 'more intense' being of
authorship, of being the author of *this* text, which so far seems entirely
coterminous with his consciousness. As the vehicle of a lost Byronism,
Harold carries a cargo of grand rhetorical inwardness, and the rest of the
stanza imagines the narrator exploiting this resource:

> I glow
> Mix'd with thy spirit, blended with thy birth,
> And feeling still with thee in my crush'd feeling's dearth.   (52–4)

This is not however the signal for retrieving the situation before 1816,
when Byron and Harold could merge into each other to create a figure
of glowing subjectivity. The stanza insists on an antithetical grammar of
'I' and 'thou'. Two distinct persons occupy its lines, and the distinction
means that only one of them demands to be properly named 'Byron', to
be identified as the figure of the author, the (openly) autobiographical
subject. Harold endows Byron with life, but only by enabling him to
extend the formless reverie of the opening lines into a third canto of
Childe Harold. Harold lets the autobiographer go on being, in the aftermath of the figure of Byron's ruin.

The first reviewers of canto III laid aside the gentlemanly scruples that
had inhibited judgements in 1812. Then, the potential confusion of
author with hero could be casually set aside: as the *Monthly Review* put
it: 'With this matter, however, the reader and the reviewer have little
concern.'[16] In 1816, by contrast, readers and reviewers scarcely pretended
to be concerned with anything else. Scott's notice in the *Quarterly* rightly
observed that this was not just because of the public's interest in Byron
personally, more acute than ever after months of gratifyingly open scandal. It is, he writes, a characteristic of the poems themselves: 'The works
before us contain so many direct allusions to the author's personal feelings and private history, that it becomes impossible for us to divide Lord
Byron from his poetry.'[17] Scott's phrasing helpfully repeats the opening
stanzas' use of the language of division and separation—from the past,
from Harold, from the figure of Byron—to produce a strongly autobiographical identification of the author as the subject of his text. Jeffrey's
article in the *Edinburgh Review* agrees that in the new canto 'it is really
impracticable to distinguish' Harold from his creator.[18] Again, this does

---

[16] *Monthly Review*, NS lxviii. 75.
[17] *Quarterly Review*, xvi. 174.
[18] *Edinburgh Review*, xxvii. 293.

not mean that the two figures merge into each other. Harold is after all a barely significant presence in canto III: he is the third-person narrative subject in stanzas viii–xvi, two lines of stanza xviii, and stanzas lii–lv, and appears nowhere else. Jeffrey's real point is that *Childe Harold's Pilgrimage* has become Lord Byron's autobiography. The subject of the new canto, he means, is Byron's personal identity, and its 'Byronic' mode of sublime self-expression now demands to be read as confessional self-writing:

as the author has at last spoken out in his own person, and unbosomed his griefs a great deal too freely to his readers, the offence would now be to entertain a doubt of their reality.[19]

Like Scott, he understands the text's demand for an autobiographical reading. His phrasing exposes the discomfort this demand always caused among the self-appointed guardians of the literary world in the Romantic period. He also recognizes that in the case of Byron in late 1816 the discomfort is aggravated: 'with the knowledge which all the world has of these subjects … not even the example of Lord Byron, can persuade us that they are fit for public discussion'.[20]

Nevertheless, a deferential silence on the subject of Byron's domestic affairs does not preclude a more general discussion of the author personally, as the evident subject of canto III. Compelled by 'the dreadful tone of sincerity, and an energy that cannot be counterfeited in the expression of wretchedness', Jeffrey is reluctantly drawn into comments on Byron's character and morality.[21] Scott takes up the challenge more resolutely. His review ends by proposing, at length, a regulatory system for the author of *Childe Harold*; a cure for Byronism, essentially. There could be no better evidence for the success of the canto's controlled transformation of the figure of Byron into Byron 'himself', the shift managed in the opening cantos from a literary inwardness to an autobiographical presence. Much less sophisticated reviews also testify to the way canto III was taken as a depiction of Byron's personal inner landscape in late 1816: 'We discern clearly that his Lordship's spirits are not raised by his separation from his country.'[22] The poem was being read in the same light as 'Fare Thee Well!' and 'A Sketch': a dangerously (but fascinatingly) direct translation of Byron's private experience into print.

Inevitably, then, *Childe Harold* III becomes involved in the same kind

---

[19] Ibid. 309. [20] Ibid. 292.
[21] Ibid. 309. [22] *Literary Panorama*, v. 410.

of complex transactions with the public sphere that so obviously attend the publication of the 'Poems On His Own Domestic Circumstances'. A review in the very short-lived London weekly *The Portfolio* unfolds all the implications of an autobiographical text of Byron's appearing late in 1816:

AS the reader will have expected, the third canto . . . is still more replete than the two preceding ones with allusions, and even direct passages, which belong to the personal circumstances of the author. Indeed, it is the real romance of that person's life, immeasurably more than the fabled one of his pen, which the public expects to find in his pages.[23]

Most revealing here is the writer's assumption of a continuing transaction between Byron's publications and their readers. The rules of this relationship apparently require the poems to expose Byron's private experience increasingly explicitly: that is what 'the public expects'. If, therefore, the strikingly intimate reverie which opens the canto introduces an autobiographical subject withdrawn in the full privacy of consciousness, that meditative self is nevertheless offered to readers in exactly the form they want. Like 'Fare Thee Well!', but this time authorized by the poet and his publishers, the lines publicize Byron's most intimate experience of the separation of 1816. The *Portfolio*'s reviewer interprets the canto's language of inwardness as a strategic intervention in the continuing scandal: 'Lord Byron seeks to gain an ascendancy over the judgment of the public, by the public profession of great tenderness of heart and strong affections.'[24] Merely using the autobiographical first person brings the new publication into the social and literary scene where the figure of Byron had risen and fallen, and so opens questions about the legitimacy and authority of the author's self-representation at this moment. Canto III is necessarily a public poem. Its careful construction of a newly personal autobiographical 'I' thus becomes at the moment of publication a new Byronic transaction with readers, an implied promise to circulate the author's personal life more unreservedly and honestly—as 'the reader will have expected'. The *Champion* article of 1816 exposed Byron as an illegitimate autobiographer by creating the same juxtaposition of private feelings with the public sphere. But, so far from confessing the fault, *Childe Harold*'s resumption that November can be (and was) read as a promise to write more, not less, intimately; to circulate the 'real' Byron, disentangled from the chicanery

---

[23] Reiman, *The Romantics Reviewed*, pt. B, 1966.   [24] Ibid. 1967–8.

of the hostile press and the misrepresentations to which the prior figure of the author had become liable.

We are trying to grasp the peculiar way in which canto III performs an autobiography which speaks the language of authentic personal consciousness while also conducting its transactions with the public sphere: the autobiography of an exile writing home, where privacy happens in public, where the very identification of the first-person subject of the text as the inward self of the author is inseparable from that subject's negotiations with the conditions of being printed. This kind of effect had always been part of the Byronic persona. In fact, the figure of Byron constructed between 1812 and 1816 might almost be defined as an objectified subjectivity. The Harold of cantos I and II often appears as a face whose expressions are traced by the narrator with fetishistic intensity ('Strange pangs would flash along Childe Harold's brow'; I. 65). In the oriental tales this becomes a basic method of narration. They lavish attention on their heroes' 'chilling mystery of mien' (*Lara*, 361). The central figures are characteristically observed from the outside; their identity is given by the theatricality of their appearance as mediated by awestruck narrators. The intricate shifts of narratorial position in *The Giaour* (1813) dissolve the hero into a collage of partial but vivid snapshots:

> Though young and pale, that sallow front
> Is scath'd by fiery passion's brunt
>
> 'Tis he—'tis he—I know him now,
> I know him by his pallid brow
>
> But once I saw that face—yet then
> It was so mark'd with inward pain
> I could not pass it by again;
> It breathes the same dark spirit now,
> As death were stamped upon his brow.   (194–5, 610–11, 793–7)

Lara and Conrad in *The Corsair* are brought under a similarly obsessive narratorial gaze, which finds itself both absorbed in and rebuffed by its object:

> His features' deepening lines and varying hue
> At times attracted, yet perplexed the view
>
> (*The Corsair*, 209–10)

The Byronic figure gains its identity and force through its power to hold attention through the eye. Like the public persona of Byron himself as it was circulated in the years following *Childe Harold* I and II, it is sustained by its ubiquitous visibility. The description of Lara's 'art / Of fixing memory on another's heart' (*Lara*, 363–4) epitomizes the figure's utterly public character:

> they who saw him did not see in vain,
> And once beheld, would ask of him again   (367–8)

He is a focus of public expectation. Hence his suitability for the prolific repetitions of Byron's narrative poetry of 1812–16; the fascinated observer cannot get enough of him. Moreover, he exists by virtue of satisfying that demand. That is what is meant by his being seen 'not . . . in vain': he gives the eye what it requires. He embodies a perfectly adapted symbiosis between representation and consumption (much to the gratification of Byron's publisher Murray).

  Childe Harold III performs these transactions too. As a continuation of the most iconic of all Byron's narratives it could not possibly do otherwise. But it also marks an important change in the relation between identity and public self-presentation—a change which I am suggesting is shaped by the conditions of Romantic-period autobiography. Jerome McGann has distinguished between the production of the Byronic figure before the separation of 1816, which he calls 'masking' (adopting a theatrical personal disguise), and the 'scenarios of masquerade' emerging in canto III and other works of later in that year (including 'Fare Thee Well!' and *Manfred*). Unlike the mask, masquerade is a performance in which the performer himself is present alongside his disguises:

Byron writes and directs the intimate dramas of his work, but he finds himself, *as writer and director*, taking part in the action, and therefore falling subject to the action.[25]

This neatly explains the altered transaction with the public, as the Haroldian figure of objectified inwardness is replaced in canto III by the autobiographical figure of Byron publishing his private self. The earlier poems encouraged identification of Byron with Harold, or Conrad, or the nameless Giaour. So Richard Westall's famous portrait of 1815 (now in the National Portrait Gallery, London) creates a poet seen as if

---

[25] Jerome J. McGann, 'Hero With a Thousand Faces: The Rhetoric of Byronism', *Studies in Romanticism*, 31 (1992), 295–313, at 308. McGann's point concentrates on the dangerous (for Byron) plurality of public interpretations openly demanded by masquerade; he focuses on the plays. The article is nevertheless very suggestive for any reading of the public quality of Byron's self-writing.

through the fetishizing eyes of the tales' narrators: a face in vividly outlined, sensuous profile, seemingly indifferent to the gaze that is invited to linger over his luminous skin, huge eyes, wayward curls, and rosy pout. But in canto III, and in the particular environment of its publication, it is Byron as *author* who becomes the object of public expectation. The introductory stanzas offer readers a public view of the historical, personal subjectivity that is working on producing itself in verse. Rather than construing Byronic identity as a face—or, as the 'Epistle to Augusta' written probably in August 1816 calls it, 'a Name' (l. 100)—they produce a 'self'. This selfhood enters the literary public sphere as the new figure of Byron, in the wake of its prior version's highly public failure.

The great theme of that self, and in fact of the whole of *Childe Harold* III, is its separateness, its self-sufficiency. 'I depart', the narrator announces in the first stanza (l. 7), and the curious present tense already mentioned gives the verb something like a performative resonance, as if the first person is removing itself through the act of writing/publishing the poem.[26] The brief passage in which Harold takes centre stage is a repetition in third-person narrative of the same stance. Harold is placed 'in desolation; which could find / A life within itself, to breathe without mankind' (ll. 107–8), and 'wanders forth again', 'Self-exiled' (l. 136). From then on the first person journeys through landscapes of ruin, each mournfully reminding him that 'true Wisdom's world will be / Within its own creation' (ll. 406–7). When at last he encounters nature in undisturbed form the effect is to emphasize and aggrandize the self's singleness. Despite the notorious Wordsworthianism of the gestures—'I live not in myself, but I become / Portion of that around me' (ll. 680–1)—the orientation of the self in nature is never towards transcendence, but rather towards a systematic contrast between sublimely solitary experience and the social world whose absence nature primarily signifies:

> And thus I am absorb'd, and this is life:
> I look upon the peopled desart past,
> As on a place of agony and strife,
> Where, for some sin, to Sorrow I was cast,
> To act and suffer   (689–93)

Compare a transition later in the canto: 'But let me quit man's works, again to read / His Maker's, spread around me' (ll. 1013–14). Nature is

---

[26] The grammar of the present tense collapses any chronological interval between the illusory moment of the line being authored and the actual moment of its being read.

metonymic for that first 'I depart'; it stands for the quitting of all human experience beyond the self (as on the field of Waterloo, where 'I stood beneath the fresh green tree, / Which living waves where thou didst cease to live', ll. 264–5). The canto reaches its climax in rhetorical ecstasies of solitude, prompted by nature but ultimately located within a purely self-regarding system of expression. First comes the supremely melodramatic stanza XCVII:

> But as it is, I live and die unheard,
>   With a most voiceless thought   (912–13)

The final statement of the theme is stanza CXIII:

> I have not loved the world, nor the world me;
> I have not flattered its rank breath, nor bow'd
> To its idolatries a patient knee,—
> Nor coin'd my cheek to smiles,—nor cried aloud
> In worship of an echo; in the crowd
> They could not deem me one of such; I stood
> Among them, but not of them   (1049–55)

In the sphere of the private self this steady dramatizing of the first person's separateness indicates (obviously enough) an intensification of privacy. The poem is stressing writing's power to sustain a meditative (or, as it might now be labelled, Wordsworthian) mode, unapologetically finding itself its own subject. As we have seen, though, *Childe Harold* III never operates in the sphere of privacy alone. In the extremely public context of its moment of publication the theme of separateness equally obviously calls attention to Byron's 'Domestic Circumstances'. It is an appropriately autobiographical stance in more than just the Wordsworthian sense, that is. Implicitly but inevitably, it also works as a narrative of past personal experience (that most literal function of auto-biography). Referring to Harold as 'Self-exiled' is bound to read as an allusion to Byron's own departure from England seven months previously, as are all the other passages expressing alienation from society and human company. With the climactic stanza CXIII it is not even a matter of allusion. The lines present themselves as a reflection on recent events as straightforwardly as do the addresses to Ada at the beginning and end of the canto, albeit in a generalized soliloquy rather than a specifically personal and sentimental mode. Their familiar pose of sublime self-defi-nition is entangled with (in Jeffrey's phrase) 'the knowledge which all the world has'. Indeed, the stanza's closing lines attribute the narrator's isolation and exile to one event in the past, the moment of a Fall (like

Manfred's or Cain's), and this autobiographical specificity is itself enough to turn the narrator's inward drama into a matter of public speculation:

> I stood
> Among them, but not of them; in a shroud
> Of thoughts which were not their thoughts, and still could,
> Had I not filed my mind, which thus itself subdued.　　　(1054–7)

The whole stance of the canto implies that this defilement ('filed') is a crime committed by the narrator against himself, in the Haroldian manner. Yet the direct reference to the first person's exile from society, as a consequence of lowering himself to the level of the 'crowd' (l. 1053), demands to be read publicly—that is, as Byron's account of his destruction at the hands of his wife and her family. Autobiographical writing has compressed together the language of privacy and the public (published) transactions between author and readers. More accurately, autobiography *occurs*, or becomes evident, as the stanza engineers the conjunction of those two spheres which its own rhetoric places in such stark opposition. Consider the stanza's notorious first line (repeated as the opening of the following stanza): 'I have not loved the world, nor the world me'. The narrator claims gloomy Haroldian isolation as his fate. But while the line parades his self-sufficiency before its readers, addressing the public in the gesture of dismissing them, the 'world' is invited to name the narrator as Byron, and to read the line as a confession. This reciprocity instantly restores the connection between 'I' and the 'world' which the line's language doubly severs. The 'I' is read as a public figure, whose relationship with the 'crowd' is a subject of continuing interest and expectation. This is, in fact, the only way that the first-person pronoun can be interpreted. Its allusion to its history ('I have not loved . . . / I have not flattered . . .') compels readers to place it in that spot in the 'world' occupied by Byron, even as it speaks of having no place. Hence the peculiar mix of sincerity and mendacity that the line transmits so unmistakably. There was no shortage of reviewers ready to assure Byron that the world had indeed loved him. At the height of his popularity no one had been so publicly and so evidently loved, or at least adulated. As the first person orchestrates its rhetoric of separation, it simultaneously evokes its readers' contradictory reply. Byron appears as both himself and his figure; both in and out of the world.

Stanza CXIII only makes obvious what the whole canto suggests. Its theme of separation has a double meaning, and the apparent contradiction between these meanings is the essence of *Childe Harold* III's autobiographical effect. Separation indicates the privacy of the narrating first person; but it also refers to the widely circulated events of Byron's life in 1816, his separation from family and country. It becomes the link between the rhetoric of subjectivity and the identity of the author. It declares that the narrator rejects all further transactions with the public, at the same time as it identifies the narrator as the inward Byron published to general view. Strikingly, the canto has taken the endemic ambivalence of autobiographical writing in the period and turned it into a kind of method. The self circulates in print in the very act of claiming not to circulate. It organizes itself around a tremendously exaggerated version of early nineteenth-century autobiography's hesitant, self-conscious traversing of the border between public and private spheres.

Nowhere is this more obvious than in the spectacular theatre of stanza XCII, the climax of the storm scene:

> Could I embody and unbosom now
> That which is most within me,—could I wreak
> My thoughts upon expression, and thus throw
> Soul, heart, mind, passions, feelings, strong or weak,
> All, that I would have sought, and all I seek,
> Bear, know, feel, and yet breathe—into *one* word,
> And that one word were Lightning, I would speak;
> But as it is, I live and die unheard,
> With a most voiceless thought, sheathing it as a sword.   (905–13)

The whole drama here is of 'expression' in the literal sense: a forcing out. A barrier is imagined between the poem's own language, apparently locked 'within', and some other 'word' possessed of the true outwardness of speech. Desire presses against this resistance, creating the spectacular rhetorical friction and energy of the stanza: the urgency of the repeated subjunctives, the compounded nouns and verbs of lines 908–10. Still, all this vocabulary of inwardness presents itself as the wrong language. The lines imagine a different mode of articulation which would display 'That which is most within me'. By frustrating their own desire to express the self they claim that the rhetoric of that desire— the actual stanza—is not expression. To say 'I live and die unheard', to describe the thought just voiced as 'voiceless', is a blatant manipulation of autobiographical writing. It creates a pathos of desire, a subjectivity energized by its striving, while at the same time denying that self-writing has actually occurred. Like the gesture 'I have not loved the world, nor the world me', it displays a self to the reader in the act of withdrawing into privacy. Nothing could be more egotistically self-dramatizing than the melodramas of inwardness evoked in these closing stanzas of the canto. Yet in stanza CXI the narrator can describe part of his purpose as 'to conceal, / With a proud caution, love, or hate, or aught,—/ Passion or feeling, purpose, grief or zeal' (ll. 1035–7). Like separation, concealment lets the first person imagine that it cannot be (or is not being) read. Byron circulates himself as a self who is not contained in his text. That is the rhetorical gesture which constitutes his subjectivity, that makes the canto read as an autobiography.

I suggested in the preceding chapter that autobiography most typically marks its presence where other kinds of transaction between text and public break down. In that light *Childe Harold* III reads as a kind of institutionalizing of Romantic-period autobiographical writing. It simulates the collapse of those transactions, and exploits the resulting pose of isolation to indulge in the language of the self; and this whole process is played out self-consciously in front of the reader. It pretends to be *The Prelude*, a text turned away from the public, withdrawn in its meditations.[27] Yet that pose itself founds the poem's relationship with the public sphere, and defines the recognizable first-person author of an autobiographical publication. The poem answers to readers' expectations, while preserving the illusion of authentic, heartfelt, private self-writing. It offers a Byron who appears both as the figure circulated among readers and as the personal consciousness of the author; yet, crucially, it does so without letting the two dissolve into each other, as did the earlier figure of Byron. Instead of a smooth synthesis of text, author, and public sphere as established by the first two cantos, canto III disrupts their interrelations (as the unauthorized publication of the 'Poems On His Own Domestic Circumstances' did). The disturbance brings us into autobiography's terrain. Remarkably, though, the poem is able to fashion a different kind of transaction with the public, even out of its stance of alienation. It offers a self that is at once private and public, in such a way that the apparent opposition between the two spheres becomes a managed reciprocity. Consider again the contrast between the situation of this text and that of Rousseau's *Confessions*. The shock of the latter came ultimately from the way it placed reader, author, and text in relation to each other. It turned the book into a window through which

---

[27] I use the comparison only to illustrate the point about Byron's poem, not to imply any invidious hierarchies of authenticity or sincerity which rank Wordsworth above Byron.

the reader was forced to witness the exposure of inwardness at its most private (erotically and psychologically intimate). So the moment of reading became an impossible juxtaposition of incompatible spheres. It made visible that which was not supposed to be seen and known; it circulated things that should have been inaccessible. In *Childe Harold* III the shock is caused by the scandalous *content* of the private sphere, and the *fact* of its (continuing) transitions into print. The text itself, however, manages this situation. With Rousseau the text compounds and epitomizes the problem—which is why so many commentators found it inexplicable. Byron's writing was in this situation in April 1816, when the *Champion* made him an autobiographer of the worst kind. In November, though, his text performs the act of exposure while establishing a place for the author exiled from the public discourse of his private life and supposedly separate from the text of the poem, in a 'here' and 'now' that can be simultaneous with the act of writing but never with the moment of reading. Canto III never presents itself as a text laid before the reader, as does the *Confessions*. Instead, the published poem becomes the medium through which 'Byron'—the figure of the first person—refers to his inaccessible inward being, while tacitly inviting readers to witness the outward or public performance of the self.

It is worth mentioning again that autobiography should not be understood as textual self-expression. *Childe Harold* III certainly gives the impression of being organized by 'the design of [Byron's] psychology' and of opening 'the hiding places of his soul'.[28] Plenty of readers in 1816 and since have treated it accordingly. As we have seen, though, any equation between the self it portrays and the personal identity of the author is worked out through the poem's negotiations with the public. There is no secret, pre-textual location where Byron and his published first person are fused together, no 'psychology' or 'soul' underpinning the 'I' of the text and expressing itself in a succession of stanzas. The 'self' of *Childe Harold* III confirms instead what our broad survey of the conditions of Romantic autobiography has indicated: self-writing is more to do with writing than selves.[29] So far we have been looking at

[28] McGann, *Fiery Dust*, 53, 77.

[29] Vincent Newey sees in cantos III and IV a progressive commitment 'to the extinction of any self prior to the word and the image', an embrace of 'living through others and in constantly changing guises' (Newey, 'Authoring the Self', in Bernard Beatty and Vincent Newey (eds.), *Byron and the Limits of Fiction* (Liverpool: Liverpool University Press, 1988), 157). Newey's argument still assumes a purely authorial drama of autobiographical methods; writing is imagined as an exclusively first-person activity. The point about the textuality of Byron's 'self' is well made, though.

passages in the canto which dwell on the inwardness of the narrator, and even there it appears that inwardness is inseparable from outwardness. More usually, though—and more in keeping with the two earlier cantos and Byron's subsequent writing generally—the 'self' appears as a reflex of literary and historical circumstances. After the most Wordsworthian of all the solitary meditations—

> Are not the mountains, waves, and skies, a part
> Of me and of my soul, as I of them?
> Is not the love of these deep in my heart
> With a pure passion? (707–10)

—there is a surprisingly abrupt self-correction:

> But this is not my theme; and I return
> To that which is immediate (716–17)

One cannot take the narrator's word for it, of course, any more than one can elsewhere in the canto. Nevertheless, the suggestion that his physical surroundings and their associations (in this case Lake Geneva and Rousseau) are 'immediate', and that by extension writing about what is in his 'soul' and 'heart' is mediated, is significant.[30] A journey structures the narrative, and though it calls itself aimless—'I depart, / Whither I know not' (ll. 7–8)—it preoccupies the first person for most of the poem. The narrator gains substance from a series of abrupt encounters.[31] Places generate his meditations: Waterloo, the Rhine valley with its ruined castles, Avenches (Roman Adventicum), Lake Geneva and the towns around it. Further, he habitually perceives places as tombs, or monuments. For all the protestations that he wants to see landscape untouched by humanity—'There is too much of man here, to look through / With a fit mind the might which I behold' (ll. 648–9)—his physical environment is mostly a living trace of dead or lost people: Frederick Howard and Napoleon at Waterloo, the addressee of the lyric 'The castled crag of Drachenfels' by the Rhine, General Marceau at Koblenz, the romantic martyr Julia Alpinula at Avenches, Rousseau at

---

[30] It has long been recognized that the meditations on nature and the natural sublime in canto III are indeed mediated—specifically, through Wordsworth via Shelley. Byron met Shelley on the shores of Lake Geneva in June 1816, during work on the canto, and the latter seems to have encouraged him to read Wordsworth sympathetically.

[31] The dialogic exchange between subjectivity and history via the medium of specific physical locations is well described in Stephen Cheeke, 'Byron, History and the *Genius Loci*', *Byron Journal*, 27 (1999), 38–50.

Geneva, Edward Gibbon at Lausanne, Voltaire at Ferney. Such ghostly figures—Ada is another—supply the occasions for the sentimental or melancholy rhetoric out of which the narrator's inwardness is most characteristically woven.

The narrator is particularly adept at occupying spaces left behind by the absence of the figures whose former presence ghosts before him. No one else actually appears in canto III; in that respect it is a much more insistently solitary kind of self-writing than anything found in Wordsworth. The exception is the quasi-presence of Harold, who is described in the opening stanzas as another ghost, a remnant of vanished thoughts and feelings, in whose vacated place the first person will establish itself. This structure is repeated in all the significant encounters of the subsequent pilgrimage. What fascinates the narrator about Napoleon or Rousseau is not just their achievements and influence, their sublime historical stature. He finds their disappearances at least equally compelling. Instead of contenting himself with the stance of a touristic observer and a historical commentator, he forces the past into direct relationship with the present, simultaneously describing the people who claim his attention and thinking about the fact that they are not 'here', 'now'. His compact summaries of Voltaire (stanza CVI) and Gibbon (stanza CVII) inevitably read as epitaphs, and so provoke in stanza CVIII a brief meditation on death ('peace be with their ashes'; l. 1004). The place of Julia Alpinula's death also inspires him to a stanza on the 'immortality' (l. 641) of fame—

> But these are deeds which should not pass away,
> And names that must not wither   (635–6)

—which focuses on the tension between endurance and decay, presence and absence. Marceau's tomb is another site where permanence meets extinction:

> he had kept
> The whiteness of his soul, and thus men o'er him wept.   (552–3)

There is an obvious thematic alignment between the narrator's funerary encounters along his pilgrimage and the first person's sense that its own 'hour's gone by' (l. 8), or (in a phrase applied to Harold) the

> knowledge that he lived in vain,
> That all was over on this side the tomb   (138–9)

His epitaphs consequently tend to round on himself. Writing about someone lost eventually brings the writing subject to its own attention, as the only figure present in the scene. Like the entire landscape of Waterloo, the lament for Frederick Howard (stanza XXIX) hinges thematically on the relation between the living writer and the absent objects of his contemplation:

> I stood beneath the fresh green tree,
> Which living waves where thou didst cease to live,
> And saw around me the wide field revive   (264–6)

On this occasion the habitual juxtaposition of presence and absence goes on to produce a splendidly exaggerated rhetorical dramatization of the theme. Stanza XXXII lingers over the idea of an emptiness which endures, a world of objects which (like Harold at the opening of the canto) testify to vacated space but also go on occupying their own vacancies. The last line unmistakably repossesses the images as a metaphor for the narrator himself.

> They mourn, but smile at length; and, smiling, mourn:
> The tree will wither long before it fall;
> The hull drives on, though mast and sail be torn;
> The roof-tree sinks, but moulders on the hall
> In massy hoariness; the ruined wall
> Stands when its wind-worn battlements are gone;
> The bars survive the captive they enthral;
> The day drags through though storms keep out the sun;
> And thus the heart will break, yet brokenly live on   (280–8)

Throughout the canto observation has this tendency to reveal itself as a mode of self-writing. Yet the self is not positioned prior to its meditations, as their governing author. It does not have a secure presence which can reflect on everything it encounters. Much more typically it emerges as the eventual *object* of the poem's descriptions and reflections, as effect of the play between absence and presence. In simplified terms, the poem uses the narrator's journey to characterize him as a figure both empty and present: 'still the more, the more it breaks' (l. 292). This is not a strategy, though. The narrator has no controlling subjective stance from which he deliberately seeks out opportunities to depict himself. Rather, the 'self' of *Childe Harold* III, for all its tremendously theatrical self-presentation, occurs mainly through its dialogues with its ruined surroundings.

This is most evident in the major epitaphic sections, on Napoleon and Rousseau. Both portraits function as self-portraits.[32] The two figures represent a polarized conjunction of success with failure, and therefore also of presence with absence (they have both left their mark and vanished without trace), 'antithetically mixt' (l. 317). Their past actions caused effects on a titanic scale, but in the 'now' of the poem's narration the effects are visible only as 'ruins' (l. 775), the enduring marks of their own effacement. In Byron's fine similes,

> Even as a flame unfed, which runs to waste
> With its own flickering, or a sword laid by
> Which eats into itself, and rusts ingloriously.   (394–6)

Napoleon and Rousseau are imagined consuming themselves in the same way that the historical forces they unleashed (the wars of conquest, the French Revolution) ended only in self-annihilating collapse. Napoleon is afflicted with 'a fever at the core, / Fatal to him who bears' (ll. 377–8), and Rousseau receives the same diagnosis: 'with ethereal flame / Kindled he was, and blasted' (ll. 735–6). Analogies with the narrator's melodramatic confession in stanza VII are obvious:

> I *have* thought
> Too long and darkly, till my brain became,
> In its own eddy boiling and o'erwrought,
> A whirling gulf of phantasy and flame   (55–8)

Nor is the identification just a matter of resonant analogies. Writing on Rousseau and Napoleon means working through observation, narrative, and commentary into a confrontation with emptiness. 'Their breath is agitation, and their life / A storm whereon they ride, to sink at last' (ll. 388–9): and having traced this arc, the first person fills the void at its end. The two self-consuming heroes become figures for an exiled autobiographical selfhood, one that exists in the form of a reflection on its absent past. They offer the narrator a vocabulary and a thematic structure for imagining something whose presence and power display themselves as ruin.

---

[32] It is a critical commonplace that Byron identifies with Napoleon and Rousseau. The aim here is to attribute the identification to the first-person subject, not to 'Byron'. Sheila Emerson argues very carefully for a strategic use of the potential parallels, whereby the canto eventually protects its own expressive capacities from falling into the self-destructive pattern modelled by Rousseau and Napoleon. (Emerson, 'Byron's "One Word": The Language of Self-Expression in *Childe Harold* III', *Studies in Romanticism*, 20 (1981), 363–82). The assumption that Byron sets out to express himself in the canto is rather different from my approach here, but the article is exceptionally sensitive to 'that configuration of exhibition and inhibition, of self-projection and self-effacement, by means of which he expresses himself in canto III' (p. 379).

Specifically, the vocabulary is historical and literary, in the most public sense. Napoleon and Rousseau are iconic figures in public discourse, talismans of early nineteenth-century culture as much as individual personalities. By writing their epitaphs the narrator again traverses public and private spheres. His meditations appear to be inward reflections, and to that extent they produce (again) the 'self' that reacts sentimentally or passionately to its surroundings and seeks relations between them and itself. Yet such relations are necessarily constructed on a far wider scale than that of the individual 'I'. In both passages the narrating self develops gradually into the spokesman for a moment in history. The Napoleon epitaph becomes surprisingly like a sermon (stanza XLV, its last, is actually a self-contained allegory, as abstractly didactic as any of Spenser's). In fact, the narrator ends up imagining the revelation of inwardness precisely as a public act:

> One breast laid open were a school
> Which would unteach Mankind the lust to shine or rule   (386–7)

Exposing Napoleon's personality becomes both a personal meditation and a lecture-hall dissection. Correspondingly, the story of his rise and fall, 'antithetically mixt' into each other, tells of both the nature of the reflecting narrator's identity and the situation of Europe after Waterloo, a place of expired convulsions and defeated energies. Rousseau is equally susceptible to this treatment. His own 'self-torturing' nature (l. 725), itself a matter of public knowledge and interest, blends with the self-annihilating work of the revolutionaries whom the narrator calls 'his compeers' (l. 768): 'They made themselves a fearful monument!' (l. 770). Out of the portrait of Rousseau thus comes a poetry which assumes the voice of 'Mankind' (l. 780). It speaks in the unmistakable language of the canto's autobiographical self-representation—

> What deep wounds ever closed without a scar?
> The heart's bleed longest, and but heal to wear
> That which disfigures it   (788–90)

—but it now means this apparently personal and utterly Byronic language of the 'heart' to refer to the endurance of revolutionary impulses among the defeated supporters of republican France. In the last line of this stanza the first person becomes, for an unsettling moment, plural: 'To punish or forgive—in *one* we shall be slower' (l. 796).

It is not so surprising that this most apparently introverted 'I' should find itself in a position to speak as 'we'. This is a self made in the public eye, and both its privacy and its publicity should be understood in relation to that defining perspective. That is, its privacy is produced by receding into the distance, drawing attention to the expanse of space between itself and the readers, while its publicity consists in the continuing currency of the figure of Byron and his texts. What *Childe Harold* III shows so vividly is how all the aspects of autobiography that seem to be to do with pure self-expression—inwardness, sincerity, authenticity, selfhood, expressiveness—are forms of a transaction with the public sphere. It would not be stretching the point too far to say that this one canto invented the complex reciprocity of private identity and public consumption which has become the generic basis of autobiographical writing today. (Another way of saying the same thing would be to call Byron the first British celebrity in the modern sense, someone whose individuality is imagined as a completely public possession.[33]) If, as I have argued in part I, the word 'autobiography' itself came into existence in a rupture of the border between opposed spheres, then canto III manages for the first time to turn the opposition into an alliance. Still, it does not matter whether the example is unprecedented. No subsequent document could do what this poem did, because no other author could have Byron's special position in November 1816, simultaneously exiled from and belonging to a huge reading public. The significant issue is the canto's articulation of the conditions of Romantic autobiography, with all its uncertainties and indeterminacies alchemically transmuted into a mode of systematic and brilliant self-writing. Being private and public together is here not impossible but fundamental.

[33] Mason's version of the same claim is that 'the Byron phenomenon suggests that the development of the modern, highly-individualized author figure is traceable in part to the late-eighteenth- and early-nineteenth-century shift from generic to brand-name products' (Mason, 'Building Brand Byron', 439–40).

8

Elia

About a year and a half after the nameless editor of Teufelsdröckh's writings labelled the 1830s 'Autobiographical times' in the pages of *Fraser's Magazine* his verdict received a kind of official sanction from the literary arm of the establishment, the *Quarterly Review*. Back in 1822 Lockhart had used this most powerful of reactionary periodicals to make a last stand against the prevailing 'belief that England expects every driveller to do his memorabilia'.[1] A piece in the issue of July 1835, overwhelmed by 'the great and increasing proportion which biography, and particularly *autobiography*, appears to bear to the general mass of publications', is reduced to the resigned comment that, 'what with increasing the quantity . . . and deteriorating the quality', life writing has become 'a mere *manufacture*'.[2] The vision of an autobiography factory seems to bear witness to the completed formation of a particular literary practice, a genre. Yet what one writer sees as a mass-produced commodity another can imagine as a canon. In the same issue of the *Quarterly* a review article imagines a library stacked with autobiographical writing. It is a place of proper comparative critical judgements, rather than industrial production and consumption. The remark is made casually, but it gives in germinal form the principle that would later found an idea of 'Romantic autobiography':

In a library of a thousand volumes you shall not find two that will give you such a bright and living impress of the author's own very soul. Austin's [St Augustine's], Rousseau's—all the Confessions on record, are false and hollow in comparison.[3]

The conventional touchstones are all here: standards of sincerity, depth, and richness ('false and hollow'), the revelation of the inward self, the equation of text ('impress') with 'soul'. The canon's founding documents

[1] *Quarterly Review*, xxxv. 149.   [2] Ibid. liv. 250, 251.
[3] Ibid. liv. 59.

are named; and while the numbering of its members is admittedly a rhetorical exaggeration, you do still feel that you could guess at a fair number of the titles that would be preserved in the imaginary library. In fact, a recent scholarly article with the phrase 'Romantic Autobiography' in its title includes a representative list of the works that by July 1835 might be thought to have found their way into a collection of expressive self-writing. The author (A. J. Harding) is referring to 'the tradition of Romantic self-exploration':

Wollstonecraft's *Short Residence*, Byron's *Childe Harold*, Hazlitt's *Liber Amoris*, De Quincey's *Confessions of an English Opium Eater*, and Wordsworth's *The Prelude*.[4]

There is no reason to assume that the *Quarterly*'s writer had those particular names in mind. Still, his collection of 'all the Confessions on record', graded by the truthfulness of their representation of the author's inner self, certainly licenses autobiography as a respectably literary act from the point of view of the mid-1830s, in much the same way that Harding's list assumes the coherence of a 'Romantic' mode of self-writing.

Which of them is it that the review in the *Quarterly* places at the very head of the genre, its transparency exceeding even Rousseau's *Confessions*? None, as it happens. The review's subject is Charles Lamb's *Last Essays of Elia* (1833), alongside the earlier volume *Elia* (1823); both titles being slightly modified collections of the essays that appeared over that signature in the *London Magazine* between 1820 and 1825, with a few published elsewhere. Lamb's Elian essays are rarely included in lists like Harding's, but the *Quarterly*'s judgement was not unusual for its time.[5] (It had been partly inspired by sentiment as well; Lamb died in December 1834, and the review is as much a valedictory as a critical notice.) In the genre of the periodical essay, which flourished so spectacularly in the 1820s, contemporaries distinguished Lamb's work for its

---

[4] Anthony John Harding, 'Wordsworth's *Prelude*, Tracey Emin, and Romantic Autobiography', *Wordsworth Circle*, 34 (2003), 59–65, at 59. I do not mean to use Harding as a straw man (the article is very interesting); more or less the same list could have been found elsewhere. I use the example merely to show how current this conception of a 'tradition' is.

[5] For studies that place the essays alongside other documents of Romantic autobiography see Gerald Monsman, *Confessions of a Prosaic Dreamer: Charles Lamb's Art of Autobiography* (Durham, NC: Duke University Press, 1984); Mary Jacobus, 'The Art of Managing Books: Romantic Prose and the Writing of the Past', in Arden Reed (ed.), *Romanticism and Language* (London: Methuen, 1984); Thomas McFarland, *Romantic Cruxes: The English Essayists and the Spirit of the Age* (Oxford: Clarendon, 1987).

expression of a highly distinctive, immediate first-person presence: the presence of Elia. By the time the first few of the essays signed with that name had appeared in the *London* Elia had become the focus of a small-scale cult of personality. Charles Elton's verse 'Epistle to Elia', printed in the magazine in August 1821, begins with an entirely typical fantasy of personal conversation with the author: 'I WOULD, that eye to eye it were my lot / To sit with thee'.[6] In contrast to the miscellaneous essays of Hazlitt, De Quincey, and other contributors to the *London*, Lamb's were read primarily as vehicles for the manner and spirit of the supposed author (rather than for their informative or polemical content, their wit, or their prose—although the quirky charm of Elia's self-consciously antiquated style was quickly identified as a central aspect of his personality).

In fact, it is more or less exactly the qualities that enabled the *Quarterly* to speak of Lamb as the most expressive and authentic of autobiographers which are in turn responsible for keeping the Elian essays out of the master-lists of Romantic autobiography (such as Harding's). For the most part they choose their explicit subjects from material that is eccentrically personal, incidental, unfamiliar, unpretentious, domestic, quotidian. When they do touch on issues of public interest or controversy, they approach them at a tangent and treat them with a deliberately unsystematic diffidence, an exaggerated evasion of serious issues—so much so that one barely notices that (for example) 'Grace Before Meat' is about freedom of religion, 'Guy Faux' ends with a rhapsody on blowing up both Houses of Parliament, and 'The Praise of Chimney-Sweepers' deals with social injustice ('the wrongs of fortune').[7] Either way, all of Elia's topics are subject to his endlessly subtle irony. Its habitual gesture of disengagement, of refusing or evading any sustained contact between writing and the things it writes about, is well described by De Quincey (though with a perhaps rather unsurprising blindness to the possibilities of understatement):

The instances are many, in his own beautiful essays, where he literally collapses, literally sinks away from openings suddenly offering themselves to flights of

[6] *London Magazine*, iv. 137. Useful surveys of the history of Lamb's critical reception can be found in Jane Aaron, 'Charles and Mary Lamb: The Critical Heritage', *The Charles Lamb Bulletin*, 59 (1987), 73–85, and, for more recent work, William Ruddick, 'Recent Approaches to Charles Lamb', *The Charles Lamb Bulletin*, 98 (1997), 50–3.

[7] E. V. Lucas (ed.), *The Works of Charles and Mary Lamb*, 7 vols. (London: Methuen, 1903–5), ii. 112. Hereafter all citations of the Elian essays in the text refer by page number to volume ii of this edition.

pathos or solemnity in direct prosecution of his own theme. On any such summons, where an ascending impulse, and an untired pinion were required, he refuses himself (to use military language) invariably.[8]

The effect is to throw the substance of the essays back on the figure of Elia himself; in De Quincey's words, 'you must sympathise with this *personality* in the author before you can appreciate the most significant parts of his views'.[9] As the objects of their attention dwindle or evaporate under irony's light touch, the authorial figure itself comes to feel like their only tangible presence (although, as we will see later, that presence is itself profoundly ironic). Elia is what they are about. Their affectionate or nostalgic observations and recollections of various places, people, and objects add up to nothing beyond a mosaic portrait of the author's peculiar cast of mind. The *Quarterly*'s article of 1835 is referring to this quality when it gives them the pre-eminent position in its autobiographical library. It has noticed that every sentence Elia writes about anything is in fact about him—a feature of miscellaneous essays in general, but taken to an extreme in this case because of the refusal to allow the ostensible topic as much attention as it ought to demand. For nineteenth-century readers Elia's very irony could be read as a kind of transparency (again, we will see later how this structure is—ironically—reversed). His evasiveness and whimsy appeared to be his character, brilliantly reiterated in each separate essay and so assembling a coherent personality. Moreover, his habitual unseriousness—earnest only in opposition to all forms of earnestness—seemed to free that personality from the more assertive egotism of, say, Hazlitt or (the extreme case) Rousseau. Elia makes other autobiographers sound 'false and hollow', as the *Quarterly* puts it, because he makes no claims on his own behalf, and is never caught in the act of trying to manipulate his readers' view of him. Reversing the usual self-aggrandizing tendencies of first-person writing, he gives the illusion of sharing an intimate, confined space with his readers, unimpeded by any tinge of Byronic self-representation, and so implying a kind of privacy whose apparent unselfconsciousness is the very sign of its authenticity.

For later readers, though, and especially for anyone interested in constructing histories of autobiography, Elia's highly restricted scope, his thorough commitment to being non-committal, disqualifies him as

---

[8] David Masson (ed.), *The Collected Writings of Thomas De Quincey*, 14 vols. (Edinburgh: A. & C. Black, 1889–90), v. 234.

[9] Masson (ed.), *The Collected Writings of De Quincey*, v. 217.

an autobiographical figure. The problem is not to do with Lamb's use of a fictional alter ego. Periodical contributions of the day were never signed with the author's name. 'Elia', like 'the English Opium-Eater', is primarily just a signature; there is no inherent implication that because he has his own name he is meant as a character in his own right, like the protagonists of first-person fictions. Contemporary readers comfortably blurrred the personality implied by the signature with the figure of the author. His identity was never a secret, despite the essays' occasional playfulness on the subject. Indeed, Lamb's thoroughly ironic treatment of all questions about Elia's identity frees the 'I' of the texts from any determinate relationship with a name. The experiences the first person narrates, and the character it articulates, belong only to the author who signs the essays, and to that extent it makes little difference whether the signature is read as Elia's or Lamb's. Nineteenth- as well as twentieth-century readers were quick to point out the correspondences between what Elia writes about himself and what Lamb elsewhere said about himself. (Virtually everything in Elia's world is 'autobiographical' in the sense that it matches identifiable features of Lamb's own experience.)[10]

The reasons Elia has not often been read as a Romantic autobiographer, then, are not formal. The problem is rather that he gives no weight, no force, to the act of self-writing. Unlike the texts on Harding's list, and unlike far less canonical documents which are aware that they might be read as autobiographies, Elia's essays do not propose the self as a site of drama, revelation, plenitude, or even understanding. The pose of conversational intimacy which so delighted Elia's admirers completely excludes any assertion of the self's value or interest. More effective still is the action of Elian irony. At the same time as it defines and individuates the author's idiosyncratic personality, it withdraws that identity out of writing's reach. It disassembles the relations between writing and truth, between text and world, so that everything brought into the orbit of the Elian first person is dissolved into a playful indeterminacy:

Reader, what if I have been playing with thee all this while—peradventure, the very *names*, which I have summond up before thee, are fantastic—insubstantial ('The South-Sea House', 7)

For Elia, this is unusually explicit (perhaps because this particular twist comes at the end of the first of the essays to appear). Although 'names'

[10] For a full list see Claude A. Prance, *A Companion to Charles Lamb* (London: Mansell, 1983).

or nouns—things and people, rather than ideas or actions—are the base
elements of his world, they are always presented as 'but shadows of
fact—verisimilitudes, not verities—or sitting but on the remote edges
and outskirts of history' ('The Old Benchers of the Inner Temple', 90).
The established conventions of autobiography require at least that the
author be seen to lay hold of his or her own experience. Instead, Elia
finds that the subjects of his writing slip out of his grasp—including the
first-person subject, 'the lean and meagre figure of your insignificant
Essayist' ('The Convalescent', 187), 'the phantom cloud of Elia' ('New
Year's Eve', 29).

However, in the light of the present effort to turn self-writing
outward, to read the public face of autobiographical transactions, the
Quarterly's judgement has to be taken seriously. In Chapter 6 I suggested
that texts of the period tend to gain a recognizably autobiographical
aspect in association with writing that exceeds narrative or polemical
functions. This goes a long way towards explaining why a contemporary
commentator might eulogize the Elian essays among the emerging
canon of self-writing. Exploiting the distinctive medium of the literary
periodical, where room could be made for ephemeral prose as long as it
was conducted with elegance and wit, Elia's writing makes no arguments
and gives no information. Its stance towards the reader is best described
as mere presence, intimacy unqualified by advocacy. 'The South-Sea
House', Elia's first essay, begins with a direct address: 'READER, . . .'
(p. 1). But the invocation initiates no more than a whimsically imaginary
scenario, one which—in the typical play of irony—knows itself to be
imaginary, winking at its fictive asumptions:

READER, in thy passage from the Bank—where thou hast been receiving thy
half-yearly dividends (supposing thou art a lean annuitant like myself)—to the
Flower Pot, to secure a place for Dalston, or Shacklewell, or some other thy
suburban retreat northerly,—didst thou never observe . . . (p. 1)[11]

—and so it goes on. Contrast the opening of De Quincey's *Confessions* in
the same magazine thirteen months later: 'I here present you, courteous
reader, with the record of a remarkable episode in my life.'[12] Here the
relation between author, reader, and text is laid out formally. The ensu-
ing narrative is submitted as valuable testimony, purposefully transmit-
ted from the first person to the 'courteous' public who (the author

---

[11] The 'Flower Pot' was a coaching inn in London.
[12] De Quincey, *Confessions*, 1.

hopes) will overlook the implied presumption and receive it as intended. Readers arrested by Elia's address are given no such clues. Their attention is demanded and then immediately dropped, as it becomes clear that writing is doing no more than playing with them. As Elia admits in 'Mackery End, in Hertfordshire', 'Narrative teazes me. I have little concern in the progress of events . . . the oddities of authorship please me most' (p. 75). In the absence of more pragmatic responsibilities to readers, the essays present only their own singular intimacy, typified by the simultaneous hospitality and irony of the speculation in 'The South-Sea House's first sentence that 'thou art . . . like myself'. Elia's only visible purpose is to be Elian, to conjure his personality out of his mannered writing. To that extent he is a figure founded on the kind of interaction between the public and the moment of publication which Romantic-period autobiographical writing so often brings into play.

The confusion for subsequent historians of autobiography largely arises from the fact that Elia's self-presentation is shaped not by the inwardness of selfhood but by the medium of publication.[13] Unlike Wordsworthian 'self-presence', or the intimacy established by Rousseau's expressive eloquence, Elia's presence is a product of the literary public sphere. Deeply as he is informed by Lamb's personal experience, Elia does not exist to give public voice to that inwardness (the process often described as Romantic autobiography's essential project). The essays in which a highly charged interiority is unveiled—'Dream-Children' and 'Old China'—achieve their astonishing effects partly because the unveiling is so unexpected; and in both cases a typically Elian retraction occurs in the last sentence. The autobiographical transaction between Elia and his readers is in fact defined by the situation of the *London Magazine*. His peculiar brand of intimacy, which made such an impression on Lamb's readers, is an extension of its publishing environment. For critics who assume that autobiography has to be the author's effort to express his or her selfhood this might be reason enough to sever Lamb from the body of Romantic autobiographical writing. In the model I am proposing, though, it makes the Elian essays a striking case of self-writing in the public sphere.

[13] This mediated, intertextual brand of identity has been suggestively—if rather elliptically—explored in the context of James Hogg's first-person writings (see Mark L. Schoenfield, 'Butchering James Hogg: Romantic Identity in the Magazine Market', in Mary A. Favret and Nicola J. Watson (eds.), *At the Limits of Romanticism* (Bloomington, Ind.: Indiana University Press, 1994)).

It is obvious enough, for a start, that one of Elia's most distinctive characteristics is a function of periodical publication. With no continuous retrospective narrative to define his identity, he is summoned into being as the observer of occasional phenomena. His world is miscellaneous, heterogeneous, ordered not by the sequences of narrative or chronology but by the multifarious accidents of a crowded city—'and what else', he writes in 'A Complaint of the Decay of Beggars in the Metropolis', 'but an accumulation of sights—endless sights—*is* a great city?' (p. 119). Elia cannot exist without the 'endless' parade of ephemera to call forth his eccentric sensibility in response. This occasional character of his subjectivity is clearly determined by the *London*'s format: brief essays, appearing at intervals, requiring no connection between one and the next other than the same signature and some uniformity of tone. Elia is above all an identity in instalments. Where the two parts of De Quincey's *Confessions* asked the *London*'s readers to bridge the gap between the September and October issues of 1821, reconstituting the split text as one autobiographical document held together by the coherence of its subject and its story, Elia's essays are self-contained nuggets of prose, responding to the subscribers' expectations of novelty and interest in each individual number of the magazine combined with a continuity of overall tone and attitude. The signature 'Elia' stands for the institutional coherence of the *London*—the annual January editorial puffs proudly claimed Lamb's articles as evidence of the magazine's sustained quality—while the quirky subjects chosen for each new essay embody the originality and freshness that were supposed to keep subscribers loyal.[14]

Elia's regular yet unpredictable appearances echoed the kind of cultured middle-class metropolitan social relations which the magazine imagined sharing with its constituency. It pictured itself as a monthly guest at its readers' tables, playing the role of a stimulating but congenial conversationalist, sharing their liberal political sympathies and their cosmopolitan intellectual pursuits. Epitomizing this stance were the articles titled 'Table Talk', treating matters of conversational interest with (at their best, in Hazlitt's contributions) an energy and erudition that made the guest both welcome and worth listening to. Elia articulates a comic version of the same attitude. His subjects are more defiantly odd and personal, and his presentation of them privileges a mannered, one-

---

[14] In fact, the *London* never managed to achieve subscription figures comparable to the periodicals it set out to compete with.

sided wit over the free exchange of opinions. Yet although the richly ironic 'Character of the Late Elia' (reprinted as the 'Preface' to the *Last Essays of Elia*) disparages his company as excessively, carelessly informal—'he gave himself too little concern what he uttered, and in whose presence' (p. 152)—his popularity with readers was always based on the image of a brilliantly entertaining and touchingly open-hearted companion. Bernard Barton's (poor) sonnet 'To Elia', in the February 1823 *London*, is a morose piece of testimony, but it captures the sense of Elia as intimate interlocutor:

> From month to month has the exhaustless flow
> Of thy original mind, its wealth revealing,
> With quaintest humour, and deep pathos healing
> The world's rude wounds, revived Life's early glow[15]

The figure of a welcome fireside companion arranges Elia's character at a fundamental level. In particular, his blend of exaggerated opinionatedness—'Whatever is, is to me a matter of taste or distaste' ('Jews, Quakers, Scotchmen, and other Imperfect Sympathies', 58)—with a mind 'rather suggestive than comprehensive'—'Hints and glimpses, germs and crude essays at a system, is the utmost [I] pretend to' (ironically from the same essay, 59)—aligns perfectly with the literary monthly's need to be at once provocative and accommodating. His 'poor antithetical manner' ('My Relations', 71), retracting its assertions and ironizing its positions, has been influentially read as an aesthetic habit essential to Lamb and fully expressed in the figure of Elia, but it can equally be understood as the condition of writing familiarly for a mass readership.[16] Elia perfectly manages the balance of engagement and disengagement implied by his medium of publication. He conjures the illusion of intimacy between the subscriber and the sheets of the periodical: 'you are now with me in my little back study in Bloomsbury, reader!' ('The Two Races of Men', 25). But his unassertiveness, his playfulness, his good humour, prevent the

---

[15] *London Magazine*, vii. 194.

[16] See Daniel J. Mulcahy, 'Charles Lamb: The Antithetical Manner and the Two Planes', *Studies in English Literature 1500–1900*, 3 (1963), 517–42. This influential article can be credited with beginning the serious study of Lamb as what in Mulcahy's day would have been called a 'Romantic artist'. Two more recent articles have made an effort to place Lamb's writing back in the context of the *London*, but in both cases this has involved replacing the ironic, distanced Elian stance with a more engaged and politicized reading of Lamb's work: Mark Schoenfield, 'Voices Together: Lamb, Hazlitt, and the *London*', *Studies in Romanticism*, 29 (1990), 257–72, and Mark Parker, 'Ideology and Editing: The Political Context of the Elia Essays', *Studies in Romanticism*, 30 (1991), 469–87. There is in fact no reason to think of Mulcahy's Lamb as irreconcilable with the essays' immediate context.

intimacy from being invasive; the reader always has the power to manage his guest, since the conversation is no more than 'solemn mockery' ('The South-Sea House', 7). Indeed, the sophistication of Lamb's irony, never permitting writing more than a tenuous or provisional hold on its own subjects, effectively matches the implied sophistication of consumers of literature for leisure, who want to be able to read or set aside the magazine as they choose.

In more straightforward ways, too, Elia is a creature of the *London*. The magazine was set up to compete against the Scottish dominance of literary periodical publication. Its models (and therefore its immediate rivals) were the *Edinburgh Review* and (especially) *Blackwood's*, founded only three years earlier. It was intended to be the capital's challenge to Edinburgh. The *Prospectus* announced that

one of the principal objects of the LONDON MAGAZINE will be to convey the very 'image, form, and pressure' of that '*mighty heart*' whose vast pulsations circulate life, strength, and spirits, throughout this great Empire.[17]

Elia writes very much as a Londoner. In an age of Romantic tourism his defiantly urban attachments are part of his quirkiness; but his metropolitanism is not so much a general aesthetic principle as a profoundly specific attachment to one city in particular. He defines himself through his sense of local belonging, his occupation of London's streetscapes. But this geography of the self belongs also to his readers. As the opening of 'The South-Sea House' (quoted above) shows, he likes to assume that the *London*'s subscribers can travel around the city alongside him. For all the sentimental intensity of his claim to his home ground—'My household-gods plant a terrible fixed foot, and are not rooted up without blood' ('New Year's Eve', 29)—it is in fact a shared space, as cities are (contrast the solitudes where Romantic sentiment more usually grounds itself). Elia's space is mapped out by the *London* as well as in his 'self'. In that sense it is as conversational, as communal, as his personality. The same metropolitanism is evident in his class (his social space). His professional is humble and unexceptional; his leisure hours are spent in comfortably ordinary middle-class pursuits (seaside vacations, reading and card-playing by the fireside, visiting, collecting old editions, going to plays). In other words, as well as writing *for* the *London*'s imagined

---

[17] Quoted in Walter Graham, *English Literary Periodicals* (New York: Octagon, 1980), 281.

constituency, Elia presents himself as one *of* them.[18] For all his singular personality, everything about his place speaks of a reciprocity between the essays and their readers.

The key interest shared between Elia, the *London*, and its subscribers is literature. As Walter Graham observes, 'the *London* began its career . . . with considerably more of its contents devoted to writers and books than is to be found in any preceding periodical of the kind'.[19] In this respect once again, Elia exactly articulates the *London*'s implied relationship with its readers. It is not just that the essays so frequently refer to literary matters, or that Elia is himself so bookish a character. More significant is his stance of amateur connoisseurship. Literature is for him not an aesthetic field (and certainly not a philosophical one) but a source of almost proprietorial gratification, a valuable commodity to be consumed with relish. His 'treasures', he writes in 'The Two Races of Men', 'are rather cased in leather covers than closed in iron coffers' (p. 25). In 'New Year's Eve' the pleasure is wittily eroticized: he apostrophizes them as 'my midnight darlings, my Folios!', and invokes 'the intense delight of having you (huge armfuls) in my embraces' (p. 30). The brilliant essay 'Detached Thoughts on Books and Reading' converts all judgements about writing into opinions of books—the material volumes.[20] Elia treats literature just as the *London* imagines its readers do: as something like a hobby, absorbing but occasional ('Much depends on *where* and *when* you read a book'; 'Detached Thoughts', 175). He plays up a dilettantism which would surely have been recognized by readers who expected the magazine to digest the literary sphere on their behalf: 'The sweetest names, and which carry a perfume in the mention, are, Kit Marlowe, Drayton, Drummond of Hawthornden, and Cowley' (p. 174). Or, at least, we can say that the *London* presents literary matters to its readers in a way which implies that reading is above all a form of cultured leisure, and that Elia's tangible pleasure in books comes from the same perspective:

Winter evenings—the world shut out—with less of ceremony the gentle Shakespeare enters. At such a season, the Tempest, or his own Winter's Tale. (p. 175)

---

[18] A more detailed, and more nuanced, reading of the essays' class ambiguities is offered in Jane Aaron, *A Double Singleness: Gender and the Writings of Charles and Mary Lamb* (Oxford: Clarendon, 1991).

[19] Graham, *English Literary Periodicals*, 271.

[20] The essay's reformulations of contemporary ideas about reading and writing are teased out with great subtlety in Newlyn, *Reading, Writing, and Romanticism*, 208–15.

Elia's bookishness goes beyond a community of interest with the *London*'s readers. Like his congeniality and his metropolitanism, the other aspects of 'his' personality which belong to the medium of his circulation, it signifies his peculiarly intertextual existence. 'Elia' is a signature appearing only in a specific publishing context.[21] (The full title of the first collected volume of essays insisted on this: *Elia. Essays Which have Appeared Under That Signature in the London Magazine.* Lamb's name was nowhere mentioned.) The games Lamb plays with Elia's merely pseudonymous being all depend on the fact that he is literally bookish, a figure of writing (or of print) only. The 'phantom cloud of Elia' ('New Year's Eve', 29) is only as substantial as its published and circulated form; in 'A Character of the Late Elia' he can look back over the interval since the first essay appeared and joke that 'a two years' and a half existence has been a tolerable duration for a phantom' (p. 151). His consumerist pleasure in the materiality of literature turns out to be unexpectedly, ironically reversible: his own material existence is nothing but literary. For all the distinctiveness of his personality, the sense of his presence, Elia is constituted by the *London* and its particular spot in the literary public sphere. He is subject to readers' interventions; their published responses (Elton's and Barton's poems, for example) appear in the magazine as part of the overall discursive field which creates him. He can also be partially overwritten by other texts. The essay 'Witches, and Other Night-Fears', which discusses the dreaming capacity and ends with a wonderfully ironic example of his own 'poor plastic power' (p. 69), appeared in the issue following the first instalment of De Quincey's *Confessions*, alongside the second instalment (which contains the most vivid transcriptions of opiate visions and nightmares). In January 1825, the first issue of a new series of the *London*, Elia contributed an explicit pastiche of De Quincey: 'Letter to an Old Gentleman Whose Education Has Been Neglected'; the earlier (June 1823) essay 'The Child-Angel: A Dream' is a gentler imitation of the same author. The 'Letter of Elia to Robert Southey, Esquire', his contribution for October 1823—part of it was reprinted in the second collected volume as 'The Tombs in the Abbey'—responds to an earlier remark of

---

[21] As the editorial and professional standards of the *London* declined, the Elian essays began to appear elsewhere (in the *New Monthly Magazine*, the *Englishman's Magazine*, and the *Athenaeum*). For the purposes of this argument, though, the signature can be understood to have been established and maintained by the *London*. Lamb's persona never established a strong footing elsewhere, and the small number of essays appearing in other magazines do not bear significantly on the body of Elia's work in general.

Southey's in the *Quarterly*, and alludes sharply to the relation between individual authors and literary coteries which gives their work its range of public meanings. Elia is always a function of the transactions between readers and writers which the periodicals of the day mediated and encouraged.

To this extent the figure of Elia is oddly analogous to Childe Harold. Though the two personalities are all but polar opposites, both represent self-writing in an explicitly public mode, not narrating experience but conjuring the expressive first person at the point where the 'I' transacts its business with the literary public sphere. Elia is the same kind of phantom as Harold: one figuring selfhood as something performed, circulated, and consumed, something as much read as written. (This explains why readers projected Elia's personality back on to Lamb, much as—on a larger scale—they created the figure of Byron in the image of Harold.) But where Byron exploits the dramatic tension between Harold's rhetoric of inwardness and his texts' public display, Lamb's essays reconcile intimacy with exposure. The Byronic vocabulary speaks of isolation from the gaze it courts. Lamb's language is all about giving the reader direct access ('come with me into a Quaker's Meeting', 45). Nevertheless, both Harold and Elia establish themselves only as the image of subjectivity. When the *Quarterly*'s article of July 1835 finds in Lamb's essays 'a bright a living impress of the author's own very soul', it is being led into the kind of reading that legions of entranced fans applied to the first two cantos of *Childe Harold's Pilgrimage*, one which takes self-writing's conformity with the public sphere as a reason to read the texts as autobiographies. Byron's writing seemed deeply confessional because it arranged the public as witness to its intimacies. So with Elia, though with an infinitely lighter touch: the impression of his 'soul' is given not by an authorial self caught in the process of unveiling its inwardness, but by a beautifully managed match between first-person writing and its audience. The Elian essays are Romantic autobiography's utopian state ('all the Confessions on record, are false and hollow in comparison'). Nowhere else in the period are the transactions between privacy and print resolved with such ease and grace.

This is not only thanks to the convenient fit between Elia's personality and the *London*'s commercial and cultural niche. The effect transcends the essays' immediate environment, and needs to be understood properly as a quality of their mode of self-writing. It is interesting nevertheless that neither of the collected volumes (*Elia* and *The Last Essays of Elia*) sold well. The significance of the *London* is that it gives an institutional shape to Elia's occasional, phantasmal presence. It effectively does the job of the apologetic and explanatory prefaces usually affixed to autobiographical publications: it gives a reason for the essays' existence, it conducts them into the literary public sphere under the cover of its own perfectly respectable pretensions to circulate. When Elia writes 'READER, . . .', the magazine has already determined who those readers are, and abolished on their behalf any scruples they might have about being addressed by an intimate first person on subjects of (to say the least) out-of-the-way interest. It has also—by virtue of the conventions of anonymous authorship—already endorsed the peculiarly ironic condition of Elia's being; at the same time as his distinctive personality writes itself it is unquestioningly accepted as a mere act of writing, a textual fiction. Nevertheless, it is Elia who addresses the reader, who writes, and it was that same first person in whose presence readers felt themselves to be. The essays themselves construct an interiority which is (like Harold) constantly in the business of circulating itself. Though the *London* finds the readers and ensures that they have the right kind of relation to the text, Elia turns his 'own' personality outwards in the distinctive discursive mode which places the reader (in the words of Elton's verse epistle) 'eye to eye' with his 'I'. His achievement is to write and circulate his personality in such a way that it appears to be evoked by other texts, by the *London*, or even by congenial readers. Instead of egotistically telling us who Elia is, his writing rearranges the relationship:

CASTING a preparatory glance at the bottom of this article . . . methinks I hear you exclaim, Reader, *Who is Elia?* ('Oxford in the Vacation', 7)

Under the conditions of Romantic autobiography the essays are utopian because the first person clearly belongs to the author and yet also seems not to antedate his signature. If the opening fanfare of Rousseau's *Confessions* epitomizes the problems of such writing, imaging the author thrusting the book into readers' hands with the declaration 'Such was I', Elia dissolves the antithesis between the world of texts and the world of selves by figuring himself as a question spoken by the reader in response to a publication. Privacy, the world of the first person, unfolds itself within, and in answer to, the literary public sphere. So the essays manage the very task whose impossibility the word 'autobiography' virtually denoted at the time: reconciling an inward selfhood with circulation and print. To answer the question 'Who is Elia?' accurately, albeit clumsily: Elia is the personality resulting from the effect of first-person writing at the moment of its reading.

Contemporary readers moved easily across the divide his writing bridges. On the one hand they understood Elia as a personality rather than a person, a figure of identity rather than a self advertising its presence to the public. At the same time, though, they read Elia as Lamb. The essays have no interest in suppressing the latter, directly autobiographical interpretation. Quite the opposite: they are willing to use the rhetoric of autobiography—personal narrative, memory, nostalgia—in relation to details that invite readers to attribute a specific historical identity to the first person. For example, 'The Old Benchers of the Inner Temple' begins 'I WAS born, and passed the first seven years of my life, in the Temple' (p. 82). This kind of straightforward personal narrative thins the distinction between the signature Elia and the verifiable historical author Lamb to transparency, leaving 'Elia' no more than a flimsy pseudonym, possessed of no substance of his own. Like everything else in the essays, this sense of simple recollected experience can be ironic. The most notable case is 'Christ's Hospital Five and Thirty Years Ago', which systematically lays claim to authenticity and sincerity while inventing memories that from Lamb's perspective at least are entirely imaginary.[22] The point is that the essays neutralize the difference between identity and its figure, between personhood and personality. Elia can be understood simultaneously as a self of his own (which might then be identified as Lamb's) and as a self in the public sphere, an image of selfhood congenial to readers, an effect of writing. In the Romantic period all autobiography is egotistical; but Lamb's writing, uniquely, empties the ego from egotism.

A simple explanation for this resolution of the conditions of Romantic self-writing would be to say that Elia is only a textual fiction (this is the line of argument that keeps the essays out of lists of the period's autobiographical monuments). That is, Lamb can reconcile the spheres of privacy and print because he never really brings the former into play. Elia (so the argument goes) belongs exclusively to the realm of writing, and therefore is indeed just a personality. To this one might justifiably reply that the relationship between Elia and Lamb is no more distant than that between the alternately effusive and reticent 'I' of the *Letters Written During a Short Residence in Sweden* and Wollstonecraft, or between the critical-philosophical narrator of the *Biographia* and

---

[22] This complex instance is dealt with at length in James Treadwell, 'Impersonation and Autobiography in Lamb's Christ's Hospital Essays', *Studies in Romanticism*, 37 (1998), 499–521.

Coleridge, and so on. As I have suggested throughout this book, though, autobiography cannot be helpfully understood in terms of that criterion. Writing has to be thought of prior to selfhood, rather than subordinating its textual first person to the being of the author. Turning to look at the essays in more detail, we can define Elia's condition more carefully. If they secure a carefully balanced transaction between the inward self and the literary public sphere, they may also reveal what is at stake when that self limits itself to its own legible form.

The first thing to notice is how prominently they thematize an absent or disappearing self. Elia's present world—family, friends, habits, surroundings—on the one hand anchors his consciousness in a particular set of attachments, but on the other remains curiously remote. He appears at the centre of a world of familiarized objects and characters, and his subjectivity emerges from his constantly amplified relations with them. His local attachments thus become substitutes for personal attributes, the more conventional means of drawing the boundaries of individuality. Elia cannot be defined by these more normal methods. He tells us a limited amount about his occupation, his family, his personal history; and yet when he does, it is only to deny that these attributes constitute his existence. We have already looked at the Christ's Hospital essay in this regard. 'Blakesmoor in H—shire', which also deals with a place from Elia's past, casts him as an interloper in the scene; he appropriates the old house for himself while admitting that he is not its rightful heir, and recognizing that what he inherits is only a ruin. 'Dream-Children' gives Elia no more than a fantasy of a family; while the welcome he receives in 'Mackery End, in Hertfordshire' is from 'out-of-date kinsfolk' who had been entirely forgotten (p. 78). As to his occupation, he explains in 'Oxford in the Vacation' that he is a clerk, or at least 'something of the sort' (p. 7). So far from being a defining attribute, however, his profession is represented as a mere hobby of Elia the essayist:

I confess that it is my humour, my fancy—in the forepart of the day, when the mind of your man of letters requires some relaxation—. . . to while away some good hours of my time in the contemplation of indigos, cottons, raw silks, piece-goods, flowered or otherwise. (p. 7)

The writing of essays is an antidote to this activity. Clerkship is not so much an occupation as an anti-occupation:

The enfranchised quill, that has plodded all the morning among the cart-rucks of figures and cyphers, frisks and curvets so at its ease over the flowery carpet-ground of a midnight dissertation. (p. 8)

The indeterminacy of such conventional attributes is heightened by the fact that Elia's relation to his world of proliferating and exaggerated objects is remarkably often one of antithesis or contradiction. This is exemplified by the essay 'Jews, Quakers, Scotchmen, and Other Imperfect Sympathies', which substitutes the arbitrary hostility of prejudice for the attributes of personality. Elia defines himself here through a series of oppositions: 'Old prejudices cling about me' (p. 61). Again, in 'My Relations' and 'Mackery End' Elia represents himself in antithesis to the subject of the essay (his male and female cousins respectively). He often appears as the voice that contradicts his ostensible material: he tentatively argues against the central figure of 'Mrs. Battle's Opinions on Whist', is victimized by the borrowers he praises in 'The Two Races of Men', replies to his cousin's nostalgia in 'Old China'.

Observing the world, Elia repeatedly disappears from it. The objects that he summons detach themselves from the consciousness at their centre, like the vanishing phantoms at the end of 'Dream-Children' or the 'eluding nereids' that conclude the essay on 'Witches, and Other Night-Fears' (p. 70). Sometimes Elia finds that he is denied access to the places he has been describing. A more subtle evaporation of consciousness occurs in the narrative structure of the essays, when personal observation gradually turns into impersonal anecdote. Elia often concludes an essay with a brief story that displaces him from the narrative centre; the first person is replaced by the third person. 'The Old and New Schoolmaster', 'Poor Relations', 'Detached Thoughts on Books and Reading', 'The Tombs in the Abbey', and 'Newspapers Thirty-five Years Ago' all exhibit this movement at their conclusion; this list does not include the numerous essays in which the first person is hardly present at all. Lamb's letters represent his 'purely local' attachments as his sustaining context, but Elia's evocation of his familiar world does not provide him with a home. It is significant that the essays' closest analogy to Elia's mode of observation belongs to an actor. The tribute to Joseph Munden ends with an account of the comedian's power to heighten the experience of quotidian reality:

Who like him can throw, or ever attempted to throw, a supernatural interest over the commonest daily-life objects? . . . A tub of butter, contemplated by him, amounts to a Platonic idea. He understands a leg of mutton in its quiddity. He stands wondering, amid the commonplace materials of life, like primæval man with the sun and stars about him. ('The Old Actors', 298)

Elia also inhabits a world where an old folio, a roast pig, a china teacup, an abandoned doorway, gain an exaggerated significance lent by his unique perspective. But, as in the case of Munden, the perspective does not reveal the individual at its source, only the presence of a subjectivity whose identity remains unfixed. Munden 'is not one, but legion': Elia notes that alone among actors he has no face 'that you can properly pin down, and call *his*' (p. 297). His unique observation of 'commonplace materials' is a performance. Elia, too, manages to describe his local attachments without being pinned down by them.

Memory's action is similarly ambivalent. The past is an even more important centre of autobiographical consciousness than the immediately present world. Elia is at his most subjective when he is being retrospective; indeed, his nostalgic, regressive, antiquarian cast of mind must be his most distinctive feature. Elia's favourite books are old books (not just old texts, but old editions); his favourite plays, old plays; and the same is true for actors, buildings, schoolmasters, beggars, and friends.[23] Nostalgia is a powerful expression of subjectivity because it is filled with the energy of an entirely introverted desire. Elia speaks of it as a compulsion, or a disease, in 'New Year's Eve': 'In a degree beneath manhood, it is my infirmity to look back upon those early days' (p. 28).[24] In the same passage he defines memory as the condition of his identity:

from some mental twist which makes it difficult in me to face the prospective ... I have almost ceased to hope; and am sanguine only in the prospects of other (former) years. (p. 28)

The sly etymological confusion here is significant; Elia's 'prospects' are retrospective. He stakes his identity not so much on the existence of a former world as on his continued ability to contemplate the past, in a succession of backward-looking essays.

Memory recalls a state that seems to be more secure, more valuable. Though Elia's picture of the past is by no means a rosy monochrome— witness the Christ's Hospital essay, or the terrors described in

[23] In a review of Hazlitt's *Table Talk* (not published until 1980), Lamb writes:'We had always thought that Old Friends, and Old Wine were the best' (Roy Park (ed.), *Lamb as Critic* (London: Routledge & Kegan Paul, 1980), 304). The review is of great interest for Lamb's comments on different forms of literary egotism in familiar essay-writing.

[24] Nostalgia is often represented in explicitly gendered language ('beneath manhood' could here imply womanhood as well as the more obvious childhood). 'Old China', Elia's most overwhelming expression of desire for the past, begins: 'I have an almost feminine partiality for old china' (p. 247). In 'Mackery End' his female cousin and alter ego Bridget astonishes him with a sudden recitation of 'a thousand half-obliterated recollections of things and persons' (pp. 78–9). On the 'feminized' quality of Elian subjectivity see Aaron, *A Double Singleness*, esp. pp. 167–83.

'Witches'—he certainly implies that old times were better times. Even in the two examples just cited the miseries of childhood have their compensations. Life at school has its freedoms—'indolence, and summer slumbers, and work like play, and innocent idleness, and Elysian exemptions' (p. 19)—that are peculiarly those of the child; while the nightmares described in 'Witches' at least signified an imaginative capability that the adult has lost ('I am almost ashamed to say how tame and prosaic my dreams are grown'; p. 69). The child is credited in various other essays ('My First Play', 'Blakesmoor', 'The Old Benchers of the Inner Temple') with a capacity for happiness that Elia remembers but no longer possesses. Even youth is a better state ('The Wedding', 'Old China'). This intimation of a happy past need not be tied to personal history; Elia is as drawn to places that represent or preserve antiquity—the University of Oxford, a Quaker meeting house, Westminster Abbey—as he is to the sites of his own memories.

The archetypal figure for all memories of a better past is Eden.[25] 'From what have I not fallen,' declares Elia, 'if the child I remember was indeed myself' (p. 28). Again, Edenic recollections are not restricted to the personal. The house and gardens of 'Blakesmoor' are the child Elia's own unfallen world (complete with fruit trees), but in 'The Old Benchers' Elia recalls simply his innocent vision: 'In those days I saw Gods, as "old men covered with a mantle," walking upon the earth' (p. 90).[26] The connection made in 'Oxford in the Vacation' between the shelves of the Bodleian and 'the happy orchard' (p. 10) simply associates antiquity with paradise, entirely free from any reference to Elia's past state.

The figure of Eden, however, also signifies the ambivalence of such an attitude to the past. Paradise is by definition lost. To associate memory with this set of images is to indicate the fragility, or even futility, of recollection. Elia is deeply affected by this ambivalence, as is evident in his constant interweaving of memory with lamentation. All his memories are memorials, recalling the past to commemorate its disappearance. In its simplest form, this structure appears in 'On the Artificial Comedy', 'A Complaint of the Decay of Beggars', 'Modern Gallantry', and

---

[25] For a full study of Edenic imagery in the essays, see James Scoggins, 'Images of Eden in the Essays of Elia', *Journal of English and Germanic Philology*, 71 (1972), 198–210. The fundamental ambivalence of such language (as a *literary*, post-Miltonic language) is explored in Lucy Newlyn, *'Paradise Lost' and the Romantic Reader* (Oxford: Clarendon, 1993), esp. chs. 2 and 6.

[26] Cf. 1 Samuel 28: 14.

'Barrenness of the Imaginative Faculty', all of which eulogize a past state of affairs only through comparison with the inferior present. Elia's praise always comes too late. Thus his character essays are virtually all obituaries: Mrs Battle, Captain Jackson, Elliston, James White (the hero of 'The Praise of Chimney-Sweepers') are all dead. Even 'Amicus Redivivus' waits for its hero's near-death before celebrating him. The most striking demonstration of the ambivalence of recollection comes in the passage already quoted, from the end of 'The South-Sea House'. The parade of the larger-than-life old clerks, all summoned 'from the dusty dead, in whom common qualities become uncommon' (p. 6), is suddenly called into question with a gesture reminiscent of Prospero dispelling his masque:

Reader, what if I have been playing with thee all this while—peradventure the very *names*, which I have summoned up before thee, are fantastic—insubstantial —...

Elia's response is to assert not their reality but merely their antiquity:

Be satisfied that something answering to them has had a being. Their importance is from the past. (p. 7)

Rather than seeking to reinforce a continuity with the present, Elia preserves the uncertainty of his memory, just as he figures the indeterminacy of authorial (present) identity. 'The Old Benchers' is a very similar essay, beginning by describing a place that has altered from the state in which Elia knew it, and proceeding to populate it with fantastical characters who are also long gone. Here, too, the very unreality of the characters is what distinguishes them, and what Elia laments:

Fantastic forms, whither are ye fled? Or, if the like of you exist, why exist they no more for me? Ye inexplicable, half-understood appearances, why comes in reason to tear away the preternatural mist, bright or gloomy, that enshrouded you? (p. 90)

Recollection reveals the unbridgeable gulf between the present and the past, realizing the value of the latter only in the process of reinforcing its inaccessibility. Buildings, like the 'melancholy looking' South-Sea House (p. 1), or the 'mere dust and rubbish' of Blakesmoor (p. 154), are ruined when Elia encounters them, his memory enacting a fantasy of reconstruction that time has already made redundant.

For Elia the past never offers what it promises. As he observes in 'Oxford in the Vacation', past time is no more than an endless sequence of deferrals, by which Elia nevertheless finds himself captivated:

Antiquity! thou wondrous charm, what art thou? that, being nothing, art every thing! When thou *wert*, thou wert not antiquity—then thou wert nothing, but hadst a remoter *antiquity*, as thou called'st it, to look back to with blind veneration; thou thyself being to thyself flat, jejune, *modern!* What mystery lurks in this retroversion? or what half Januses are we, that cannot look forward with the same idolatry with which we for ever revert! The mighty future is as nothing, being every thing! the past is every thing, being nothing! (p. 9)

Though Elia exists largely in the process of memory, what he remembers cannot secure his identity—just as his relation to his local environment failed to supply a means of identifying him. It is interesting to find Lamb writing as early as 1797 of memories 'in the recollection of which I feel I have no property'.[27] Elia's past will not account for his present.

Hence his pervasive feeling that he is 'SUPERANNUATED' (p. 270). Without a past he can call his own, yet constantly looking back to the past, Elia often describes himself as being in an indeterminate limbo. The situation of 'New Year's Eve'—between one year and the next—typifies this state, and provides an apt context for Elia's admission that 'the child Elia—that "other me," there, in the back-ground' is not recognizably himself (p. 28). The discontinuity of time is felt again in 'The Superannuated Man', which describes the occasion of retirement as 'like passing out of Time into Eternity'. The result is that 'I could scarce trust myself with myself' (p. 195). Likewise, in 'Distant Correspondents' Elia's jokey musings on the distortions of truth involved in writing a letter which takes months to reach its destination turn suddenly into a realization of lost time. Regretting his distant friend's departure from the Temple, he asks 'Why did you ever leave that quiet corner?—Why did I?' (p. 108). His attendance at the marriage of a friend's daughter in 'The Wedding' evokes in him a vicarious sense of youth, ironically inappropriate for the elderly bachelor: 'On these occasions I am sure to be in good-humour for a week or two after, and enjoy a reflected honeymoon' (p. 239). Life comes to Elia only at one remove. The most extreme statement of his superannuation is in the fourteenth of the 'Popular Fallacies', a series of occasional pieces submitted to the *New Monthly Magazine* between January and September 1826 and included in the 1833 *Last Essays of Elia*. This startlingly morbid paragraph consists of a series of variations on the assertion that Elia has no life at all:

[27] E. V. Lucas (ed.), *The Letters of Charles and Mary Lamb*, 3 vols. (London: J. M. Dent, 1935), i. 110.

We were never much in the world. Disappointment early struck a dark veil between us and its dazzling illusions . . . We have asked no more of life than what the mimic images in play-houses present us with . . . We once thought life to be something; but it has unaccountably fallen from us before its time. Therefore we choose to dally with visions. The sun has no purposes of ours to light us to. (270–1)[28]

Forever engaged with an elusive past, Elia is again in the indeterminate position that characterizes the role: suspended between subjectivity and displaced identity. That this suspension is the consequence of memory is apparent in 'My First Play'. Recalling his childhood experience of the theatre, Elia remembers the innocent vision which did not distinguish between reality and illusion: 'Gorgeous vests, gardens, palaces, princesses, passed before me. I knew not players' (p. 99). Returning to the theatre as an adult, for a performance of the same play, Elia encounters exactly the same objects. Now, however, the reality of illusion has turned into the familiar theatrical illusion of reality:

The same things were there materially; but the emblem, the reference, was gone!— The green curtain was no longer a veil, drawn between two worlds . . . but a certain quantity of green baize . . . The lights—the orchestra lights—came up a clumsy machinery. The first ring, and the second ring, was now but a trick of the prompter's bell—which had been like the note of the cuckoo, a phantom of a voice.

Memory cannot retain the 'reference' that authenticates the theatrical world. In the absence of this unspecifiable faculty of the child—which can be remembered but not re-experienced—the adult achieves a new understanding of theatre:

Comparison and retrospection soon yielded to the present attraction of the scene; and the theatre became to me, upon a new stock, the most delightful of recreations. (p. 100)

The vision of the child is thus replaced by a 're-creation', an act of memory that fails to achieve what it recalls and so reinterprets it as theatre. The adult's delight is in the suspension of disbelief (as in the

---

[28] The bitterly gloomy tone is rather uncharacteristic of Elia (although the overall stance of the passage is absolutely in keeping with his sensibility as developed in the *London* essays), and it is interesting that Lamb asked Charles Ollier, an editor at the *New Monthly*, to have the 'Popular Fallacies' signed 'L.', 'and reserve *Elia* for Essays *more Eliacal*' (Lucas (ed.), *Letters of Lamb*, iii. 30). This particular piece is more reminiscent of the slightly hysterical personae of Lamb's essays contributed to Leigh Hunt's *Reflector* in 1811 and 1812. By 1826, though, anything publicly identifiable as the product of Lamb's pen was inescapably '*Eliacal*'.

essay 'Stage Illusion'); this becomes Elia's new state, substituted for the pure fantasy of the child. He is re-created as an illusory figure, without a 'reference' to the past. Memory recalls realities, but in doing so can only discover that they have become performances. Autobiography repeats the process; it recalls identity, but the recollection itself displaces that selfhood, never securing the link between author and narrative.

So Elia is written as a personality in place of a self-identifying first person. Accommodated by the medium of the *London Magazine*, he effectively joins the reader on the public side of the autobiographical divide, finding himself given by writing rather than presenting himself egotistically. I described this situation as utopian because it resolves the central difficulty of publishing the self. It seems, though, that selfhood— an inward, impassioned privacy, claimed by the author—endures instead in the form of its own silhouette. Again, there is an analogy with Childe Harold. Byron's writing also takes the position that life 'has unaccountably fallen from us before its time' (p. 271). Its first person sustains itself by meditating on the self's collapse. Like Harold, Elia is fascinated by relics, traces, ruins. His first essay, 'The South-Sea House', prophetically introduces the tendency. It remembers one of the most notorious phantoms of all, 'that famous BUBBLE' (p. 2), the epitome of a presence that turned out to be no more than its own figure. Yet the very nothingness of the bubble leaves its mark, enduring in the form of an emptiness writ large: 'Silence and destitution are upon thy walls, proud house, for a memorial!' (p. 2). The more Elia dwells on things that are lost, the more his central, archeytpal loss—the loss of himself—becomes a similarly tomb-like monument overshadowing the essays.[29] If his egotism lacks an ego, and so smoothes the troubled relation between self-writing and the public sphere, the 'I' that remains is nevertheless haunted by that lack.

Hazlitt's essay on Lamb in *The Spirit of the Age* (1825) captures the effect in a telling image:

That touches him most nearly which is withdrawn to a certain distance, which verges on the borders of oblivion:—that piques and provokes his fancy most, which is hid from a superficial glance . . . a page of his writings recalls to our fancy the stranger on the grate, fluttering in its dusky tenuity, with its idle superstition and hospitable welcome![30]

---

[29] Seamus Perry has described Elia as 'a bundle of recollected absences' (Perry, 'Charles Lamb and the Cost of Seriousness', *Charles Lamb Bulletin*, 83 (1993), 78–89, at 88). The article gives a fine account of the reciprocity between the essays' comic and elegiac tendencies.
[30] P. P. Howe (ed.), *The Complete Works of William Hazlitt*, 21 vols. (London: J. M. Dent, 1930–4), viii. 245.

As readers of Coleridge's 'Frost at Midnight' know, the 'stranger on the grate' refers to a thin film of flame appearing intermittently over the surface of a glowing fire. Coleridge's note explains what Hazlitt means by the 'superstition' and the 'welcome': 'In all parts of the kingdom these films are called *strangers* and supposed to portend the arrival of some absent friend.'[31] Hazlitt understands perfectly that the welcome offered by Lamb's essays is contingent upon a purely phantasmal presence. Elia invites readers into his private sphere—'you are now with me' (p. 25)—but the 'me' whom we join is in fact a 'stranger', a ghostly sign of someone not yet present. Indeed, it would be a characteristic Elian irony if the superstition revealed its double meaning. The stranger may portend an arrival, but by the same token it signifies an absence. Likewise, the Elian personality creates a hospitable community between writer and reader, but also marks the loss of the inward, private self which (as with all Romantic autobiography) would have disrupted that relationship.

We can, therefore, name the guest whose imminence—but absence—the 'stranger' Elia signals. He is Lamb, the autobiographical first person, the owner of Elia's narrated experience, the self that claims authentic personhood rather than printed and circulated personality. By disappearing from his own autobiographical writing he has left a legible personality in his place. The number of his contemporaries who write about Lamb as if he was Elia is a sign of this manoeuvre's unusual success. There is a cost, though, or at least a reverse side. Elia is perpetually shadowed by the absence of his 'self'. His preoccupation with loss amounts to a kind of recollection of 'that "other me," there, in the background', and of the chasm that separates them. Thus even as autobiography is displaced on to the phantom of Elia it finds itself still performing a shadowy self-writing, tracing the silhouette of the absent author. For some critics the process looks like a psychological repression. Gerald Monsman has traced Lamb's self-effacement in the figure of Elia to a guilt inherited from the 'day of horrors' in September 1796 when his sister killed their mother during a bout of insanity.[32] Because such a trauma cannot be written, but also cannot be forgotten, autobiography (it is claimed) can only be a shadow of the author's experience, circling around an absent centre. But I think the ghostliness of Elian autobiography can be understood without reference to biographical material, which is always a problematic recourse for readings of autobiographical

---

[31] Coleridge, *Poetical Works*, i. 240.
[32] Gerald Monsman, 'Charles Lamb's Art of Autobiography', *ELH* 50 (1983), 541–57.

material.[33] We can approach it as an effect of writing rather than something speculatively located in the author's self. In fact, it is embedded in the stance writing adopts towards itself and its contents. The condition of self-writing in the essays, where the 'I' makes its presence felt as a personality while also making its absence felt as a (missing) person, is equally the condition of irony.

Irony is both double-voiced—earnest and satirical together, denying what it asserts—and two-faced, substituting the Elian mask and the supposedly authentic inward self for each other in a dizzyingly endless series of dislocations.[34] In the essays it becomes the figure of figuration itself. Negating writing's referentiality, the simulation of truthfulness, it redefines the apparently historical, narrative mode of self-writing as a series of self-consciously fictional representations. Hence in 'New Year's Eve' it appears (on first reading rather startlingly) as the climax of a list of typically Elian *things*, one of those parades of particularity that give him his illusion of material existence. The sentence mimes Elia's fondness for amassed objects—'an accumulation of sights' (p. 119)—as it depicts that world of sensual attachments in which he seems to anchor himself, until the list remembers (ironically) that all these pleasures are contingent and temporary:

Sun, and sky, and breeze, and solitary walks, and summer holidays, and the greenness of fields, and the delicious juices of meats and fishes, and society, and the cheerful glass, and candle-light, and fire-side conversations, and innocent vanities, and jests, and *irony itself*—do these things go out with life? (p. 29)

Irony is the condition of all the other Elian delights, because (as the final rhetorical question both confesses and hopes to deny) they exist on the verge of their own absence, as Elia himself does. The text that unsays itself in the process of saying is the appropriate vehicle for an autobiography which describes an inaccessible world, recalls an irretrievable past, and outlines an absent self.

Elia's phantom identity is a favourite subject for ironic humour both within and outside the essays. In a postscript to 'A Chapter on Ears' he vigorously asserted his authenticity against Leigh Hunt's accusation that

---

[33] The reasons for resisting 'a privileged notion of referentiality' (p. 18) are explained comprehensively in Jay, *Being in the Text*, 14–21.

[34] The effect is analysed with remarkable precision and force in Jacobus, 'The Art of Managing Books'. Jacobus concentrates on Lamb's (and Hazlitt's and De Quincey's) bookishness, but her attention to 'the ironic disguise that liberates and authorizes self-representation through the dissimulation of writing' (p. 235) results in the best account of Elian autobiography as a whole that we have.

he was Lamb's pseudonym: 'Good heavens! that a plain man must not be allowed *to be*' (p. 332).[35] The banter continued in 'Elia to his Correspondents', printed a few months later, in which he claims that he is allowed to vary autobiographical information according to his mood, and reply to questions according to the questioner's merits, rather than limiting himself to historical consistency. He ends by invoking the liberation of textual existence:

> he [Elia] hath not so fixed his nativity (like a rusty vane) to one dull spot, but that, if he seeth occasion, or the argument shall demand it, he will be born again, in future papers, in whatever place, and at whatever period, shall seem good unto him. (p. 340)

In a brief autobiographical sketch written in 1827, and published posthumously, Lamb says that his 'true works' are in the hundreds of East India House ledgers he filled as a clerk, while the Elian texts have an existence independent of his authorship: he is 'rather better known from that name without a meaning, than from anything he has done or can hope to do in his own'.[36] All these ironies of identity are concentrated in the 'Character of the Late Elia' purportedly contributed by 'Phil-Elia' to the *London* for January 1823. (Naturally, the announcement of Elia's death was no hindrance to the printing of 'Rejoicings Upon the New Year's Coming of Age' in the same issue.) The obituary works to confirm Elia's real existence, in so far as it describes him as a real person with a distinct personality, but at the same time it both denies that existence—by saying that he is dead—and explains that his autobiographical writing is not in fact about himself: 'what he tells us, as of himself, was often true only (historically) of another' (p. 151). The irony is then compounded by the rest of the essay, which reverses this assertion by tracing the characteristics of his writing to his historical experience, again implicating selfhood in the text. At this point, though, it becomes apparent that these repeated displacements and substitutions of identity merge unexpectedly into something like confessional autobiography, replacing the pseudo-biography of Elia with an account that describes writing as the manifestation of a historical author's real 'weaknesses' (p. 153). At first the obituary describes Elia as a figure of communal, congenial personality, 'making himself many, or reducing many unto himself'. Defending him against the charge of egotism, it then asks an interesting question:

---

[35] A particularly neat touch in the note comes when Elia retorts that 'Leigh Hunt' is widely known to be a pseudonym.
[36] Lucas (ed.), *Works of Lamb*, i. 376.

And how shall the intenser dramatist escape being faulty, who doubtless, under cover of passion uttered by another, oftentimes gives blameless vent to his most inward feelings, and expresses his own story modestly?   (p. 151)

The idea that a dramatist might express the truth through the masking role hints at Elia's potential transparency. The preface goes on to call him 'a singular character' (p. 152), contradicting the multiplicity asserted earlier. The ironic context unfixes the identity of Elia; the biographical portrait that forms the rest of the essay comes instead to describe the 'singular' author of the essay, the 'intenser dramatist', Lamb. The first person, we are told, is a fiction; but the third person, in which the preface is increasingly narrated, is able to uncover the facts behind the masquerade, and so expose the direct link between writing and history denied at the beginning. Describing 'His' resistance to the approach of death, the preface concludes:

He did not conform to the march of time, but was dragged along in the procession. His manners lagged behind his years. He was too much the boy-man . . . The impressions of infancy had burnt into him, and he resented the impertinence of manhood. These were weaknesses; but such as they were, they are a key to explicate some of his writings.   (p. 153)

That the 'he' of the 'Preface' should gain the autobiographical authenticity that the 'I' of all the other essays evades is profoundly ironic; yet it is a direct consequence of this kind of writing. Irony's two-facedness is (ironically) reversible: when the text says 'I', the context gives no identity, but when the text purports to give an account of the phantom author it ends up describing the real author.[37] Indeed, it interprets the author's writing as a manifestation of his desire to be rooted in his past experiences. Instead of Elian indeterminacy we have a real fear of extinction: writing holds out hope of securing a fragile and tenuous identity, through the autobiographical procedure of reverting to the past and reading the self there.

Irony always contains a latent power to expose authorial presence, because it depends on a consciousness of some overviewing perspective that is to a degree detached from the text.[38] It implies a voice which

[37] Aaron interestingly analyses this aspect of irony in terms of its threat to recuperative Elian 'play' (Aaron, *A Double Singleness*, 190–7).

[38] For German Romantic theorists of irony it 'hovers over the entire work' (Friedrich Schlegel, in his 1798 essay 'On Goethe's *Meister*'); it is the 'one all-embracing glance' that 'hovers over everything' (Karl Solger, from his 1816 tract on aesthetics *Erwin*. Cited by Kathleen Wheeler (ed.), *German Aesthetic and Literary Criticism: The Romantic Ironists and Goethe* (Cambridge: Cambridge University Press, 1984), 67, 146.

might be articulated through the Elian persona rather than from it, like the dramatist whose 'inward feelings' are apparent 'under cover of passion uttered by another' (p. 151). It creates a sense of authorial detachment from writing—as in Lamb's hoaxing letters, where one side of a sheet would be devoted to terrible lies, and the joke would be revealed as the reader turned the page. Hence the 'Character of the Late Elia's accusation that 'He too much affected that dangerous figure—irony' (p. 152). The danger is that it will implicate the author in the world of the text and make him appear as the subject to which his otherwise indeterminate 'I' refers.

There are two essays—both among the most extraordinary achievements of Romantic-period prose, arguments enough in themselves for giving Lamb greater prominence in critical histories of the age—in which ironic structures suddenly seem to reveal a voice speaking through the Elian 'I'. In 'Dream-Children' Elia comes up with an unusually dramatic fiction. He depicts himself telling stories to his imaginary children. The story he tells them is itself a fantasy of family life. It describes the domestic happiness of Elia and his brother at the great mansion where their grandmother was housekeeper (Lamb's Blakesware, or Elia's 'Blakesmoor', not named in the essay). The children participate in this fantasy, themselves imagining places and people they have never seen: all of the people Elia remembers as he speaks are dead, including the children's mother, 'the fair Alice W—n'. As often in the essays, Elia's marvellously detailed and poignant recollections are placed in a context that emphasizes their contingency. Here, however, the ironic tension between the reality of a lost past and the fantasy of memory is amplified by the figures of the children, who represent an illusory inheritance from the dead family, and the promise of a future. At the climactic moment the depth of the irony interrupts Elia's narration and replaces it with a distant, sourceless voice that unambiguously reveals the sense of loss underpinning the dream:

when suddenly turning to Alice [the imagined daughter], the soul of the first Alice [the mother] looked out at her eyes with such a reality of re-presentment, that I became in doubt which of them stood there before me, or whose that bright hair was; and while I stood gazing, both the children gradually grew fainter to my view, receding, and still receding till nothing at last but two mournful features were seen in the uttermost distance, which, without speech, strangely impressed upon me the effects of speech; 'We are not of Alice, nor of thee, nor are we children at all . . . We are nothing; less than nothing, and dreams. We are only what might have been . . .'—and immediately awaking, I found myself quietly seated in my bachelor arm-chair, where I had fallen asleep, with the faithful Bridget unchanged by my side—but John L. (or James Elia) was gone for ever. (p. 103)

The precise moment when the fantasy exposes itself as fantasy—the moment of fullest irony—is the point at which Elia's loss, mediated by his capacity for illusory restoration, surrenders to an authentic realization of the impossibility of recovering the past. James Elia (who is elsewhere Elia's cousin) is actually identified as 'John L.', Lamb's brother, who did indeed die in 1821 ('Dream-Children' appeared in January 1822). The invention of the children is Elia's most extreme compensatory fiction, a complete rewriting of the past and an explicit use of writing's fictions to fill the void memory finds there. It gives him the living inheritance his nostalgia so urgently misses and regrets. The fiction is exposed, and so exploded, by a voice 'without speech', an unidentifiable person writing the historical truth: the 'voice' of autobiography, articulated through (but not by) the vanishing faces, which at once reveals the irony and tells the history that irony figures, making explicit the implied contrast between fiction and the real story.

Like 'Dream-Children', 'Old China' is structured by a powerful contrast between aesthetic illusion and the reality of privation. Elia and his cousin Bridget (the essays' figure for Mary Lamb) debate the happiness of their past over a china teacup populated by 'old friends—whom distance cannot diminish' (p. 248—whole worlds of pathos lie beneath the simple parenthetical clause). Uncircumscribed by either space, time, or identity ('the same lady, or another—for likeness is identity on teacups'), the figures on the china seem to inhabit the ideal Elian environment. In their 'world before perspective' (p. 248) they are unaffected by the perspectival problems Bridget raises in the long nostalgic speech that takes up most of the essay. Her voice supplies 'Old China's narrative substance, listing events and objects from the past, while regretting that Elia's relative wealth has since dulled their enjoyment of everyday things. Her argument is a typically ironic one (wealth destroys the pleasure of possessions), and the narrative ironies—giving Elia's memories to another speaker, associating recollection with loss, setting Elia's diminished present against the permanence of the figures painted on the china—are also characteristic of the essays. What complicates the familiar Elian displacements is the fact that he replies, in his 'own' voice, to his cousin. The perspective of the reply is markedly different from Bridget's. Whereas her narrative balances the pleasures of memory with the sense of distance from the remembered world, the counter-argument is resigned to the bare present: 'Competence to age is supplementary youth; a sorry supplement indeed, but I fear the best that is to be had' (p. 251). As in 'Dream-Children', the ironic structures of displacement and contrast give way to a startlingly direct confrontation with the present reality of loss. The replying voice supplies the essays' only hint of a reference to the events of the 'day of horrors': 'That we had much to struggle with, as we grew up together, we have reason to be most thankful. It strengthened, and knit our compact closer' (p. 251). Because Bridget's speech is the vehicle for Elia's memories, his reply reads like a more personal voice, separate and corrective, belonging to the present author rather than the figure of recollection. This speaker's desire to reinhabit the past world has an intensity unmatched in the essays:

Yet could those days return—could you and I once more walk our thirty miles a-day—could Bannister and Mrs. Bland again be young, and you and I be young to see them—could the good old one shilling gallery days return—they are dreams, my cousin, now—but could you and I at this moment, instead of this quiet argument, by our well-carpeted fireside, sitting on this luxurious sofa—be once more struggling up those inconvenient stair-cases, pushed about, and squeezed, and elbowed by the poorest rabble of poor gallery scramblers . . . I know not the fathom line that ever touched a descent so deep as I would be willing to bury more wealth in than Crœsus had, or the great Jew R— is supposed to have, to purchase it.

Instantly the text reverts to Elia's characteristically muted, neutral, ironic tone:

And now do just look at that merry little Chinese waiter holding an umbrella, big enough for a bed-tester, over the head of that pretty insipid half-Madona-ish chit of a lady in that very blue summer house.   (p. 252)

The extreme contrast of tone suggests a corresponding contrast of voices, one expressing the Elian free equilibrium of the teacup or other such illusory utopias, including the utopia of Elia's congenial circulation among the *London*'s readers, the other bound to the privations of the temporal process; one inhabiting the world of personality and print, the other speaking through the text to reveal authorial presence captured in autobiographical writing.

   The 'Character of the Late Elia' hinted that when Elia's writing is to do with the self as author it exposes the author's 'weaknesses' (p. 153). 'Dream-Children' and 'Old China' confirm the link between afflicted selfhood and autobiography. They are haunted by Hazlitt's 'stranger', a figure invoked by writing but at the same time placed out of its range, absent from it. In both essays it is this phantasmal absentee only who possesses experience. The first-person writer, Elia, can only simulate that possession, in what turns out to be a poignantly ironic shadow of autobiography. In 'Dream-Children' he narrates his own acts of autobiographical narrative: the essay is constructed out of a simple iteration, 'Then I went on to say . . . And then I told how . . . Then I told . . . Then in somewhat a more heightened tone, I told how . . .' (pp. 101–2). 'Old China' puts an equivalent grammar of narration into Bridget's mouth: 'Do you remember . . . Do you remember how . . . Then, do you remember . . . Do you remember when . . .' (pp. 249–50). The repetitions allow the texts to accumulate a wealth of narrated detail, recollections of past experience laden with an intensely expressive and nostalgic particularity. But in each case the burgeoning writing of Elia's past pulls it further and further out of his reach as it gathers pace. The children to whom Elia tells his own childhood in 'Dream-Children' are not there, so no act of telling is taking place; in 'Old China' Bridget ventriloquizes his past only in order to remind him that none of its pleasures belong to him any more. The brilliance of both essays is how they let the ironies accumulate their tension right to the breaking point: the texts go on and on narrating the lost past as they come steadily closer to the inevitable moment when they will have to unmask their own autobiographical impulse as a fiction. When the break occurs, it speaks with a blank finality: 'We are nothing; less than nothing, and dreams' (p. 103); '[those days] are dreams, my cousin, now' (pp. 249–50). This is autobiography's last word: that which it writes into being is not there, that which it narrates as history is 'nothing'. So, too, both essays silently observe, with the autobiographer. Elia is the self of a fictional self-writing; when he confesses Lamb's 'weaknesses' (his childlessness and the death of his brother in 'Dream-Children', his imprisonment within nostalgia in 'Old China') he turns him into a 'phantom' too, or writes his obituary.

This brings us to the fullest of full stops. But, reversing irony's direction once again, writing 'nothing' is here also writing autobiographically: as Philippe Lejeune famously observes after wrestling with the theoretical problems of the genre, 'In spite of the fact that autobiography is impossible, this in no way prevents it from existing.'[39] Even as it allows us to see the fictions that sustain it, Elia's self-writing transcribes (in the *Quarterly*'s words) an 'impress' of 'the author's own very soul'. If we can

[39] Lejeune, *On Autobiography*, 132.

in the end name that 'author' neither Elia (the publicly circulated personality) nor Lamb (the self who both writes and is written), the indeterminacy itself tells us most of what we need to know about the condition of autobiographical writing in the period. In studies of this sort the last example always risks being misread as some kind of epitome of the whole field. Here, as throughout the preceding chapters, we have to avoid the temptation to read the situation of a specific work as if it answered the questions raised in a wider perpective. Individual documents cannot comprehensively read their moment in literary history, any more than a fully historicized context can comprehensively read a given text. Still, there is no better guide than Elia to the complexity of the transactions between autobiographical writing and the sphere where it is named and circulated. Only in those transactions can we properly understand what Romantic autobiography involves.

Bibliography

The Bibliography is in two sections: I. autobiographical writings, and editions containing texts of autobiographical writings; II. other primary and secondary material.

I. AUTOBIOGRAPHICAL WRITINGS, AND EDITIONS CONTAINING TEXTS OF AUTOBIOGRAPHICAL WRITINGS

ALEXANDER, MARY, *Some Account of the Life and Religious Experience of Mary Alexander* (York: C. Peacock, 1811).

ANON., *Genuine and Authentic Memoirs of a Well-Known Woman of Intrigue* (London: James Ridgway, 1787).

ARCHER, ANN, *Authentic and Interesting Memoirs of Miss Ann Sheldon*, 4 vols. (London, 1787).

ASHE, THOMAS, *Memoirs and Confessions of Captain Ashe* (London, 1815).

Autobiography. A Collection of the Most Instructive and Amusing Lives Ever Published, Written by the Parties Themselves, 34 vols. (London: Hunt and Clarke, 1826–33).

BAMFORD, SAMUEL, *An Account of the Arrest and Imprisonment of Samuel Bamford* (Manchester: George Cave, 1817).

BELLAMY, GEORGE ANN, *An Apology for the Life of George Ann Bellamy*, 5 vols. (London, 1785).

BELOE, WILLIAM, *The Sexagenarian*, 2 vols. (London: F. C. and J. Rivington, 1817).

BRASBRIDGE, JOSEPH, *The Fruits of Experience* (London, 1824).

BRISTOW, JAMES, *A Narrative of the Sufferings of James Bristow* (London: J. Murray, 1793).

BRYDGES, SIR SAMUEL EGERTON, *The Autobiography, Times, Opinions, and Contemporaries of Sir Egerton Brydges*, 2 vols. (London: Cochrane and McCrone, 1834).

BYRON, LORD, *Lord Byron: The Complete Poetical Works*, ed. Jerome J. McGann, 7 vols. (Oxford: Clarendon, 1980–93).

CAMPBELL, ARCHIBALD, *A Voyage Round the World*, ed. James Smith (Edinburgh: Archibald Constable, 1816).

CARLYLE, THOMAS, *Sartor Resartus*, ed. Kerry McSweeney and Peter Sabor (Oxford: Oxford University Press, 1987).

CARY, CATHERINE, *Memoirs of Miss C. E. Cary*, 3 vols. (London: T. Traveller, 1825).

CLARE, JOHN, *John Clare's Autobiographical Writings*, ed. Eric Robinson (Oxford: Oxford University Press, 1983).

COBBETT, WILLIAM, *The Life and Adventures of Peter Porcupine* (1796; London: J. Wright, 1797).

COGHLAN, MARGARET, *Memoirs of Mrs. Coghlan*, 2 vols. (London: G. Kearsley, 1794).

COIGLY, JAMES, *The Life of the Rev. James Coigly* (Derry: Valentine, 1798).

COLERIDGE, S. T., *Biographia Literaria*, ed. James Engell and W. J. Bate, 2 vols. (Princeton, NJ: Princeton University Press, 1983).

CRADOCK, JOSEPH, *Literary and Miscellaneous Memoirs*, 4 vols. (London: J. B. Nichols, 1828).

CUMBERLAND, RICHARD, *Memoirs of Richard Cumberland* (London: Lackington, Allen, 1806).

DE QUINCEY, THOMAS, *Confessions of an English Opium Eater and Other Writings*, ed. Grevel Lindop (Oxford: Oxford University Press, 1985).

DIBDIN, CHARLES, *The Professional Life of Mr. Dibdin*, 4 vols. (London, 1803).

DIBDIN, THOMAS JOHN, *The Reminiscences of Thomas Dibdin*, 2 vols. (London: Henry Colburn, 1827).

EDGEWORTH, RICHARD LOVELL, *Memoirs of Richard Lovell Edgeworth, Esq.*, 2 vols. (R. Hunter, 1820).

EQUIANO, OLAUDAH, *The Interesting Narrative of the Life of Olaudah Equiano*, 2 vols. (London, 1789).

FRANKLIN, BENJAMIN, *Benjamin Franklin's Memoirs*, ed. Max Farrand (Berkeley, Calif.: University of California Press, 1949).

GALT, JOHN, *The Autobiography of John Galt*, 2 vols. (London: Cochrane & McCrone, 1833).

GED, WILLIAM, *Biographical Memoirs of William Ged* (London: J. Nichols, 1781).

GIBBON, EDWARD, *The Autobiography of Edward Gibbon* (1796; London: J. M. Dent, 1932).

GOETHE, JOHANN WOLFGANG VON, *The Autobiography of Johann Wolfgang von Goethe*, trans. John Oxenford, 2 vols. (Chicago, Ill.: University of Chicago Press, 1974).

GOOCH, ELIZABETH SARAH, *An Appeal to the Public on the Conduct of Mrs. Gooch* (London: G. Kearsley, 1788).

——, *The Life of Mrs. Gooch*, 3 vols. (London, 1792).

GRONNIOSAW, JAMES ALBERT UKAWSAW, *A Narrative of the Most Remarkable Particulars in the Life of James Albert Ukawsaw Gronniosaw, An African Prince* (Bath: W. Gye, 1770).

HAGGART, DAVID, *The Life of David Haggart*, 2nd edn. (Edinburgh: W. & C. Tait, 1821).

HARRIOTT, JOHN, *Struggles Through Life*, 2 vols. (London: J. Hatchard, 1807).

HAYDON, BENJAMIN ROBERT, *The Autobiography and Journals of Benjamin Robert Haydon*, ed. Malcolm Elwin (London: MacDonald, 1950).

HAYLEY, WILLIAM, *Memoirs of the Life and Writings of William Hayley*, ed. John Johnson, 2 vols. (London: Henry Colburn, 1823).

HAZLITT, WILLIAM, *Liber Amoris* (1823; Oxford: Woodstock, 1992).

HOGG, JAMES, *Memoirs of the Author's Life and Familiar Anecdotes of Sir Walter Scott*, ed. Douglas S. Mack (Edinburgh: Scottish Academic Press, 1972).

HOLCROFT, THOMAS, *Memoirs of the Late Thomas Holcroft* (1816; Oxford: Oxford University Press, 1926).

HUME, DAVID, *The Life of David Hume* (1777; Altrincham: J. Martin Stafford, 1987).

HUNT, HENRY, *Memoirs of Henry Hunt, Esq.*, 3 vols. (London: T. Dolby, 1820).

IRELAND, WILLIAM HENRY, *An Authentic Account of the Shaksperian Manuscripts* (London: J. Debrett, 1796).

——, *The Confessions of William Henry Ireland* (London: Thomas Goddard, 1805).

JEMMAT, CATHERINE, *The Memoirs of Mrs Catherine Jemmat*, 2 vols. (London, 1772).

JOHNSTONE, JULIA, *Confessions of Julia Johnstone* (London: Benbow, 1825).

LACKINGTON, JAMES, *Memoirs of the First Forty-Five Years of the Life of James Lackington* (London, 1791).

——, *Confessions* (London, 1804).

LUCAS, E. V. (ed.) *The Works of Charles and Mary Lamb*, 7 vols. (London: Methuen, 1903–35).

MARRANT, JOHN, *A Narrative of the Lord's Wonderful Dealings With John Marrant* (London: Gilbert and Plummer, 1785).

MARTIN, JONATHAN, *The Life of Jonathan Martin* (Barnard Castle: Thomas Clifton, 1826).

MOORE, MARK, *Memoirs and Adventures of Mark Moore* (London: J. W. Myers, 1795).

NICOL, JOHN, *The Life and Adventures of John Nicol, Mariner* (Edinburgh: W. Blackwood, 1822).

O'KEEFFE, JOHN, *Recollections of the Life of John O'Keeffe*, 2 vols. (London: H. Coburn, 1826).

OWENSON, SYDNEY, LADY MORGAN, *The Book of the Boudoir*, 2 vols. (London: Henry Colburn, 1829).

PHILLIPS, PHEBE, *The Woman of the Town* (London: J. Roe, 1801).

PLACE, FRANCIS, *The Autobiography of Francis Place*, ed. Mary Thrale (Cambridge: Cambridge University Press, 1972).

POLWHELE, RICHARD, *Traditions and Recollections*, 2 vols. (London: John Nichols, 1826).

PRESTON, THOMAS, *The Life and Opinions of Thomas Preston, Patriot and Shoemaker* (London, 1817).

PRINCE, J. H., *The Life, Adventures, Pedestrian Excursions, and Singular Opinions of J. H. Prince* (London, 1807).

ROBINSON, MARY, *Memoirs of the Late Mrs Robinson*, 2 vols. (London: Richard Phillips, 1803).

ROUSSEAU, JEAN-JACQUES, *The Confessions of J. J. Rousseau, Citizen of Geneva: Part the First*, 2 vols. (London, G. G. J. and J. Robinson, 1790).

——, *The Confessions of J. J. Rousseau, Citizen of Geneva: Part the Second*, 3 vols. (London, G. G. J. and J. Robinson, 1790).

SAXBY, MARY, *Memoirs of a Female Vagrant* (Dunstable: J. W. Morris, 1806).

SCOTT, THOMAS, *The Force of Truth* (1779; London: G. Keith and J. Johnson, 1808).

SEMPLE, J. G., *The Life of Major J. G. Semple Lisle* (London: W. Stewart, 1799).

SHIPP, JOHN, *Memoirs of the Extraordinary Military Career of John Shipp*, 3 vols. (London: Hurst, Chance, 1829).

SMITH, AARON, *The Atrocities of the Pirates; Being a Faithful Narrative of the Unparalleled Sufferings Endured by the Author During His Captivity* (London: G. & W. B. Whittaker, 1824).

STOCKDALE, PERCIVAL, *The Memoirs of the Life, and Writings of Percival Stockdale*, 2 vols. (London: Longman, Hurst, Rees, and Orme, 1809).

SUMBEL, LEAH, *Memoirs of the Life of Mrs. Sumbel, Late Wells*, 3 vols. (London: C. Chapple, 1811).

THICKNESSE, PHILIP, *Memoirs and Anecdotes of Philip Thicknesse* (Dublin: William Jones, 1790).

TOLD, SILAS, *An Account of the Life, and Dealings of God with Silas Told* (London: Gilbert and Plummer, 1786).

TRELAWNEY, EDWARD JOHN, *Adventures of a Younger Son*, ed. William St Clair (Oxford: Oxford University Press, 1974).

VAUX, JAMES HARDY, *Memoirs of James Hardy Vaux*, 2 vols. (London: W. Clowes, 1819).

WAKEFIELD, GILBERT, *Memoirs of the Life of Gilbert Wakefield*, 2 vols. (London: J. Johnson, 1804).

WARNER, RICHARD, *Literary Recollections*, 2 vols. (London: Longman, Rees, Orme, Brown, and Green, 1830).

WATSON, RICHARD, RT. REVD, *Anecdotes of the Life of Richard Watson, Bishop of Landaff*, 2 vols. (London: Cadell & Davies, 1818).

WILKINSON, TATE, *Memoirs of His Own Life*, 4 vols. (York: Wilson, Spence, and Mawman, 1790).

WILLIAMS, HELEN MARIA, *Letters Written in France in the Summer 1790* (1790; Oxford: Woodstock, 1989).

WILSON, HARRIETTE, *Memoirs of Harriette Wilson*, 4 vols. (London: J. J. Stockdale, 1825).

WOLLASTON, FRANCIS, *The Secret History of a Private Man* (London, 1795).

WOLLSTONECRAFT, MARY, and GODWIN, WILLIAM, *A Short Residence in Sweden and Memoirs of the Author of 'The Rights of Woman'*, ed. Richard Holmes (Harmondsworth: Penguin, 1987).

WOODARD, DAVID, *The Narrative of Captain David Woodard* (London: J. Johnson, 1804).

WORDSWORTH, WILLIAM, *The Prelude, 1798–1799*, ed. Stephen Parrish (Ithaca, NY: Cornell University Press, 1977).

——, *The Prelude: 1799, 1805, 1850*, ed. Jonathan Wordsworth, M. H. Abrams, and Stephen Gill (New York: W. W. Norton, 1979).

II. NON-AUTOBIOGRAPHICAL AND SECONDARY MATERIAL

AARON, JANE, *A Double Singleness: Gender and the Writings of Charles and Mary Lamb* (Oxford: Clarendon, 1991).

——, 'Charles and Mary Lamb: The Critical Heritage', *The Charles Lamb Bulletin*, 59 (1987), 73–85.

ABRAMS, M. H., *Natural Supernaturalism: Tradition and Revolution in Romantic Literature* (New York: W. W. Norton, 1971).

ANDREWS, WILLIAM L., *To Tell a Free Story: The First Century of Afro-American Autobiography, 1760–1865* (Urbana, Ill.: University of Illinois Press, 1986).

BARRELL, JOHN, *The Infection of Thomas De Quincey* (New Haven, Conn.: Yale University Press, 1991).

BAXTER, EDMUND, *De Quincey's Art of Autobiography* (Edinburgh: Edinburgh University Press, 1990).

BENSTOCK, SHARI (ed.), *The Private Self: Theory and Practice of Women's Autobiographical Writings* (London: Routledge, 1988).

BEAUDRY, CATHERINE, *The Role of the Reader in Rousseau's 'Confessions'* (New York: Peter Lang, 1991).

BRADY, FRANK, and WIMSATT, W. K. (eds.), *Samuel Johnson: Selected Poetry and Prose* (Berkeley, Calif.: University of California Press, 1977).

BRUSS, ELIZABETH W., *Autobiographical Acts* (Baltimore, Md.: Johns Hopkins University Press, 1976).

——, 'Eye for I: Making and Unmaking Autobiography in Film', in James Olney (ed.), *Autobiography: Essays Theoretical and Critical* (Princeton, NJ: Princeton University Press, 1980), 294–312.

BRYDGES, SIR EGERTON, *Imaginative Biography*, 2 vols. (London: Saunders and Otley, 1834).

BUCKLEY, JEROME H., *The Turning Key* (Cambridge, Mass.: Harvard University Press, 1984).

BURKE, EDMUND, *A Letter From Mr. Burke to a Member of the National Assembly* (London: J. Dodsley, 1791).

——, *Reflections on the Revolution in France*, ed. J. G. A. Pocock (Indianapolis, Ind.: Hackett, 1987).

BURNETT, JOHN, MAYALL, DAVID, and VINCENT, DAVID (eds.) *The Autobiography of the Working Class: An Annotated Critical Bibliography, i., 1790–1900* (Brighton: Harvester, 1984).

BUTLER, MARILYN, 'Satire and the Images of Self in the Romantic Period: The Long Tradition of Hazlitt's *Liber Amoris*', in G. A. Rosso and Daniel P. Watkins (eds.), *Spirits of Fire: English Romantic Writers and Contemporary Historical Methods* (London: Associated University Presses, 1990).

BYGRAVE, STEPHEN, 'Land of the Giants: Gaps, Limits and Audiences in Coleridge's *Biographia Literaria*', in Stephen Copley and John Whale (eds.), *Beyond Romanticism* (London: Routledge, 1992).

CAFARELLI, ANNETTE WHEELER, *Prose in the Age of Poets* (Philadelphia, Pa.: University of Pennsylvania Press, 1990).

CHARTIER, ROGER (ed.), *A History of Private Life, iii. Passions of the Renaissance*, trans. Arthur Goldhammer (Cambridge, Mass.: Harvard University Press, 1989).

CHASE, CYNTHIA (ed.), *Romanticism* (London: Longman, 1993).

CHEEKE, STEPHEN, 'Byron, History and the *Genius Loci*', *Byron Journal*, 27 (1999), 38–50.

CHRISTENSEN, JEROME C., *Coleridge's Blessed Machine of Language* (Ithaca, NY: Cornell University Press, 1981).

——, 'Coleridge's Marginal Method in the *Biographia Literaria*', *PMLA* 92 (1977), 928–40.

——, *Lord Byron's Strength* (Baltimore, Md.: Johns Hopkins University Press, 1993).

CLEJ, ALINA, *A Genealogy of the Modern Self: Thomas De Quincey and the Intoxication of Writing* (Stanford, Calif.: Stanford University Press, 1995).

COBURN, KATHLEEN (ed.), *The Notebooks of Samuel Taylor Coleridge*, 4 vols. (London: Routledge & Kegan Paul, 1957–90).

COLERIDGE, S. T., *Complete Poetical Works*, ed. E. H. Coleridge, 2 vols. (Oxford: Oxford University Press, 1912).

——, *The Friend*, ed. Barbara E. Rooke, 2 vols. (Princeton, NJ: Princeton University Press, 1969).

COOKE, M. G., '*Quisque Sui Faber*: Coleridge in the *Biographia Literaria*', *Philological Quarterly*, 50 (1971), 208–29.

CURTIS, PAUL M., 'Rhetoric as Hero: "A Most Voiceless Thought" ', *Byron Journal*, 19 (1991), 104–13.

DANAHAY, MARTIN A., *A Community of One* (Albany, NY: SUNY Press, 1993).

DARLEY, GEORGE, *The Errors of Ecstasie* (London: G. and W. B. Whittaker, 1822).

DARNTON, ROBERT, *The Great Cat Massacre* (Harmondsworth: Penguin, 1985).

DART, GREGORY, *Rousseau, Robespierre and English Romanticism* (Cambridge: Cambridge University Press, 1999).

D'ISRAELI, ISAAC, *Miscellanies; or, Literary Recreations* (London: T. Cadell, 1796).

DUFFY, EDWARD, *Rousseau in England* (Berkeley, Calif.: University of California Press, 1979).

EDWARDS, PAUL, *Unreconciled Strivings and Ironic Strategies* (Edinburgh: Centre of African Studies, Edinburgh University, 1992).

EILENBERG, SUSAN, *Strange Power of Speech: Wordsworth, Coleridge, and Literary Possession* (New York: Oxford University Press, 1992).

EMERSON, SHEILA, 'Byron's "One Word": The Language of Self-Expression in *Childe Harold III*', *Studies in Romanticism*, 20 (1981), 363–82.

FAVRET, MARY A., *Romantic Correspondence* (Cambridge: Cambridge University Press, 1993).

FELSKI, RITA, *Beyond Feminist Aesthetics* (Cambridge, Mass.: Harvard University Press, 1989).

FLEISHMAN, AVROM, *Figures of Autobiography* (Berkeley, Calif.: University of California Press, 1983).

FOGEL, DANIEL MARK, 'A Compositional History of the *Biographia Literaria*', *Studies in Bibliography*, 30 (1977), 219–34.

FOLKENFLIK, ROBERT (ed.), *The Culture of Autobiography* (Stanford, Calif.: Stanford University Press, 1993).

FOSTER, JOHN, *Essays in a Series of Letters to a Friend*, 2 vols. (London: Longman, Hurst, Rees, and Orme, 1805).

FOTHERINGTON, THOMAS, 'Utterly Wet and a Weed: Saturation in Canto III of *Childe Harold's Pilgrimage*', *Journal of European Romantic Studies*, 9 (1984), 111–29.

GARBER, FREDERICK, *The Autonomy of the Self from Richardson to Huysmans* (Princeton, NJ: Princeton University Press, 1982).

——, *Self, Text, and Romantic Irony* (Princeton, NJ: Princeton University Press, 1988).

GRAHAM, WALTER, *English Literary Periodicals* (New York: Octagon, 1980).

GREBANIER, BERNARD, *The Great Shakespearean Forgery* (London: Heinemann, 1966).

GRIGGS, E. L. (ed.), *Collected Letters of Samuel Taylor Coleridge*, 6 vols. (Oxford: Clarendon, 1956–71).

GROSS, JONATHAN, 'Hazlitt's Worshiping Practice in *Liber Amoris*', *Studies in English Literature 1500–1900*, 35 (1995), 707–21.

GUSDORF, GEORGES, 'Conditions and Limits of Autobiography', in James Olney (ed.), *Autobiography: Essays Theoretical and Critical* (Princeton, NJ: Princeton University Press, 1980), 28–48.

HABERMAS, JÜRGEN, *The Structural Transformation of the Public Sphere*, trans. Thomas Burger with the assistance of Frederick Lawrence (Cambridge, Mass.: MIT Press, 1989).

HAMILTON, PAUL, *Coleridge's Poetics* (Oxford: Blackwell, 1983).

HANEY, JANICE L., ' "Shadow-Hunting": Romantic Irony, *Sartor Resartus* and Victorian Romanticism', *Studies in Romanticism*, 17 (1978), 307–33.

HARDING, ANTHONY JOHN, 'Wordsworth's *Prelude*, Tracey Emin, and Romantic Autobiography', *Wordsworth Circle*, 34 (2003), 59–65.

HAYDEN, JOHN O., 'De Quincey's *Confessions* and the Reviewers', *Wordsworth Circle*, 6 (1975), 273–9.

HAYTER, ALETHEA, *Opium and the Romantic Imagination*, rev. edn. (London: Crucible, 1988).

HOFKOSH, SONIA, 'A Woman's Profession: Sexual Difference and the Romance of Authorship', *Studies in Romanticism*, 32 (1993), 245–72.

HOWE, P. P. (ed.), *The Complete Works of William Hazlitt*, 21 vols. (London: J. M. Dent, 1930–4).

JACKSON, H. J., 'Coleridge's *Biographia*: When is an Autobiography not an Autobiography?', *Biography*, 20 (1997), 54–71.

JACOBUS, MARY, 'The Art of Managing Books: Romantic Prose and the Writing of the Past', in Arden Reed (ed.), *Romanticism and Language* (London: Methuen, 1984).

——, *Romanticism, Writing and Sexual Difference* (Oxford: Clarendon, 1989).

JAUSS, HANS ROBERT, *Toward an Aesthetics of Reception*, trans. Timothy Bahti (Brighton: Harvester, 1982).

JAY, PAUL, *Being in the Text: Self-Representation from Wordsworth to Roland Barthes* (Ithaca, NY: Cornell University Press, 1984).

JONES, C. B., *Radical Sensibility* (London: Routledge, 1993).

KAVANAGH, THOMAS M., *Writing the Truth* (Berkeley, Calif.: University of California Press, 1987).

KEARNS, SHEILA M., *Coleridge, Wordsworth, and Romantic Autobiography* (Madison, Wis.: Fairleigh Dickinson University Press, 1995).

KEEN, PAUL, *The Crisis of Literature in the 1790s* (Cambridge: Cambridge University Press, 1999).

KLANCHER, JON, *The Making of English Reading Audiences, 1790–1832* (Madison, Wis.: University of Wisconsin Press, 1987).

KOENIGSBERGER, KURT M., 'Liberty, Libel, and *Liber Amoris*: Hazlitt on Sovereignty and Death', *Studies in Romanticism*, 38 (1999), 281–309.

LEASK, NIGEL, *The Politics of Imagination in Coleridge's Critical Thought* (London: Macmillan, 1988).

——, ' "Murdering One's Double": De Quincey's *Confessions* and Coleridge's *Biographia*', in Peter J. Kitson and Thomas N. Corns (eds.), *Coleridge and the Armoury of the Human Mind* (London: Frank Cass, 1991).

LEJEUNE, PHILIPPE, *On Autobiography*, ed. Paul John Eakin, trans. Katherine Leary (Minneapolis, Minn.: University of Minnesota Press, 1989).

LIU, ALAN, *Wordsworth: The Sense of History* (Stanford, Calif.: Stanford University Press, 1989).

LOESBERG, JONATHAN, 'Autobiography as Genre, Act of Consciousness, Text', *Prose Studies 1800–1900*, 4 (1981), 169–85.

LUCAS, E. V. (ed.), *The Letters of Charles and Mary Lamb*, 3 vols. (London: J. M. Dent, 1935).

MCDONAGH, JOSEPHINE, 'Opium and the Imperial Imagination', in Philip W. Martin and Robin Jarvis (eds.), *Reviewing Romanticism* (New York: St Martin's Press, 1992).

——, *De Quincey's Disciplines* (Oxford: Clarendon, 1994).

McFARLAND, THOMAS, *Romantic Cruxes: The English Essayists and the Spirit of the Age* (Oxford: Clarendon, 1987).

——, *Romanticism and the Heritage of Rousseau* (Oxford: Clarendon, 1995).

McGANN, JEROME J., *Fiery Dust: Byron's Poetic Development* (Chicago, Ill.: University of Chicago Press, 1968).

——, 'Hero With a Thousand Faces: The Rhetoric of Byronism', *Studies in Romanticism*, 31 (1992), 295–313.

MAGNUSON, PAUL, *Coleridge and Wordsworth: A Lyrical Dialogue* (Princeton, NJ: Princeton University Press, 1988).

MANIQUIS, ROBERT M., 'Lonely Empire: Personal and Public Visions of Thomas De Quincey', in Eric Rothstein and J. A. Wittreich (eds.), *Literary Monographs, viii* (Madison, Wis.: University of Wisconsin Press, 1976).

MANNING, PETER J., '*Childe Harold* in the Market Place', *Modern Language Quarterly*, 52 (1991), 170–90.

MARCUS, LAURA, *Auto/biographical Discourses* (Manchester: Manchester University Press, 1994).

MASON, NICHOLAS, 'Building Brand Byron', *Modern Language Quarterly*, 63 (2002), 411–40.

MASSON, DAVID (ed.), *The Collected Writings of Thomas De Quincey*, 14 vols. (Edinburgh: A. & C. Black, 1889–90).

MATTHEWS, WILLIAM, *British Autobiographies* (Berkeley, Calif.: University of California Press, 1955).

MILLS, SARA, 'Written on the Landscape: Mary Wollstonecraft's *Letters Written During a Short Residence in Sweden, Norway and Denmark*', in Amanda Gilroy (ed.), *Romantic Geographies* (Manchester: Manchester University Press, 2000).

MITCHELL, W. J. T., 'Influence, Autobiography, and Literary History: Rousseau's *Confessions* and Wordsworth's *The Prelude*', *ELH* 57 (1990), 643–64.

MONSMAN, GERALD, *Confessions of a Prosaic Dreamer; Charles Lamb's Art of Autobiography* (Durham, NC: Duke University Press, 1984).

——, 'Charles Lamb's Art of Autobiography', *ELH* 50 (1983), 541–57.

MORLEY, EDITH J. (ed.), *Henry Crabb Robinson on Books and their Writers*, 3 vols. (London: J. M. Dent, 1938).

MORRIS, JOHN N., *Versions of the Self* (New York: Basic Books, 1966).

MOSKAL, JEANNE, 'The Picturesque and the Affectionate in Wollstonecraft's *Letters from Norway*', *Modern Language Quarterly*, 52 (1991), 263–94.

MOTTOLESE, WILLIAM, ' "Almost an Englishman": Olaudah Equiano and the Colonial Gift of Language', in Greg Clingham (ed.), *Questioning History* (Lewisburg, Pa.: Bucknell University Press, 1998), 160–71.

MUDGE, BRADFORD, 'Bibliography of English Romantic Autobiography and Biography', *A/B: Auto/Biography Studies*, 2 (1986), 45–55.

MULCAHY, DANIEL J., 'Charles Lamb: The Antithetical Manner and the Two Planes', *Studies in English Literature 1500-1900*, 3 (1963), 517–42.

MULVIHILL, JAMES, 'The Anatomy of Idolatry: Hazlitt's *Liber Amoris*', *Charles Lamb Bulletin*, NS 70 (1990), 195–203

MYERS, MITZI, 'Wollstonecraft's *Letters Written . . . in Sweden*: Towards Romantic Autobiography', *Studies in Eighteenth-Century Culture*, 8 (1979), 165–85.

NANGLE, B. C., *The Monthly Review, Second Series, 1790–1815* (Oxford: Clarendon, 1955).

NEGT, OSKAR, and KLUGE, ALEXANDER, *Public Sphere and Experience*, trans. Peter Labanyi, Jamie Owen Daniel, and Assenka Oksiloff (Minneapolis, Minn.: University of Minnesota Press, 1993).

NEUMAN, SHIRLEY (ed.), *Autobiography and Questions of Gender* (London: Frank Cass, 1991).

NEWEY, VINCENT, 'Authoring the Self', in Bernard Beatty and Vincent Newey (eds.), *Byron and the Limits of Fiction* (Liverpool: Liverpool University Press, 1988).

—— and SHAW, PHILIP (eds.), *Mortal Pages, Literary Lives* (Aldershot: Scolar, 1996).

NEWLYN, LUCY, *'Paradise Lost' and the Romantic Reader* (Oxford: Clarendon, 1993).

——, *Reading, Writing, and Romanticism* (Oxford: Oxford University Press, 2000).

NUSSBAUM, FELICITY, *The Autobiographical Subject* (Baltimore, Md.: Johns Hopkins University Press, 1989).

OGDEN, J., 'A Note on "Autobiography" ', *Notes and Queries*, 206 (1961), 461–2.

O'NEILL, MICHAEL, *Literature of the Romantic Period: A Bibliographical Guide* (Oxford: Clarendon, 1998).

PARK, ROY (ed.), *Lamb as Critic* (London: Routledge & Kegan Paul, 1980).

PARKER, MARK, 'Ideology and Editing: The Political Context of the Elia Essays', *Studies in Romanticism*, 30 (1991), 469–87.

PERRY, SEAMUS, *Coleridge and the Uses of Division* (Oxford: Clarendon, 1999).

——, 'Charles Lamb and the Cost of Seriousness', *Charles Lamb Bulletin*, 83 (1993), 78–89.

PETERS, GERALD, *The Mutilating God: Authorship and Authority in the Narrative of Conversion* (Amherst, Mass.: University of Massachusetts Press, 1993).

PETERSON, LINDA H., *Victorian Autobiography* (New Haven, Conn.: Yale University Press, 1986).

——, *Traditions of Victorian Women's Autobiography* (Charlottesville, Va.: University Press of Virginia, 1999).

PORTER, DENNIS, *Rousseau's Legacy* (New York: Oxford University Press, 1995).

PRANCE, CLAUDE A., *A Companion to Charles Lamb* (London: Mansell, 1983).

RAJAN, TILOTTAMA, and WRIGHT, JULIA M. (eds.), *Romanticism, History, and the Possibilities of Genre* (Cambridge: Cambridge University Press, 1998).

READY, ROBERT, 'The Logic of Passion: Hazlitt's *Liber Amoris*', *Studies in Romanticism*, 14 (1975), 41–57.

REIMAN, DONALD H. (ed.), *The Romantics Reviewed*, 3 pts. (New York: Garland, 1972).

RIEDE, DAVID, 'Transgression, Authority, and the Church of Literature in Carlyle', in Jerome J. McGann (ed.), *Victorian Connections* (Charlottesville, Va.: University Press of Virginia, 1989).

RUDDICK, WILLIAM, 'Recent Approaches to Charles Lamb', *The Charles Lamb Bulletin*, 98 (1997), 50–3.

RUST, MARION, 'The Subaltern as Imperialist', in Elaine K. Ginsberg (ed.), *Passing and the Fictions of Identity* (Durham, NC: Duke University Press, 1996).

RUTHERFORD, ANDREW (ed.), *Byron: The Critical Heritage* (London: Routledge, 1970).

SABINO, ROBIN, and HALL, JENNIFER, 'The Path Not Taken: Cultural Identity in the *Interesting Life* of Olaudah Equiano', *MELUS*, 24 (1999), 5–19.

SCHNEIDER, MATTHEW, *Original Ambivalence: Autobiography and Violence in Thomas De Quincey* (New York: Peter Lang, 1995).

SCHOENFIELD, MARK, 'Voices Together: Lamb, Hazlitt, and the *London*', *Studies in Romanticism*, 29 (1990), 257–72.

——, 'Butchering James Hogg: Romantic Identity in the Magazine Market', in Mary A. Favret and Nicola J. Watson (eds.), *At the Limits of Romanticism* (Bloomington, Ind.: Indiana University Press, 1994).

SCOGGINS, JAMES, 'Images of Eden in the Essays of Elia', *Journal of English and Germanic Philology*, 71 (1972), 198–210.

SHAFFER, E. S., 'The Hermeneutic Community: Coleridge and Schleiermacher', in Richard Gravil and Molly Lefebure (eds.), *The Coleridge Connection* (London: Macmillan, 1990).

SMITH, SIDONIE, *A Poetics of Women's Autobiography* (Bloomington, Ind.: Indiana University Press, 1987).

——, 'Performativity, Autobiographical Practice, Resistance', *A/B: Auto/Biography Studies*, 10 (1995), 17–33.

SPACKS, PATRICIA MEYER, *Privacy: Concealing the Eighteenth-Century Self* (Chicago, Ill.: University of Chicago Press, 2003).

SPENGEMANN, WILLIAM C., *The Forms of Autobiography* (New Haven, Conn.: Yale University Press, 1980).

STANFIELD, JAMES, *An Essay on the Study and Composition of Biography* (Sunderland: George Garbutt, 1813).

STAROBINSKI, JEAN, *Jean-Jacques Rousseau: Transparency and Obstruction*, trans. Arthur Goldhammer (Chicago, Ill.: University of Chicago Press, 1988).

STELZIG, EUGENE L., *The Romantic Subject in Autobiography* (Charlottesville, Va.: University Press of Virginia, 2000).

STROUT, ALAN L., *A Bibliography of Articles in 'Blackwood's Magazine', 1817–1825* (Lubbock, Tex.: Texas Technical College Library Bulletin, 1959).

STULL, HEIDI I., *The Evolution of the Autobiography from 1770–1850* (New York: Peter Lang, 1985).

SWAAB, PETER, 'Romantic Self-Representation: The Example of Mary Wollstonecraft's *Letters in Sweden*', in Vincent Newey and Philip Shaw (eds.), *Mortal Pages, Literary Lives: Studies in Nineteenth-Century Autobiography* (Aldershot: Scolar, 1996).

THORSLEV, PETER L., JR., *The Byronic Hero* (Minneapolis, Minn.: University of Minnesota Press, 1962).

TODD, JANET, *Sensibility: An Introduction* (London: Methuen, 1986).

——, 'Mary Wollstonecraft and Enlightenment Desire', *Wordsworth Circle*, 29 (1998), 186–91.

TREADWELL, JAMES, 'Impersonation and Autobiography in Lamb's Christ's Hospital Essays', *Studies in Romanticism*, 37 (1998), 499–521.

—— 'The Legibility of *Liber Amoris*', *Romanticism on the Net*, 17 (2000), <http://www.non.umontreal.ca/>, accessed March 2004.

VINE, STEVEN, 'To "Make a Bull": Autobiography, Idealism and Writing in Coleridge's *Biographia Literaria*', in Peter J. Kitson and Thomas N. Corns (eds.), *Coleridge and the Armoury of the Human Mind* (London: Frank Cass, 1991).

VOISINE, JACQUES, *J.-J. Rousseau en Angleterre à l'époque romantique* (Paris: Didier, 1956).

WALLACE, C. M., *The Design of 'Biographia Literaria'* (London: Allen & Unwin, 1983).

WANG, ORRIN N. C., 'Romancing the Counter-Public Sphere', *Studies in Romanticism*, 33 (1994), 579–88.

WARD, WILLIAM S., *A Bibliography of Literary Reviews in British Periodicals, 1798–1820*, 2 vols. (New York: Garland, 1972).

——, *Literary Reviews in British Periodicals 1821–1826: A Bibliography* (New York: Garland, 1977).

——, *Literary Reviews in British Periodicals 1789–1797: A Bibliography* (New York: Garland, 1979).

WEINTRAUB, KARL J., *The Value of the Individual: Self and Circumstance in Autobiography* (Chicago, Ill.: University of Chicago Press, 1978).

WHEELER, KATHLEEN M. (ed.), *German Aesthetic and Literary Criticism: The Romantic Ironists and Goethe* (Cambridge: Cambridge University Press, 1984).

WILLIAMS, HUNTINGDON, *Rousseau and Romantic Autobiography* (Oxford: Oxford University Press, 1983).

WILSON, FRANCES (ed.), *Byronism* (London: Macmillan, 1999).

YOUSEF, NANCY, 'Wollstonecraft, Rousseau and the Revision of Romantic Subjectivity', *Studies in Romanticism*, 38 (1999), 537–57.

Index